D0984624

ATTACHMENT-FOCUSED
FAMILY THERAPY

A Norton Professional Book

ATTACHMENT-FOCUSED FAMILY THERAPY

DANIEL A. HUGHES

W. W. Norton & Company
New York • London

For information about permission to reproduce
selections from this book, write to
Permissions, W. W. Norton & Company, Inc.,
500 Fifth Avenue, New York, NY 10110

Manufacturing by: Quebecor World, Fairfield Graphics
Book design by: Pine Tree Composition
Production Manager: Leeann Graham

Library of Congress Cataloging-in-Publication Data

Hughes, Daniel A.
   Attachment-focused family therapy / Daniel A. Hughes.
       p.   cm.
   "A Norton professional book."
   Includes bibliographical references and index.
   ISBN-13: 978-0-393-70526-3 (hardcover)
   ISBN-10: 0-393-70526-9 (hardcover)
   1. Family psychotherapy. 2. Attachment behavior. I. Title.
   [DNLM: 1. Family Therapy. 2. Object Attachment. WM 460.5.O2
   H893a 2007]
RC488.5.H827 2007
616.89'156—dc22   2006038471

ISBN 13: 978-0-393-70526-3
ISBN 10: 0-393-70526-9

W. W. Norton & Company, Inc., 500 Fifth Avenue, New York, N.Y. 10110
www.wwnorton.com

W. W. Norton & Company Ltd., Castle House, 75/76 Wells St.,
London W1T 3QT

0   9   8   7   6   5

To my parents
Marie Collier Hughes
William Anthony Hughes (deceased)

To my siblings
James W. Hughes (deceased)
Mary Pat Sullivan
Kathleen English
William R. Hughes
John M. Hughes
Michael V. Hughes

CONTENTS

ACKNOWLEDGMENTS

While this work has certainly been influenced by various works of family therapists, its primary impetus has been the depth and breadth of knowledge that has emerged within the theory and research associated with attachment and intersubjectivity. These fields of child development have greatly facilitated our understanding of how human beings develop (neurologically, affectively, cognitively, socially, and behaviorally) through their close interactions with members of their families. These interactions permeate all aspects of healthy human development. They serve as excellent guides for both the modification of family interaction patterns that are conflict-ridden and deficient as well as for facilitating new patterns that will engender optimal growth.

I am indebted to many individuals who are not family therapists but who have greatly influenced my thinking in utilizing attachment and intersubjectivity for the practice of family therapy. These individuals are a varied group and they include Diana Fosha, Allan Schore, Dan Siegel, and Colwyn Trevarthen, as well as the writings of John Bowlby, Dante Cicchetti, Mary Dozier, Stanley Greenspan, and Alan Sroufe.

Within the family therapy field itself I am most indebted to the work of Murray Bowen, Milton Erickson, Barry Ginsberg, Jay Haley, Susan Johnson, and Carl Whitaker.

Of course much gratitude always goes to those many colleagues with whom one exchanges ideas, concerns, problems and successes, day after day, year after year. Finally there are the families themselves who have willingly allowed me to join them for a time, experiencing their conflicts, separations, and pain, as well as their joy, hopes and love. To each family I am grateful for having been able to both give and receive so much during our many moments of vibrant intersubjectivity.

And a final thanks to Andrea Costella and colleagues at W. W. Norton whose relaxed competence has enabled this process to be much easier than it might have been.

ATTACHMENT-FOCUSED FAMILY THERAPY

Introduction

INDIVIDUALS, FAMILIES, AND THE THERAPEUTIC RELATIONSHIP—THE INTERPLAY OF ATTACHMENTS

The gifts we treasure most over the years are often small and simple. In easy times and in tough times, what seems to matter most is the way we show those nearest us that we've been listening to their needs, to their joys, and to their challenges. —*Fred Rogers,* The World According to Mr. Rogers

So much of what gives meaning and purpose in our lives involves our relationships—and especially our relationships within our old and new families. These relationships are different from those that we have with our casual friends and acquaintants, our colleagues and neighbors. These family relationships contain the interwoven features of attachment security and intersubjectivity. It is these features that are central to attachment-focused family therapy.

The therapeutic relationship is central to all models of psychotherapy, including, I believe, those which are evidence based, and at the same time are found by clinicians to be truly effective (Norcross, 2001). When the therapeutic relationship is at its best it contains the same characteristics of attachment and intersubjectivity that are present in good family relationships. It is within attachment and intersubjectivity that therapy is able to provide both the safety and also the exploration that is necessary for progress.

From an attachment perspective, a central purpose of the family is to facilitate the development of both its members and also the functioning of the family as a whole. This is achieved through providing a secure base/safe haven in which and from which each member is able to begin to form a coherent autobiographical narrative. Family members' narratives, to a significant extent, become increasingly coherent through being engaged by the intersubjective experiences that are generated within the family. Intersubjectivity, in turn, tends to occur more fully, frequently, and spontaneously when family members are feeling safe with one another. The affective states of each member of the family are being coregulated within these same intersubjective experiences. This process of affective coregulation is necessary for children in order for them to be able to adequately regulate the more intense or difficult positive and negative affective states that occur during development. Similar intense affective states naturally emerge—and need to be coregulated—within the context of all ongoing attachment relationships.

Parents provide a safe setting for their children. Partners provide a similar safe setting for each other. Within such secure attachments, the members of the family are able to attain relationships that provide the opportunity to coregulate a full range of affective states and cocreate an equally wide range of meanings. Within such relationships, the members of the family are also given the freedom to develop their own autonomous interests, beliefs, and activities apart from the other members of the family. Such a family is able to uniquely blend the human desires for autonomy and intimacy and to demonstrate to each member that one does not have to sacrifice the self when one loves another, nor sacrifice a relationship with the other while developing the self.

THE ROLE OF FAMILY THERAPY IN ATTACHMENT SECURITY

In this model of family therapy the therapist applies perceptions and interventions that flow from the twin theories of attachment and intersubjectivity in working with the members of the family. She does this by increasing each member's ability to relate to each other in ways that facilitate attachment security. The therapist's role varies. Moving from the individual to the family and back again, she demonstrates how to foster both individuality and intimacy. The therapist facilitates secure attachment patterns and behaviors among the members of the family so that they are able to become engaged with each other in a manner similar to how she is engaged with them.

This model of family therapy utilizes the interwoven theories of attachment and intersubjectivity to provide guides for interpersonal interactions that facilitate safety and trauma resolution, neuropsychological development, affect regulation, narrative integration, emotional communication, conflict resolution, and the experience of joy. Such goals do not seem to be too grand when one considers that parents have similar goals in their respective relationships with their child. Nor are they too grand when we consider that attachment relationships are uniquely suited to be successful in attaining such goals.

The therapist's treatment stance is congruent with the dyadic reciprocal communications that occur frequently between parents and their young children. It is an active stance, affectively varied and attuned with each individual's affective state. It is a stance in which the therapist openly communicates her own intersubjective experience of the subjective and intersubjective experiences of the members of the family. The therapist's frequent goal is to identify and bring into expression the subjective and intersubjective experiences—which are often confusing, frightening, shameful, and nameless—in the day-to-day life of the members of the family.

This process is best done when the therapist is fully aware of how well-functioning parents have engaged in the same process with their young children for generations. Within families characterized by attachment security, the parent is continuously discovering and giving meaning to the interplay that she experiences between herself and her child, between herself and her partner, or between her child and the world. At the same time, the parents are coregulating the affect that emerges during the process. The parents take the lead in this joint endeavor of coregulating affect and cocreating meaning, but their children are active participants. In a similar manner in therapy, the therapist enters the intersubjective matrix with the members of the family and takes the lead. But the meaningful affective states are not generated from within the mind of the therapist, but rather are cocreated and coregulated by all present. The therapist enters and participates in the family's intersubjective space. It is in this intersubjective stance, evolving over the centuries, that human development has occurred. Therapists are wise to take advantage of the intersubjective process that truly is the foundation of our humanity.

The distinction between affect and cognition is often not apparent within the lived experience of this model of family therapy. During this treatment the therapist and family become fully engaged in a conversation about past memories and current experiences, including both reflective and affective states that are relevant to the developing narratives of each family member. These conversations are not verbal dialogues alone. Nonverbal communication is central to all emotional communication and is central to this model of family therapy as well. The nonverbal and verbal forms of communication are constantly interwoven and so insure that the affective experience of the dialogue will be coregulated and the meaning of the dialogue will be cocreated. When the nonverbal and verbal are not congruent, this disparity is addressed and understood. Most often, aspects of the verbal train of thought that are associated with the affect of greatest vitality, are followed. Planned discussions are set aside when they seem to lack a lived meaning in the present. Or the fact that they do not have a lived meaning in the present may become the theme of the next dialogue. At the same time, catharsis is not seen as a therapeutic goal. Affect has a role in understanding and giving expression to the meaning of an experience and its current memory. The simple expression of isolated affect—such as screaming or hitting a pillow as techniques to make one more comfortable with anger—is considered to be of little lasting value.

Thus, this attachment-focused family therapy involves the process of facilitating the abilities of parent and child to engage in an affective/reflective (a/r) dialogue with the therapist and with each other. Within such reciprocal states of affective communication, the focus of attention, whatever it may be, is more able to be accessed and assume a part in the narratives of the family members, becoming an aspect of their coherent autobiographies. As the child and parent increase their abilities to engage in this process, past events associated with anxiety and shame are now more able to fully enter into the narrative as particular experiences among many varied affective/cognitive experiences.

In this treatment model the therapist is a part of the intersubjective process, she is not standing aside attempting to take an "objective" stance from which she can convey "the truth." She is experiencing with the family the full meaning of a theme, both what the theme means to the family members as well as what it means to her. Being engaged in the intersubjective process means that it has an impact on her as well as on her clients: the therapist's heart and mind are affected by the intersubjective experience. The parent–child relationship is again the closest analogy to this process. Whereas in most instances the child is affected more than the parent, the parent is nevertheless affected by being this child's parent in this situation. The child needs to experience the parent as being affected by the event or it will have less meaning to the child. If such a failure in making the child's experience intersubjective with the parent happens often enough, the meaning the child gives to herself will be similarly restricted. She will become a child who does not carry much meaning for her parent. Therapy becomes much more likely to be transformative when the client knows affectively that he or she has meaning in the therapist's life.

An attachment-focused family treatment differs from some models of working with the family in various ways.

1. The therapist continuously maintains an atmosphere characterized by safety and repair. The therapist insures safety for the parents while the therapist and parents together provide safety for the children. The moment in treatment when the parents are not insuring safety for their children (i.e., when they relinquish their roles as attachment figures), the therapist addresses what is occurring with the parents either alone or in the presence of the children.

2. In order for the parents to feel safe and then be in a position to insure safety for their children, the therapist meets alone with the parents for a number of sessions before involving the children in the treatment. The therapist's goal is to develop an alliance with the parents through experiencing empathy and understanding for them, understanding their parenting and attachment histories, discovering their strengths and vulnerabilities, and presenting to them this model of treatment and parenting.

3. The here-and-now nonverbal communications serve as the foundation of the coregulation of affect and cocreation of meanings that are at the core of the treatment. The verbal aspect of the dialogue always rests upon and is congruent with nonverbal expression of the vitality affect.

4. The therapist assumes an active, intersubjective stance in treatment, communicating to the family verbally and nonverbally the impact that they—and the treatment process—is having on her. She actively models and coaches the family in the affective/reflective dialogue that she is trying to facilitate, and she ensures the structure and momentum of the dialogue. She does not place herself in a "professional chair" that lies outside of the family, but rather sits within the family's intersubjective matrix.

5. The therapist frequently "speaks for" and "speaks about" the children—and at times the parents—in guiding the dialogue into the underlying themes that are creating dysregulating affective states and hindering the development of coherent narratives. Often family members who seek treatment have only a partial awareness of the thoughts, feelings, and intentions that become manifest in their behaviors. Many cannot "find the words" in the presence of a therapist's receptive stance, and then benefit more quickly and fully from the therapist sharing her experience of the other's experience, though in a tentative and respectful manner. Speaking for the child in the first person often deepens the meaning of the words within the child's experience and enables him or her to both understand and express the experience more fully in the future.

6. When children enter the treatment sessions they become active participants in the dialogue. This treatment model assumes that children have a significant capacity to learn to be receptive, and give expression to emotional words that reflect their inner lives. The therapist actively facilitates the development of this crucial skill of "emotional intelligence."

Many parents, and professionals as well, are infrequently engaged with children in the intersubjective a/r dialogues that will be presented in this work. When we are able to become present with children in this way, we are providing them with experiences of primary intersubjectivity which will impact their self-narrative in ways that are transformative. When we provide both parent and child with the skills to engage in such a/r dialogues, attachment security is facilitated. The narratives of both parent and child thus become more coherent and the family is better able to function in an effective way.

ORIGINS OF ATTACHMENT-FOCUSED FAMILY THERAPY

This model of family therapy was developed for the treatment of abused and neglected children and youth who were living in foster and adoptive homes. It became know as Dyadic Developmental Psychotherapy (Becker-Weidman & Shell, 2005; Hughes, 2004, 2006). Many of these children manifested features consistent with the classification of attachment disorganization. They manifested no clear patterns of relying on their adoptive or foster parents for safety, guidance, affect regulation, or meaning making. The attachment-focused interventions described in this book were ideally suited to facilitate the development of patterns of secure attachments with their adoptive or foster parents.

In more recent years this model has been successfully employed where one or both of the biological parents is parenting the child. With these families the interventions are directed both toward the past attachment behaviors and intersubjective patterns that existed within the family, as well as contemporary patterns. Seeds of a secure attachment, embedded in the original relationship, can be elicited and utilized in developing new patterns. At the same time, activated maladaptive attachment patterns from the past need to be actively modified so that they do not impede the emergence of new patterns.

Attachment-focused family therapy has vivid parallels with Accelerated Experiential Dynamic Psychotherapy (AEDP) developed by Diana Fosha (2000, 2003). Dr. Fosha's model of treatment has striking similarities with the principles and interventions presented here. Her treatment is for individual adults rather than for children and their parents in a family setting. As a result she does not utilize the various principles for facilitating parent–child communication and for engaging children that are central to this work. However, her treatment goal for the individual mirrors my goal for the family:

> The goal [of therapy] is to help the patient weave a meaningful narrative: integrating affect and cognition, informed by understanding the contributions of self and other, always through the lens of empathy toward the self, a coherent autobiographical

tale, a narrative not fractured by defensive exclusion, can un-
fold. (Fosha, 2000, p. 270)

There are also strong similarities between this model and Emotionally
Focused Therapy (EFT) developed by Susan Johnson (2002, 2004)
and Les Greenberg (2002a, 2002b) for both individuals and couples.
Much of their work involves couples, rather than families, and when
it does involve families, preadolescent children tend not to be engaged with the dialogue described in this book. The intersubjective
stance of the therapist is also not stressed to the degree that it is in the
present work. Readers may also note some parallels with the interventions and stance of Milton Erickson, Carl Rogers, and the Gestalt
and Narrative schools of therapy. There are clear similarities between
this model of family therapy and Relationship Enhancement Family
Therapy (RE; Ginsberg, 1997). What all of these models have in common is the priority given to the focus on experience, and especially that
of the here-and-now experience, often including the therapeutic relationship. This stance is more common in individual treatment than in
family treatment, and more common with adults than it is with children. The theoretical works of Allan Schore (1994, 2001) and Dan
Siegel (1999, 2001) provide the most comprehensive framework, I believe, for attachment-focused family therapy as well as aspects of the
above treatment models.

ORGANIZATION OF THE BOOK

This book is divided into two main parts: theory and application. Part I
consists of Chapter 1, which provides the theoretical foundations of
attachment and intersubjectivity that serve as the basis of this treatment model. Part II, which consists of Chapters 2 through 9, describes
the application of these theoretical foundations in this treatment
model. Chapter 2 presents an overview of the application of the theory in family treatment. The primary therapeutic stance, which consists of playfulness, acceptance, curiosity, and empathy (PACE), is
described in Chapter 3. Chapter 4 details the nature of the therapeutic
dialogue that is the central activity of the family treatment. Chapter 5
focuses on one of the central features of this treatment model, namely
having the initial stage of treatment involve the parents without their

children. The purpose of this treatment component is to ensure that the parents are able to provide attachment security for their children by first experiencing safety themselves with the therapist. Chapter 6 focuses on another central feature of this model, namely, the manner of being engaged with and communicating with children. Managing shame, an often overlooked emotion, but one which is often pervasive within families who seek treatment, is presented in Chapter 7. Chapter 8 explores the crucial ingredients of relationship breaks and repair, which are central both in the development of the family's problems as well as in the treatment meant to resolve them. Chapter 9 focuses specifically on childhood trauma and the means of providing treatment for traumatized children within a family treatment modality. An Epilogue points to possible future directions in family therapy, based on current research and related clinical practice.

There are three appendices, two actual case studies and one composite case that demonstrate this treatment model.

Some readers may choose to review the theory before considering its application, while others may become impatient with the theory until after first having been exposed to how it is applied. This is most likely a matter of personal preference. Reading the theory is not crucial for an initial understanding of the treatment interventions, though it is likely to be necessary in any efforts to more thoroughly understand the treatment rationale.

Finally I would like to make a brief reference to an aspect of Martin Buber's profound teachings. By seeing and bringing forth each family member's unique qualities the therapist is taking a stance that is similar to what Martin Buber described as "imagining the real." By this phrase, Buber is referring to:

> not a looking at the other, but a bold swinging—demanding the most intensive stirring of one's being—into the life of the other . . . The realm of my action is . . . the particular real person who confronts me, whom I can attempt to make present to myself . . . in his wholeness, unity, and uniqueness, and with his dynamic centre which realizes all these things ever anew. (1965, p. 81)

Buber adds that for him to "imagine the real" it is necessary to be in a "living partnership" with another person and then "to expose myself vitally to his share in the situation as really his share . . . If mutuality stirs, then the interhuman blossoms into genuine dialogue" (p. 81).

Buber is speaking of something more than empathy and more than imagination. He is describing "a bold swinging" into the subjective experience of the other, so that it is now an aspect of one's own subjective experience as well, enabling one to understand the other "from the inside out." In doing so, this subjective experience—"real" but often unseen and unintegrated into the family member's narrative—is "real" to the therapist as well. It is experienced by the therapist intersubjectively and expressed back to the child and parent, nonverbally and verbally, so that they can now better develop their own subjective experiences, first within the therapist's nonverbal and verbal manifestation of it and then within the meaning-making context that the therapist brings to it. The event or object confronting the family member has taken a journey within the subjectivity of the therapist, through the intersubjective matrix, and now is back to the child and parent, having taken on new meanings and ways of being identified, regulated, and expressed. It is now more able to find a place within the narratives of the child, parent, and family as a whole.

PART I
THEORY

Chapter 1

ATTACHMENT AND INTERSUBJECTIVITY

I didn't care about anything on this earth except the way her face was tipped toward mine, our noses just touching, how wide and gorgeous her smile was, like sparklers going off. She had fed me with a tiny spoon. She had rubbed her nose against mine and poured her light on my face . . . I was loved. —Sue Monk Kidd, The Secret Life of Bees

Attachment and intersubjectivity (A&I) represent the double helix of the psychological birth and development of the human being. This is very evident in the daily life of the young child. A&I permeate the child's day with discovery, mystery, joy, and an intense immediacy of emerging affect and meaning. However, the importance of A&I remains throughout the life span, often becoming very clear again when one begins to face the immediacy of death.

In speaking of attachment security I will be referring to the pattern of behaviors manifested by the child and parent. These are the behaviors by which the child attains physical and psychological safety through proximity with a parent who is available, sensitive, and responsive to the child's various self-expressions, while also repairing any relationship breaks that might threaten the felt sense of safety. Within attachment security the parent serves as a secure base, which provides the child with the safety needed to begin to explore and interact with the world. Within attachment security the parent serves as a "safe haven" to whom the child can return when the novel and strange features of the world create fear. Attachment security enables the child to regulate fears in order to be free to learn from novel objects and events in the environment. As the child matures, physical proximity becomes less necessary while psychological availability remains crucial throughout childhood if the child is to successfully proceed through the developmental milestones (Cassidy & Shaver, 1999).

In speaking of intersubjectivity I am referring to those moments when the parent and child are in synch: When they are affectively and cognitively present to each other; when the vitality of their affective states are matched; their cognitive focus is on the same event or object; and their intentions are congruent. As will be indicated throughout this book, when two individuals are engaged intersubjectively their affect is being coregulated and they are cocreating the meaning of the objects or events that they are attending to.

Attachment and intersubjectivity are felt by some to be two distinct motivating factors in human development (Stern, 2004; Trevarthen, 2001). In this discussion, I will adopt that position, reserving the term *attachment bond* for a highly specific type of *affectional bond* that is characterized by an individual seeking security and comfort (Cassidy, 1999, p. 12). *Intersubjectivity* represents a fundamental interpersonal activity that exists within all affectional bonds. Whether considered to be distinct or not, they are nevertheless interwoven to such an extent that when one speaks of their respective influences, one is often describing the same themes twice, each time from a slightly different perspective. Without intersubjectivity, attachment security would be limited in its organization and meaning. Without secure attachment figures, intersubjective experiences would be limited in their developmental range and power to influence what we know and who we become.

When a parent is engaged with her child intersubjectively, she remains an attachment figure. Her intention during the act of engagement is to coregulate her child's experience and cocreate its meaning. Her commitment to be available, sensitive, and responsive to her child makes intersubjective experiences more available and central in his or her development. Her commitment is also to patiently accept, and when necessary, repair, the periodic breaks that occur within their relationship. This quality of repair is crucial if the child is to feel safe in the belief that the relationship will persist in spite of the breaks.

I will now focus on five central developmental processes and attempt to make clear how A&I contribute to them. The five themes selected are safety and exploration; the sequence of breaks and repairs within attachment relationships; the coregulation of affect; the cocreation of meaning; and the development of a coherent self. These themes are central principles in the model of family treatment that will be presented.

SAFETY AND EXPLORATION

Infants are born without the abilities necessary for them to be safe alone (Bowlby, 1969/1982). If they are to survive they need to have one or more adults who are willing and able to assume the responsibility for their safety. The infant's primary skills involve a readiness and ability to elicit and maintain the attention of adults so that they will notice what he or she needs (be sensitive) and meet the needs that are present (be responsive). Infants' primary skill for eliciting such attention is crying. When infants are entering a dysregulated physiological state or an unresponsive environment, they cry. Infants have a variety of cries, based on the unique quality of distress that they are experiencing. Their sensitive and responsive parents are often quickly able to identify the need through the unique expression of each cry. The infant is in distress, communicates it, and the child's parents respond appropriately. The better the communication of the infant the quicker (and better) the response. The infant, from birth, will be safer when he or she is able to both give expression to the distress, but also do so in a manner that communicates the unique need. The success of the infant's communication requires first that she has a variety of ways to express distress depending upon its nature. But success also requires that the infant has specific caregivers who become sensitive to her unique expressions. Thus, infants' safety is enhanced as they improve their communication skills and also have specific adults who get to know their unique expressions (be sensitive) so that the adults can respond more efficiently.

From birth, infants prefer their parents before other adults. They are familiar with the parents' odor and voice. During their early months infants prefer being with any adult to being alone. Adults other than their parents are also able to help them to become calm, keep them warm, fed, and dry. Infants like being close to other humans who will keep them safe in a variety of ways. And when infants are close to caretakers, they want to communicate with them. The better infants are at communicating with those who care for them, the safer they will feel.

Infants initially prefer the parent because her odor and voice are familiar. This preference deepens when the parent is the primary person who meets the infant's needs for food, warmth, touch, and a calm, regular, soothing environment. The preference deepens further when the infant's primary social engagement activities, which lead to intersubjective experiences, occur with his parents. The infant and his parents are developing their own unique dance that becomes a primary source of comfort, communication, shared affective states, and learning about self, other, and the objects and events of the world. This unique dance is pivotal in making the parent unique to the infant, and the infant unique to the parent.

The infant's preference becomes stronger still with time, so that early in the second half of the first year, the infant begins to show a very strong desire to be with his parent over others, becoming anxious when the parent is not present, and anxious when he is with a stranger. This is because infants have learned at this point that the parent is the primary source of safety. A sense of safety involves having the parent meet the infant's needs for food, warmth, and protection from what is "strange." Safety also involves engaging in intersubjective experiences with the parent in which they both communicate and learn about their respective inner lives. Physical proximity with a sensitive and responsive parent becomes a building block for the attachment behaviors that become strong in the second half of the first year. Successful, repeated, intersubjective experiences between infant and parent are additional building blocks to further strengthen attachment security. Both, together, facilitate the young child's optimal development.

The infant wants to interact with others. He engages in "proto-conversations" with the other person long before expressive or even receptive verbal language has been mastered. Together, the infant and adult enter a state of intersubjectivity whereby their affect becomes matched, they are focused on each other, and they are sharing the same intentions to communicate with and enjoy each other, as well as to learn about and enjoy or avoid the events and objects of the world.

Another way of describing this crucial developmental path is to focus on the interwoven nature of safety and exploration behaviors (Marvin, Cooper, Hoffman, & Powell, 2002). When infants feel safe (a secure base), they become very interested in exploring their world. When, during the course of exploration, they do not feel safe for whatever reason, the exploration needs are set aside and their attachment needs (a safe haven) are activated again. What is fascinating during the first several months of life, is that both infants' safety-seeking and many of their exploration behaviors are directed toward their caregivers. When they begin to explore the world they are the most interested in exploring their parents. They want to become engaged with them intersubjectively and so learn about self and other (primary intersubjectivity) (Trevarthen, 2001). They learn about the world (secondary intersubjectivity) through reciprocal affect, attention, and intentions—the intersubjective triad—being directed toward an object or event in the world. When their attachment behaviors are active, infants want their parents to protect and comfort them (often through coregulating their affective states). When their exploration behaviors are active they want their parents to engage in joint discovery and meaning making. The two pathways both alternate and are interwoven.

The first joint parent–child activity to create a sense of safety and connectedness most likely involves the joint regulation of the infant's physiological state (Field, 1996). The parent's calm and soothing presence enables the infant's physiology to match that of the parent. The infant cannot self-soothe, but rather is soothed by the parent's calming presence, which sensitively responds to the more agitated, irregular presence of the infant. Within this joint physical/affective state, the opportunity for attuned engagement occurs. The parent repeatedly matches the vitality of the infant's nonverbal expressions. The rhythm, beat, intensity, duration, contour, or shape of the infant's expression is being matched by that of the parent (Stern, 1985). However, whereas the infant's affective experience may be dysregulated, the parent's consistently remains regulated. As their affective states become congruent, the parent's regulated quality becomes absorbed by the child. The child's affect is being coregulated through the joined connection with the parent. The parent is also

17

communicating that the infant's expression has been noticed and given meaning and by doing so the infant is increasingly able to notice and give meaning to his or her own expressions. The parent's response is contingent upon the infant's unique expression. The infant is learning that her expression is having an effect on the parent. As the vitality of the infant's expression changes, so too does the parent's response.

Whereas at first the parent will often match her infant's vocal expression with a similar vocal expression, or the child's arm movement with a similar movement of her own, gradually the parent begins to match the vitality of the expression with varying nonverbal responses. Thus, if the infant is manifesting a facial expression with a certain degree of intensity, contour, and duration, the parent may match this expression with her vocal tone with similar vitality (intensity, contour, or duration). This "cross-modality" matching (Stern, 1985) is very important for the development of the range and depth of the communication that is occurring between infant and parent and hence for the skill by which the parent is able to keep her infant safe. By using another modality, the parent is demonstrating that she is responding to the child's communication about his inner affective state. In so doing, she is helping her infant become aware of actually having an inner affective state. The infant's inner state can be expressed through various nonverbal modalities. The specific nonverbal modality is not what is important in the interaction. The parent's act of responding to the nonverbal expression is not as important as the act of communicating that the child's nonverbal expression is connected to the child's inner affective state. The parent is making clear the particular state that she has noticed and is responding to. The parent is communicating empathy and understanding for her child's inner state, not simply for his or her nonverbal behavioral expressions.

As the parent responds to the child's inner state of subjective experience with an expression of her own inner state of subjective experience, the joint communication becomes an intersubjective experience. The infant is experiencing the parent's subjective experience of her own subjective experience. Parent and child are not simply imitating behaviors. The infant's inner state exists *within* the parent's inner state. It is noticed, valued, accepted, and given meaning while existing in the parent's subjective experience. Through this intersubjective experience, infants become aware of their own subjective experience which they otherwise would not be able to identify and value as important. Such subjective experiences, through being experienced intersubjectively, are the initial building blocks for infants' development of a coherent sense of self. Experiences that are not noticed or valued by the parent are not as likely to become mastered by the child. Experiences that are not noticed or valued by the parent are likely to remain outside of a coherent narrative.

Through intersubjective experience we become more able to identify, regulate, and express our affective life. Through such experiences, we are able to develop empathy for others and to successfully engage in shared, reciprocal, social experiences. Through intersubjectivity we are able to understand the thoughts, wishes, and intentions of others just as we become able to identify and express our own. The inner lives of others become a central part of our own inner life. We are able to share our inner worlds, thus making our subjective worlds much more vital and interesting as well as making it possible for us to relate effectively within and about these worlds.

Throughout this book, intersubjectivity will be described as representing psychological processes beginning in infancy, which have been described in detail by both Trevarthen and Aiken (2001) and Stern (2004). Trevarthen and Aitken (2001) state: "the infant is born with awareness specifically receptive to subjective states of other persons" (p. 4).

Trevarthen (2001) offers details of this process when he says:

Human conversation is a brain–brain regulation, mediated by an exceptionally elaborate array of special expressive movements (postural, gestural, vocal, and facial signaling powers) that instantly reflect motives. It engages dynamic purposes, interests, and feelings between participants, and it does so according to innate parameters of timing and expressive morphology that are built into the motive activity of all human brains. (p. 112)

Daniel Stern (2004) states that he and many other researchers agree that,

infants are born with minds that are especially attuned to other minds as manifested through their behavior. This is based in

19

large part on the detection of correspondences in timing, intensity, and form that are intermodally transposable. The result is that from birth on, one can speak of a psychology of mutually sensitive minds. (p. 85)

Stern goes on to say that from 7 to 9 months of age, the infant's "sharable mental states start to include goal-directed intentions, focus of attention, affects and hedonic evaluations, and, as before, the experience of action" (2004, p. 86). He then describes three domains that are developing: participation in the other's feelings, ability to share the focus of attention, and ability to read the intentions of the other.

During moments of intersubjectively facilitated by the parent, children:

1. Experience self and parent (primary) or self and object/event (secondary) at the same time as experiencing the parent's experience of the same.
2. Are able to regulate the affect associated with the experience through being joined with the parent's affective experience of self/other or the object/event.
3. Are able to reexperience self/other or the object/event through experiencing the parent's experience of it and cocreating a meaning influenced by both.
4. Are able to experience self/other or an event/object with less fear or shame.
5. Experience self, in the context of self-and-other, in a more integrated, coherent way.
6. Develop the capacity to maintain acceptance, curiosity, and empathy toward self, with a readiness to integrate past and present events into the self-narrative. Aspects of self associated with certain experiences are not "off-limits."
7. Develop the capacity to enter into similar intersubjective experiences with others, coregulating affect and cocreating meaning.
8. Are within the "zone of proximal development" (Vygotsky, 1962) whereby the intersubjective experience facilitates an emerging mastery of their social/emotional/cognitive/behavioral realities.
9. Begin to relate with the other in a manner in which both are subjects to each other. Neither is an object to the other in which the other's experience is not relevant.

Focusing now on the parent, during moments of intersubjectivity:

1. The parent's central intention is to focus on the experience of her child. Her affect, attention, and intentions are fully engaged with her child.
2. The parent resonates with the initiatives and responses of her child.
3. The parent, by resonating with her child's vitality affect, is able to coregulate her child's affective state.
4. The parent maintains an accepting, curious, and empathic affective/reflective state directed toward the subjective experience of her child.
5. The parent allows her child to have an impact on her mind and heart.
6. The parent often gives nonverbal/verbal expression to the impact that her child is having on her.
7. The parent experiences the uniqueness of her child. She responds in a unique manner to her child's nonverbal expressions of his or her subjectivity.
8. The parent actively discovers an aspect of her child that was not known/experienced before in the same unique way. She facilitates self-discovery in her child.
9. The parent actively accepts her child's current functioning while encouraging her child to take the next step in mastering his or her potential skills.
10. The parent experiences a deeper and broader sense of self through the intersubjective presence of her child within her own subjective narrative.

The importance and relevance of these features—for both child and parent (and therapist as well)—with regard to psychotherapy will become evident to the reader throughout this work.

Within families that are not characterized by secure attachments, the members of the family gradually become hesitant to initiate intersubjective experiences with one another. They do not feel safe enough to do so. They may want to resonate with reciprocal affect, share the same focus of attention, and engage in the cooperative behaviors that flow from joint intentions. However, in these families such experiences often lead to failure. As a result, there is a gradual decrease in their openness to being influenced and affected intersubjectively by one another. Initial orientation to one another with eye contact, curiosity, and a readiness to fully communicate becomes less likely to occur. In defending the self, intersubjective experiences are now suspect. The family members begin to anticipate that intersubjectivity will create shame and other negative affective states. Initially, the person may have been receptive to an intersubjective experience, but as soon as that experience created a sense of being judged negatively—as soon as it brought with it a threat to the self—the experience was abruptly stopped. When that sequence became the pattern rather than the exception it no longer became desirable to share affect, attention, and intentions; rather, such sharing was to be actively avoided or approached with great caution. In this way, intersubjectivity—the cradle of reciprocal joy and family intimacy—became a threat to the developing self-narrative. For this reason, the door through which the other is best able to impact the self—intersubjectivity—is often likely to be closed.

CONTINUITY IN RELATIONSHIPS: COMMITMENT, BREAKS, AND REPAIR

The continuity of a relationship is crucial if it is to function as a source of safety and at the same time facilitate the emergence of intersubjective states that facilitate the development of a coherent self. Within attachment security, trust in such continuity becomes strong. Separations are temporary. Physical separations always lead to reunion. Psychological separations always lead to repair (Kobak, 1999).

It is characteristic of attachment security that parents' commitment to their child is unconditional. Parents communicate by word and deed that when their child needs them, they will be there. Nothing will take priority over the well-being of their child. The parents will remove any threat to their child. If they cannot remove the threat, they will face it with their child. Their child will not face it alone. Parents also communicate by word and deed that whatever differences, conflicts, or misunderstandings they experience will never be a threat to the relationship. Differing goals, wishes, affective states, or interests will be integrated into the relationship—possibly with strain—and will not break it.

Within the parent–infant relationship, parents insure that the infant's experience of separation from them is brief. When the child is in distress, they come close to him or her, address the distress, it becomes resolved, or, if they cannot reduce the distress they remain with the child. They offer comfort and thus coregulate the negative affective state that their child is experiencing. When he or she is receptive to interactions, they interact with the infant, facilitating his or her intersubjective skills while coregulating positive and negative affective states. Extended separations lead to both physical and psychological distress that the infant finds difficult to regulate alone. Thus, parents who provide attachment security are habitually available, sensitive, and responsive to their infant, who is safe, and whose physical and intersubjective needs are routinely being met.

At times the parent–infant dancers are out of step with each other. This may be due to either member of the dyad misreading the other. This happens routinely and inadvertently and when it does, the other member of the dyad waits momentarily for the first to "catch his feet" and the dance resumes. At other times, one member decides to take a brief break from the dance. Again, the other member often simply waits for the first to "catch his breath" and the dance resumes, or a subsequent one, begins. Finally, at times one member decides to introduce a new step into the dance. The other member takes his or her cue from the first and they jointly develop a different rhythm to their dance.

When they discipline their toddler, parents are introducing another break into the attachment relationship. With discipline the infant's parents are not simply misattuned to the child's expressed intention, rather their deliberate intention is to not respond to the infant's desires. This new parental intention is confusing to the infant who has come to expect that the parent will at least try to respond as the infant wants her to respond.

The challenge for the infant now is to understand the parent's motive for her intention not to respond. The infant's behavior demonstrates an intention to engage in a particular activity and the parent then restricts that behavior. The important question for the infant is "Why?" The infant struggles to know the parent's motives in placing the limit. A parent can greatly assist this internal process when she makes a brief effort to explain her motive while at the same time communicating empathy for the toddler's intention to do the opposite. What is being limited is the toddler's behavior, not his or her intention to engage in it. Thus, a parent may say, "Oh, you really want to play with your brother's game, you really do! But you can't play with it sweetie, it is easy to break and your brother would be very upset if it broke."

It is fortunate that by the time that discipline is necessary—when infants begin to crawl—infants' intersubjective skills are sufficient to enable them to be able to grasp the parent's motives for the act of discipline as well as the parent's empathy for the child's original motives to engage in the act. In Chapter 7, which focuses on shame, I will explore circumstances in which this joint process of communicating and understanding the motives of both the child and parent do not develop that well.

There are still other breaks that are even more difficult than those caused by brief separations, misattunements, or discipline. These breaks include the various times that the child wants to engage in an activity with a parent and the parent refuses, as well as times when the parent's anger and irritability have nothing to do with discipline. One example includes times when the parent is engaged with the infant's sibling and the younger child has to wait. In essence, we are referring to the fact that whereas meeting the young child's primary needs is a top priority for the parent, meeting his or her routine wishes is a lower priority, and requires that at times the child waits, and at other times that the child's wish is denied. We are also referring to the fact that the parent is not always available, sensitive, and responsive. There are some times when the parent is preoccupied with other worries and responsibilities and is not ready as often for intersubjective engagement with her child. The young child's affective state is mildly dysregulated and the parent is not ready to coregulate that state—or the parents may also be in a dysregulated state. At these times the parent's presence may make an anxious child more anxious rather than serve as the source of soothing.

Such breaks in the intersubjective dance represent a temporary crisis in the relationship that must be seen, accepted, and repaired. When they are repaired, they represent an opportunity—the other side of the crisis—to expand both the relationship as well as the subjective realities that can be explored within the dyad. The relationship is expanding in that it becomes one in which brief separations, misattunements, differing intentions, or discipline can be present and not destroy the relationship. When such dimensions are added to the relationship, it may well become stronger, rather than more fragile. The child becomes aware that these breaks will always be repaired. Any distress inherent in these breaks will be regulated and transient. Breaks that are neither too long nor too frequent, and that are consistently repaired, enable the child's sense of safety to deepen. He need not fear breaks because they are never a threat to attachment security.

Researchers speak of interactive repair as the process whereby the parent and child initiate a state of reattunement with each other following these various breaks (Beebe & Lachmann, 2002; Tronick, 1989). The parent and young child are motivated by the strong desire to reassure each other that the relationship is still secure. Behaviors involved in attachment security are still important to both. Brief differences in attention, affective states, or intentions are not a threat to the relationship. Interactive repair demonstrates that relationship breaks are simply a natural part of the relationship rather than being a sign that the relationship may end.

Interactive repair is also valuable in facilitating attachment security and intersubjective skills when it focuses on the child's negative affect that is associated with the breaks. Repairs communicate that the child's anger or anxiety associated with discipline or other breaks will be understood and accepted and the affect will be coregulated by the parent. The parent is communicating that the child's negative affect *toward the parent herself* need not be denied. The child's anger at the parent is not a threat to the attachment security. The child's anger at the parent can itself enter the intersubjective focus of the relationship. It does not have to be excluded and hence, it is much more able to become integrated into the child's developing narrative.

Often interactive repair is initiated by the parent. The child is in a dysregulated, disconnected state and the parent remains or becomes present with her child, inviting him or her into the intersubjective state. Her regulated affect, focused attention, and her intention to repair their relationship all invite her child to return into an intersubjective experience that will regulate the affect associated with the break and create meaning that will place the break in the context of their permanent relationship. The child is safe again and their interactive dance can continue.

25

If the parent does not invite her child into this state of repair, or if she rejects his or her efforts to repair, the breaks will represent a threat to the ongoing continuity of the relationship and leave the child in a state of anxiety or despair. This sequence is more likely to occur if the behaviors of the child activate unresolved aspects of the parent's own attachment history. Repair often occurs infrequently or efforts to repair are limited and ineffectual in families that seek treatment.

COREGULATION OF AFFECT

We have seen how the newborn infant's most basic physiological states of arousal are able to be coregulated by the parent's more regulated and integrated affective/physiological state when she holds the child, sways gently, and speaks lovingly to him or her. The rhythm of her movements and voice tone, the familiarity of her odor and voice, and the calmness of her immediate bodily presence, all embrace the infant's poorly integrated, often dysregulated, moment-to-moment bodily states. Within these dyadic moments, the mother's integrated affective states are being absorbed by her infant and used as a template for the child's early movements toward regulation and organization of his or her own affective/physiological states (Jaffe, Beebe, Feldstein, Crown, & Jasnow, 2001; Schore, 1994; Sroufe, 1995; Stern, 1985).

Through countless repetitions of this process, infant and parent truly get to know each other. The parent becomes a master at identifying the various affective/physiological states of her infant and matching her own affective/bodily response so that it is most effective in coregulating her infant's state. The infant becomes equally adept at identifying and responding to the parent's affective/bodily rhythms and arousal states. The dyadic presence that emerges is unique and serves as an excellent template for the emergence of differential attachment behaviors and intersubjective activities. The infant seamlessly moves from this basic arousal regulation experience to the more complex coregulation of various affective states. He or she does this by remaining close to the parent, and being receptive to her calming and soothing presence when the child is frightened. The infant is repeatedly reassured that the parent will keep him or her safe and he discovers his own congruent response to the parent's calming presence. They are now intersubjectively present. As the infant gives expression to an inner state, the parent notices it and responds affectively in a manner that matches the state. Her affective response guides the child's affective experience of the state, enabling it to be regulated conjointly.

As the infant notices the parent's response, she notices the infant noticing her, and she affectively responds to his or her interest in her, which guides the child's affective state that is associated with noticing her. This same process occurs as the infant begins to notice and they jointly respond to objects in their immediate environment, whether they are a colorful toy, a dog, music, or a button. Their affective experience is reciprocal.

"Attunement" as defined by Daniel Stern (1985) involves the "intersubjective sharing of affect" (p. 141). Attunement permeates the intersubjective experience so that infants' attention as well as their intentional actions within the intersubjective experience will be greatly influenced by their associated affects. The matched affective states of the parent and child enable parents to "hold" infants' attention, extending their attention span while they focus on the parent or while the two together focus on a separate object or event. As infants' nonverbally expressed wishes are noticed, given meaning, and responded to by the parent, they develop an interest in their own inner life, their parent's inner life, as well as in acquiring the communication skills needed to understand the other and be understood by her.

Coregulation of affect, occurring naturally in intersubjective experiences, refers both to helping children to increase minimal affective states and also to decrease maximal affective states. This process occurs for both positive and negative affective experiences, making both more understandable, more able to be contained, and more validated and shared. Alan Sroufe (1995) has referred to secure attachment as being "the effective dyadic regulation of emotion in infancy" (p. 189).

When the parent maintains attunement during positive experiences children are enabled to experience reciprocal joy and delight, and their capacity for enjoyment and excitement becomes enhanced. Children can elicit delight in their parents' eyes—they can cause their parents to experience happiness. The child's parents are discovering and responding to a positive quality that involves who the child is, and over time the child discovers that he or she can have a similar, positive impact on others as well. Without the parent matching this positive affective state with her own more animated and playful state, the child's state would be in danger of moving from excitement to agitation and anxiety.

When the parent maintains attunement during negative affective experiences she prevents her child from entering into a state of affective, behavioral, and cognitive dysregulation. When the distress is caused by a separation from the parent, it is resolved by the support and comfort provided by the parent when they reunite. When the distress is caused by the parent limiting or being nonresponsive to the infant's behaviors, resolution again comes when the parent nonverbally reassures the infant or toddler that, even if a particular behavior is not permitted, he or she is accepted and special to her, and can elicit empathy in her eyes. Thus, the child experiences the parent as resonating with his or her affect, and finds that the affect is being contained. The child's affect is becoming associated with new meaning that conveys a new sense of self and other—a common meaning is being established. It is fundamentally an intersubjective experience for both parent and child. Attunement enables the child to begin to access, identify, and make conceptual the ongoing affective states that comprise his or her developing sense of self, including expanding symbolic abilities.

THE COCREATION OF MEANING

Within the safety created by attachment security and the development of intersubjective skills, within the continuity of the attachment relationship which incorporates separation and reunion, breaks and repair, and within the dyad that coregulates the emerging affective experiences, infant and parent are actively cocreating the meaning of their worlds. The infant is actively discovering who he or she is, who the parents are, and the nature of the events and objects he or she encounters by the child. The parents are actively discovering their infant as well as themselves as parents. As Peter Fonagy (2003) has suggestsed: "A major selective advantage conferred by attachment on humans was the opportunity it afforded for the development of social intelligence and meaning making" (p. 225).

Before infants take an active interest in the world, their first heightened interest is in mother and father. Infants are especially interested in the parents when they are being interested in him or her. Infants want to see themselves reflected in their parents' eyes, face, voice, movements, touch, timing, and rhythm of affective expressions. They want to see the impact that they are having on the parents. How infants affect their parents will tell them who they are. The enjoyment, interests, acceptance, love, and delight that they see in their parents' eyes will tell infants that they are enjoyable, interesting, acceptable, lovable, and delightful.

The term *primary intersubjectivity* (Trevarthen, 2001) refers to this interactional process in which children's view of self emerges from their experience of what their parents are recognizing and responding to. When parents fully respond to an aspect of a child's expressions with acceptance, joined attention, matched affect, and curiosity, it becomes part of the child's subjective experience that then becomes integrated into his or her early sense of self. The meaning that parents find and respond to within the child's nonverbal expressions becomes the core meaning that he or she gives to those expressions.

The infant is able to know that mother's expressive eyes are also representative of a response to him or her, rather than solely reflecting a quality in the parent. The child knows this because the moment-to-moment expressions in her face and eyes are highly contingent on the moment-to-moment expressions that the child is making. The child's expressions reflect his or her emerging inner affective states and the mother's contingent responses make the child aware that she is noticing these states and responding to them with enjoyment, interest, acceptance, and delight (Fonagy, 2003). As mother notices these states and responds to her child's affective expressions, the child herself is more likely to notice them. The nature of her response will give her child a first definition of him- or herself. The parent provides a different contingent response based on the nature of the affective state that the child is expressing. She may respond to his or her smiling exuberance with enjoyment, delight, and a matched degree of vitality affect. Or when the child is quiet and less focused on her, the parent may become quiet too, accepting the "wish" to reduce the affective states that are elicited by his or her interactions with the mother, who remains attuned with the child as he or she sets the tone and pace.

Infants in states of primary intersubjectivity with their parents are experiencing a sense of self-efficacy that is empowering. They have the ability to elicit joyful, enthusiastic, and captivating responses from their parents. They have the ability to make the parents deeply engaged with them in discovering who infants are, what they like, and what they are capable of doing. Whatever infants express and experience their parents respond to and experience with them. The meaning that parents most often give to these intersubjective experiences with infants is one of all-encompassing joy and interest. Infants discover again and again that there are wonderful qualities about and within them that deeply affect their parents. Infants are able to have a profound impact on their parents, and they are indeed very special to them.

It is now evident that experiences of primary intersubjectivity affect both infants and parents. Just as infants discover themselves in the eyes of their parents, parents discovers themselves as parents in the eyes of their infants. A significant part of the joy of parenthood comes from those intersubjective experiences with one's child where his or her nonverbal responses to the parent convey interest, delight, and joy. When, as an adult, one chooses to be a parent, that aspect of self—namely, self-as-parent—becomes central to one's core identity. The felt meaning of self-as-parent comes in major ways from the experience that a parent's child has of her as his or her parent. During those moments of the attuned dance between parent and child, *both* are being impacted deeply at the core of their sense of self.

During the breaks in the relationship the parent, it is hoped, will be able to experience the break with much less anxiety than does her child. The parent is likely to be more able to see the break as being temporary and having no relevance to the security of the relationship. However, these breaks will be more challenging for the parent if they represent for her features of her own attachment relationships with her parents that were unresolved. In that case the breaks may be experienced as a threat to the relationship and a threat to her experience of herself-as-parent. In this way attachment patterns are passed from generation to generation.

The meaning of these breaks is also likely to place both the parent and child at risk when the breaks are intense, frequent, and often unresolved. In those situations, both parent and child are likely to experience shame in association with the perceived threats to the relationship. It is in such situations that parents seek family treatment.

Thus, the clinician need not be surprised at the quality of defensiveness and resentfulness that both parent and child manifest when they arrive for the first appointment.

During intersubjective states the infant is being *experienced, not evaluated,* as being worthwhile and lovable. The parents are not sitting back and forming a judgment about their infant's worth. Within the intersubjective state they are *discovering* his or her worth, delightfulness, resilience, and unique, meaningful qualities. These qualities are within the child and the parents are simply discovering and responding to them. Thus, they are not giving their child these qualities that they could just as easily take away. These qualities are innate to the child and discovered within the parents' loving gaze, not added to the child as a gift by the parents' love.

Infants who have parents experience and discover their innately positive qualities are profoundly different from infants whose parents evaluate them as being lovable. In describing how infants discover themselves in their parents' eyes, we often fail to focus on this act of discovery and instead focus on how important it is for infants that they see these positive qualities in their parents' expressive eyes. The crucial question is how the infant's characteristics found their way into the parents' eyes. Most parents have no choice in the matter when they are intersubjectively present with their infant. They perceive their infant as they experience their infant as he is giving expression to his inner life. They are not evaluating the infant and giving him or her qualities based on their judgment and their needs. The qualities emerge from the child, rather than being imposed on him or her. This is not to say that parents do not "step back" and reflect on their infant and "evaluate" him from a more distant perspective. Rather, it is to emphasize that even such reflections are secondary to the primary knowledge of their infant which is experiential. Also, their infant's primary experience of self emerges intersubjectively, rather than from his parents' more reflective, secondary knowledge of him, unless that knowledge affects their intersubjective experience.

Since infants' emerging sense of self is being discovered by their parents, rather than being presented to them by the parents, they are free to give expression to who "they" are, continuously discovering qualities of "themselves" being reflected by the significant people in their lives as well as by the effects of their initiatives on objects. Infants' sense of self is not endangered by others' evaluations—others do not define their worth. They are inherently worthwhile and when others are not able to "see" those positive qualities in them, there is a deficiency in others' vision, rather than in the infants.

During the second half of the first year infants are increasingly interested in learning about the world. This knowledge too comes primarily from their experience with their parents and has been referred to as Secondary Intersubjectivity (Trevarthen, 2001). Children's parents are continuously giving meaning to the objects and events in their shared world and communicating these meanings nonverbally to their children. If parents respond to a stranger with fear, the stranger is experienced as being fearful to the child. When toddlers see something that makes them curious, they will often point to it or bring it to the parents to see how they respond to it. When children are doing something new, they will often look to their parents to see if they think that the children's actions will lead to something pleasant or unpleasant. Particular events and objects that parents most notice and respond to become the objects and events that infants are most likely to notice and respond to. The particular aspects of these events and objects that are most relevant to parents are likely to become most relevant to children.

As with primary intersubjectivity, the meaning-making activity is a mutual one. The parent is not reflecting on the meaning of an object and presenting it as an accomplished fact to her infant. Rather, she is experiencing the object herself, then she is experiencing her infant's experiencing of the object, and she then begins to give expression to what both she and her infant seem to be experiencing. The two, parent and infant, are mutually creating the meaning of the object or event. While it may often be that her meaning making is the more dominant, the infant's contribution is always present as well. With the parent experiencing the object or event along with the young child, the child becomes more able to experience the object from various perspectives, with less fear, less shame, and is more able to perceive deeper meanings in the object and achieve a greater sense of mastery over it.

Through countless acts of primary and secondary intersubjectivity the infant and toddler are forming templates for their primary experiences of self and other, dogs and toys, new events and potential interests. These events and objects may or may not enter into the young child's subjective experience and to his or her emerging sense of self. If they do become part of the child's subjective experience, they may or may not become integrated with other subjective experiences. Whether they enter into the child's narrative with labels of "good" or "bad" will depend in large part on the intersubjective context in which he or she becomes engaged with them.

The cocreation of meaning does not stop when the child leaves infancy. Rather, the cocreation of meaning proceeds throughout the life span and becomes more complex and diverse. With words, child and parents are able to identify and express nuances of subjective experiences that were not accessible intersubjectively prior to the child's ability to use words. The focus of their intersubjective present can now extend much more easily into the past and future. As the parents use words to describe their own subjective experiences, the child becomes able to understand their state of mind more fully and accurately. Sharing inner states is often a never-ending interest of preschool children and their parents. With the success of each stage of developmental mastery the child is able to more fully approach these new mastered events in a more intersubjective manner. Also as children mature, they are exposed to an increasing number of people with whom they are very motivated to become engaged in meaning-making activities. As their sphere of safety extends outside the family, so too does their desire to be influenced by, and influence, others within intersubjective experiences extending into the community.

As children engage increasingly well in meaning-making activities, they begin to identify with the significant others in their lives, again beginning with their parents. They want to be like them, not just in behavior, but also in interests and values, beliefs and wishes, thoughts and feelings (Hobson, 2002). Children's identifications tend to be the strongest with their attachment figures. Within dyads that are characterized by attachment security, the individuals tend to be the most able to coregulate their affective states, to communicate nonverbally with the most precision, and to cocreate meaning the most comprehensively.

As children's identification with their attachment figures guides the organization of their experience and the meaning that they give to events, it also guides their developing skills and their ability to achieve mastery in their interactions with the world. These interactive states are at the core of children's "zone of proximal development," whereby their parents accept their current level and gently encourage them to further increase their abilities.

The reciprocal nature of meaning making is more clearly seen in the parent–child dyad as the child develops throughout childhood. The child and adolescent become increasingly able to differentiate their meaning-making activities from those of their parents. They are able to perceive that their parents have another perspective and they begin to know that their parents retains the child's worth whether or not they accept the parents' perspective. Children are able to enter their parents' subjective states and become like them, or they can emphasize differences between the children's state and the parents' state. When parents are able to recognize and accept these experiential differences between themselves and their children, they are facilitating their children's ability to integrate their needs for autonomy and intimacy. The children do not have to sacrifice their unique subjective experience in order to enter into intersubjective states with their parents. They are able to develop a coherent autobiographical narrative and still maintain attachment security. Given the nature of both phenonmena, there really is no other possibility.

Families who seek treatment frequently have difficulty accepting differences in meaning-making experiences. Differences in judgments, perceptions, feelings, and thoughts are often seen as inappropriate or wrong. Rather than accepting differences in each other's experiences, these differences are seen as being a threat to the relationship. Rather than simply evaluating behaviors, the self of the other in the dyad is often evaluated. Differences are experienced as a threat to the worth of the self or a sign of disrespect. At other times the meaning given to the motives of the other in the dyad is predominately negative. Efforts to clarify and understand the inner life of the other become secondary to judgments that are made in response to the behaviors of the other. Intersubjective experiences become infrequent and the individuals become more isolated, unsafe, and noncommunicative.

THE DEVELOPMENT OF A COHERENT SENSE OF SELF

Infants' subjective experiences, which primarily become organized within states of primary and secondary intersubjectivity, gradually form into an increasingly differentiated and hierarchically integrated sense of self. The integrated self is defined here as the comprehensive, coherent, continuous, and comprehensive organization of subjective experiences. With this definition, self is not a rigid entity, but rather an open, flexible, actively integrating, and unique creator of experiences through engagements with others as well as the objects and events of the world (Siegel, 1999). Attachment security and intersubjective states are the stem cells of subjective experiences that become organized into a coherent sense of self. The parents' subjective experiences of their child's nonverbal expressions of his or her inner states, cocreates the meanings of these expressions. This act of cocreation is not a one-time process. The meaning of events and objects is continuously being cocreated, created alone, and recreated again intersubjectively or alone. As self and other are increasingly differentiated within the parent–child dyad, on his own, the child is increasingly able to create circumstances of safety, repair breaks, regulate affect, and create meaning. However, it is important to stress that the child—and adult—is not fully alone. The presence of "virtual others" remains a part of one's experiences throughout the course of a lifetime.

In a fundamental way, attachment security and a coherent self are two sides of the same coin. Leading researchers describe the securely (or "autonomous") attached adult as having a coherent autobiographical narrative. Within attachment security, the child or adult is able to remain open to whatever event or object that she or he encounters, regulate or coregulate the affect associated with it, create or cocreate meaning from it, and integrate it into her or his autobiographical narrative. Events and objects become subjective experiences that become organized within the differentiation and integration of the developing self. They do not have to be denied or distorted. They do not threaten the sense of self with fragmentation or dissociation. As a result, the "self" is able to remain continuous, comprehensive, and organized in a coherent manner.

It is apparent from the above discussion that in the world of family relationships, there is no such thing as objective experience. There may be "objective" events and objects which are able to be measured in a standard manner. But the meanings of these events and objects, which change them into experiences, is always unique, always "subjective," and primarily created by intersubjectively means. When parents are able to recognize this psychological truth and place value on the uniqueness of their child's experience, they provide intersubjective experiences that demonstrate acceptance and curiosity about the meaning-making activities of their child. These parents do not discourage their toddler from having a subjective experience that differs from their experience. They make it clear in their intersubjective presence that there are a wide range of feelings, desires, attitudes, and intentions about many objects and events that are equally acceptable. By doing so, they are encouraging the development of a subjective self that is curious, open to new experiences, comfortable with differences, and ready to create and cocreate meaning from the events and objects that pass before one. (There are certainly some necessary behavioral limitations that parents must apply to specific objects and events. While limiting the behavior, the parents are still well advised to grant their child the freedom to develop his or her own unique meaning regarding that same object or event.)

In summary, I wish to emphasize the enormous importance of attachment security and intersubjective experiences in the psychological development of all members of the family, and especially the child. The impact of these twin experiences permeates the child's physical, affective, behavioral, cognitive, and social development. When they are compromised, all aspects of the child's development are placed at risk. Each parent's sense of self may also be compromised, especially with respect to her identity as parent, which is central to her own autobiographical narrative. The goal of this model of family treatment is to restore the "joyful dialogic companionship" (Trevarthen, 2001), which was more likely to have been present within their relationships during the early years. The goal is to openly gaze beneath the behavioral difficulties being expressed within and among the family members. The goal is to discover together the core, reciprocal, intentions that lie under the difficulties, to accept these intentions, and to communicate with each other in ways that facilitate understanding, empathy, and interactive repair.

PART II

APPLICATION

Chapter 2

FAMILY TREATMENT:
AN OVERVIEW

Communication involves affecting and being affected by someone else. The transaction involves the transmission of feelings, thoughts, or whatever between two minds. Therefore sharing—and, if my argument is correct, sharing implicates feelings—is at the root of all communication and all intentions to communicate. —P. Hobson, The Cradle of Thought (2002)

The concepts of attachment and intersubjectivity have been slow to enter the field of family therapy. Attachment theory itself has not been applied in many areas nearly to the extent that would be expected from its deep and comprehensive research base. Intersubjectivity, with its frequent focus on the dyad, has a more natural fit with individual psychotherapy. The relationship between two partners, between parent and child, or between therapist and client often serves as the template for our understanding of this experience. It is hard to engage in reciprocal eye gaze with more than one person at a time, yet the intersubjective experience is not restricted to the dyad. All present within the parent–child–therapist triad are able to engage in inter-subjective experiences as well.

The therapist models her stance with the child or parent on the attuned interactions that occur between a parent and infant or toddler. It is an active, affectively varied, dyadic interaction that interweaves moments of affect and reflection. The basic therapeutic stance involves acceptance and curiosity, empathy and playfulness. This stance applies to the client's initiatives and responses, to his resistance and to his deep engagement. The therapist's intersubjective presence is always available as the therapist follows and leads and follows, exploring confidence and fear, doubt and certainty, pride and shame. Again and again the therapist is coregulating emerging affect, developing with those present more coherent representations for these poorly integrated affective states, and establishing a common meaning now accessible to those present. Again and again the therapist is repairing the relationship as needed so that the intersubjective process can continue to flow and produce its therapeutic effects. The therapist's active engagement in the intersubjective process guides the members of the family into the same process with her and with each other. She strives to remain intersubjectively present with all members of the family, together or separately, while focused on themes that have prevented the family members from being intersubjectively present with one another at home.

ATTACHMENT

According to John Bowlby, the father of attachment theory, the role of the therapist is similar to a mother "who provides her child with a secure base from which to explore" (1988, p. 152). Bowlby goes on to elaborate:

> This means, first and foremost, that he accepts and respects his patient, warts and all, as a fellow human being in trouble and that his over-riding concern is to promote his patient's welfare by all means at his disposal. To this end the therapist strives to be reliable, attentive, empathic, and sympathetically responsive, and also to encourage his patient to explore the world of his thoughts, feelings, and actions not only in the present but also in the past. (p. 152)

The fundamental reason for attachment behaviors—a feeling of safety—is continuously insured by the therapist and it applies to all participants of the treatment session. Most often when the family comes for treatment none of its members is feeling safe. The parents are likely to be experiencing a sense of failure in this central aspect of their identities as adults. They are anticipating that they will be judged negatively and blamed for any problems that their child may be manifesting. They fear that they will be told that their child's difficulties are either being caused by their behaviors or that their inability to solve the problems demonstrates a clear parental deficiency. The children also are not likely to feel safe. They are likely to have been told that they are all going to family treatment because of their behaviors. If it were not for their "problems" there would be no need for treatment. They are likely to fear that the therapist will find fault with them and tell them to change their behaviors in a manner similar to what their parents may have been saying.

The therapist's first task is to facilitate a sense of safety among all members of the family. To be more specific, she first establishes safety with the parents, and then she and the parents jointly provide safety for the children. Her intention is similar to that held by therapists throughout the field, whether it be called "joining," "engaging," "developing an alliance," or "relationship building." This intention at its core is to enable everyone in the session to feel safe. The family therapist facilitates this sense of safety in the following ways:

1. She maintains an attitude of relaxed engagement that includes the qualities of playfulness, acceptance, curiosity, and empathy (PACE); see Chapter 3. Safety is immediately enhanced when the family members experience this nonjudgmental foundation along with a very clear commitment to understand each person's narrative and to coregulate any emerging stressful affective states while assisting in reorganizing the experiences associated with these states so that they become less stressful.

2. She reduces ambiguity about her intersubjective experience of all members of the family by openly communicating her empathy and interest nonverbally with her facial expression, voice tone, gestures, posture, touch, and timing of response. She is making clear the impact that the family members are having on her. This impact is overwhelmingly positive. If a family member is having a negative impact on her, then her intention will be to get to know that person at a deeper level that will elicit a positive response from her. By communicating clearly where each person "stands" with her, the therapist is reducing the ambiguity that often generates anxiety.

3. She matches the vitality of the affective expressions of the members of the family, creating for each a sense of being deeply understood.

4. Her intention is to understand the respective experiences of every member of the family. A related intention is to communicate that there is no "right" or "wrong" experience. All experiences are valid, all will be heard. A third intention is to assist the family in creating a safer place for the expression of all experiences so that differences between experiences may be understood, resolved, or integrated into their joint narratives.

5. She demonstrates clearly that she respects the basic values and traditions of the family that reflect its cultural, national, religious, racial, and generational heritage. If she perceives difficulties within or between family members she will openly ask how these difficulties might be addressed within the framework of their heritage.

6. She provides basic information about attachment and intersubjectivity theory, child development, and family process so that this information will help members of the family to understand the reasons for her interventions and recommendations, as well as help them to anticipate "what's coming next."

7. She develops a sense of safety for the parents first, so that together they can provide safety for the children. She addresses openly the shame and doubt that they are likely to feel upon seeking family treatment and opens a space where she—and they—are able to experience their strength as parents, including their motivation to provide for the needs of their children.

While it is necessary for the therapist to provide a sense of safety for both parents and children, this does not reduce the parents' need to provide a similar sense of safety for their children. Throughout the family sessions, the parents need to remain the attachment figures for their children. In the area of attachment, the relationship between parent and child remains one-directional. The child turns to the parent for safety, not vice versa. While the intersubjective process is reciprocal, the parent's intention must include a commitment to insure the safety of their child, whereas a similar commitment is not expected from the child. (When a child is frequently worried about the well-being of the parents, the therapist is likely to address this worry.)

This reality—that attachment behaviors associated with safety are one-directional—is addressed with the parents alone at the onset of the treatment. It is presented as being a central feature of the parental role that includes providing both physical and psychological safety for their children. The therapist will be explicit that her role will be to both provide a sense of safety for parent and child in the session and also to facilitate the parents' ability to provide a sense of safety for their children.

As was stated in the last chapter, once individuals feel safe, the reciprocal nature of intersubjectivity becomes more active and evident. They are much more likely to begin to explore each other or a separate event through their joint perspectives. Such explorations generate the greatest amount of discovery when they are intersubjective. The success, in turn, of these intersubjective explorations facilitates a sense of safety between and among those who are engaged with one another in this manner. Within intersubjective experiences each knows/is known, feels/feels felt, senses/is sensed, gives/receives. Each of these dyads generates increased psychological safety in the presence of the other. While the intersubjective "figure" is primarily the experiences of the family members—separately or together—the "ground" of the therapist's experience is always present as well.

Safety for "everyone" also includes the therapist. For her to feel safe she needs to begin to make progress toward getting to know the individuals and the family system and to establish a rhythm within the session so that she is able to feel confident as the "conductor" of the symphony. She also needs to discover effective ways of being with each and all the members of the family, separately and together. If she experiences dysregulating anxiety, anger, hopelessness or shame in the session, her stance is likely to be compromised so long as she remains in those affective states. She will be less able to provide an attuned response and coregulate the affect of the family member(s). Her dysregulated affect is likely to cause all members to be more anxious. Not feeling safe, her ability to reflect on the treatment experience is likely to be restricted or distorted. Her openness to whatever verbal or nonverbal communications are being expressed may be limited.

The following factors represent how safety issues can be addressed throughout the course of treatment.

1. Children's functioning often reflects a lack of a felt sense of safety. Examples of this will be presented to parents prior to the onset of treatment. The attitude of PACE will actively facilitate the child's and parent's sense of safety during the sessions. The family will learn through the intersubjective experiences of the treatment session how to maintain this sense of safety while addressing conflicts and various states of shame. This is especially addressed in Chapter 3 on "PACE."

2. Parents do not feel safe when interactions with their child activate unresolved issues from their own attachment history. The nature of this process will be presented to the parents and their attachment history will be explored. When aspects from their history become activated in their present family relationships, they will be addressed. This is explored in Chapter 5, "Treatment Onset."

3. Certain child-rearing principles, influenced by attachment theory, facilitate a child's sense of safety. These principles will be shared with the parents first and then with the entire family. These principles will be explored in Chapter 5, "Treatment Onset."

4. The affective state of shame greatly undermines one's sense of safety. Information regarding shame and guilt will be presented to family members, and when shame is evident in the session it is identified and responded to within the framework of PACE. This is explored in Chapter 7, "Managing Shame."

5. Breaks and repair is a crucial sequence that will occur frequently throughout successful treatment sessions. Families who seek treatment will often experience considerable difficulty integrating conflicts, misattunements, discipline, and differences into the continuity of their relationships. Family therapy itself will, at least in part, be focusing on these relationship breaks and in so doing is likely to activate a here-and-now break within some of the relationships. The therapist needs to identify these breaks and initiate interactive repair whenever they occur. She will be facilitating the family's ability to repair similar breaks when they occur at home. This process is explored further in Chapter 8, "Breaks and Repair."

6. If the therapist is not able to consistently feel safe herself during the session, due to either treatment failures that elicit shame or

else to activated, unresolved, issues in her own attachment history, she will address this through reflection, supervision, or psychotherapy for herself.

INTERSUBJECTIVITY

While Bowlby does not use the term *intersubjectivity* in describing the role of attachment and communication within therapy, his description of the process is quite similar to what I am proposing for this model of family treatment. He places the emphasis on the therapist being more in the role of "a companion for his patient in the latter's exploration of himself and his experiences," and "less on the therapist interpreting things to the patient" (1988, p. 151). He further stresses what I would call the intersubjective reciprocal nature of the interactions between the therapist and patient:

> There are, in fact, no more important communications between one human being and another than those expressed emotionally, and no information more vital for constructing and reconstructing working models of self and other than information about *how each feels towards the other* . . . Small wonder therefore, if, in reviewing his attachment relationships during the course of psychotherapy and restructuring his working models, *it is the emotional communications between a patient and his therapist that play the crucial part.* (pp. 156–157; emphasis added)

When Bowlby is stressing the importance of "how each feels towards the other" and "emotional communications between a patient and his therapist," he certainly is questioning the role of a "neutral stance" in therapy, and he is asking therapists to consider the value and ways to communicate, how they "feel towards" their client. Allan Schore, who brings a neuropsychological perspective to Bowlby's theory, states that "deficits in subjectivity and intersubjectivity are repaired in therapeutic contexts that optimize intersubjective communication and interactive regulation." (2005, p. 835).

Intersubjective experiences are certainly able to be initiated and maintained across three people's minds and hearts, just as they are across two, or even four or five, or a symphony! The intersubjective

45

triad is frequently present when the therapist is reciprocally engaged with two or more of the family at the same time. At other times the focal intersubjective experience may exist within a dyad, while others present are participating within the background (a dyad within a triad). The other(s) are also sharing the same affective state, joint attention, and congruent intentions of the dyad. Within a triad or a dyad-within-a-triad it is often the rhythm of the voices, more than the eyes and facial expressions, that provides the level of coherence necessary to hold all members of the triad in the same intersubjective space. The metaphor of a symphony in describing this process remains quite appropriate.

The intention of psychotherapy—whether individual or family—is to create experiences in the present that will influence experiences from the past and generate hope for more healing and integrative experiences for the future. There is nothing more suited for this endeavor than is intersubjectivity. Within intersubjectivity, the therapist—from a position of safety—strives to join her experience of each person with the person's experience of self. In so doing she is influencing the self-experience and being influenced by the other, and cocreating a new experience of self (primary intersubjectivity). The client's new experience of self includes features such as courage, honesty, resilience, openness, delight, compassion, persistence, competence, and a motive toward health that were discovered by the therapist through the impact that the person was having on her. Discovered by the therapist, these features can now be seen and experienced by the client. Within family treatment, when the therapist discovers these features in one member of the family, the other members are also likely to experience those same features within their child, parent, or sibling.

As this state of primary intersubjectivity deepens, and with it the experiences of safety and openness to discovery, the therapist invites the attention of the client to go toward the events of the past (secondary intersubjectivity). She experiences those past events—in the present—with the client conveying his experience of those same events. She is now with him, in the past, experiencing those events with him. She is now able to coregulate any affect associated with those events. Being together reexperiencing the past events, the events are certain to contain less fear and less shame. The events now hold another perspective, new meanings can be cocreated, and the client is able to acquire an emerging sense of mastery of the event.

As this experience of secondary intersubjectivity deepens, the client's original dysregulating or traumatic experience starts to dissipate and the client begins to experience it again through the experience of the therapist. Within the safety that the therapist's experience of the event generates, the client begins to autonomously reorganize the experience of it again. In so doing, the client is able to hold the therapist's experience along with his or her new experience, so that the emerging meaning of the event is being cocreated.

This new meaning—without the prior affective states of fear and shame and with the new intersubjective perspective—is able to be assimilated into the person's autobiographical narrative. It is an event now, like other events that influence the development of one's narrative. It is able to influence and be influenced by these other events and in so doing the overall narrative becomes more coherent.

I wish to now turn my attention to the three qualities of intersubjective experience—matched affect, joint attention, and congruent intentions—which exist within each treatment session, with the therapist being an active participant in the dyad or triad.

Attunement

*First, matched vitality affect—or attunement—*among those present is necessary in order to facilitate an intersubjective matrix within the family session. It becomes possible to develop new meaning of the event because the intersubjective experience that is being attended to involves two or more matched states of affective vitality. This provides the child or parent with the ability to coregulate the emerging present vitality affect associated with the categorical affect of the past event. Alone, while being frightened or ashamed, the individual most likely was not able to sufficiently regulate the intensity of the experience, and hence was not able to give the event a subjective meaning that could be truly integrated into the self. The event existed in a frozen place in the person's mind, which placed the narrative at risk for becoming fragmented and incoherent. The flow of matched affect is central to moving frozen memories into intersubjective experience. The affect is being coregulated and the event is being more fully experienced. It is able to enter the person's narrative in a coherent manner for the first time. As this is happening, the narratives of those present are also being affected. The therapist is clear, not ambiguous, about her affective/reflective experience of both the individuals and the event. If there is a lack of clarity in therapeutic intention, the family member, though in the therapist's office and removed from the original event by time and space, is still attempting to regulate the affect and construct the meaning of the event alone. Ambiguity does not facilitate the joint process of coregulation of affect and cocreation of meaning.

Attending to the Same Event/Object

Second, within the intersubjective experience the family members and therapist are *attending* to the same event (or object) and one or more of their experiences of it. Together they are focusing on that event from their unique perspectives. The multiple perspectives provide different ways of experiencing the same event, making it clear that the experience of the event is not the same as the event itself. It is equally clear within intersubjectivity that there are as many ways of experiencing that event as there are subjective presences. Experience itself becomes experienced as an active, constructive process that one's consciousness brings to an event. Emerging meanings are a result of the cocreation of the meanings of the event during the intersubjective activity. In this way, for example, an event that was originally felt alone by the child as traumatic, may now be experienced with the therapist and parent as being stressful. An event that had been experienced by a parent as shameful, is now experienced with the therapist, the other parent, and the child as being a mistake that can be corrected. This is possible because when we focus our intersubjective attention on an event this enables each participant to create new meanings about the event through the recognition and possible integration of the various ways of experiencing it.

It is important to stress that in therapy the primary focus of attention is not on the event itself, but rather, the client's experience of the event. In this way their respective experiences are being reorganized, new meanings of the event are able to be cocreated by all, and the event as experienced by each is now able to be welcomed into each member's narrative.

Congruent Intentions

The *third* quality of intersubjectivity is *congruent intentions*. The therapist and family may, for a time, share joint attention and affect, but if their intentions in engaging in this intersubjective experience are not congruent, then the experience will be incomplete and brief. At some level of awareness, the therapist and family need to jointly communicate that their intentions are congruent. When the therapist is intending to work with the family in understanding an event, the family needs to be intending to work to understand the event also. If the therapist intends to communicate that she completely accepts and is curious about the family's experience, at some level of awareness the family needs to accept and be curious about the same experience. If the family fails to do so, the therapist's acceptance and curiosity do not enter into the intersubjective experience. The family may fail to do so because the therapist did not make her intention clear and the family failed to recognize it. Or the family may fail to do so because, though recognizing the therapist's intention, one or all of them did not want to accept it fully.

The intention of the therapist is crucial in determining whether or not the family will enter into the intersubjective experience with her. If the therapist's intention is to help the child to solve particular problems, such as angry outbursts directed toward his or her parents, many children will refuse to match the therapist's intention with a complementary one that accepts such help. If, instead, the therapist's intention is simply to understand the child's inner life of affect and thought, combined with an intention to enter into a dialogue about this inner life, the child may have a complementary intention of helping the therapist to understand him by communicating with her about his inner life. The former intention—to solve a particular problem—may be experienced by the child as an effort to "fix" him, and to participate would mean that the child agreed that he needed to be "fixed." The latter intention—to understand through dialogue the child's inner life—is more likely to be experienced by the child as being much less threatening. The same holds true for the parent.

How is change facilitated, if the therapist's primary intention is not to facilitate change? *Personal and family development* (a more accurate term than *change*) occurs because the intersubjective experiences of reciprocal enjoyment, acceptance, curiosity, and empathy inherently facilitate such developments within the human being. The therapist trusts that the intersubjective process of therapy—in a manner similar to the intersubjective process of the parent–child relationship, or the reciprocal attachment relationships between adults—will facilitate development within the members of the dyad or triad. If the intersubjective process is active, the therapist will also experience personal or professional development. "Change" is certainly the intention that lies on the distant horizon. The immediate intention is simply to coregulate the present affective states and to cocreate new meanings of the events being explored.

The intersubjective dialogue being described necessarily involves both the heart and mind of all participants (*all* includes the therapist). This dialogue is both affective and reflective and it is expressed nonverbally and verbally. It is integrated as both implicit and explicit awareness into our sense of self. The continuity of our self over time becomes our autobiographical narrative. Throughout the remainder of this book I will speak of intersubjective dialogue as affective/reflective (a/r) dialogue. In all such dialogues, the therapist is fully engaged with the family members both nonverbally and verbally. She is assisting in the reorganization of experiences through the coregulating affect and cocreating of meaning. She brings the focus of the dialogue from the past into the present and back again. She communicates nonverbally and verbally her unwavering intention to accept, try to understand, and have empathy for the events of the family members' lives, how they experienced these events, and the effects of these experiences on their sense of self and their historical narrative. Throughout the course of treatment, she allows this intersubjective experience to have an impact on her also. If she fails to do so, the intersubjective experience does not occur.

Intersubjective a/r dialogue is not "just talking." This is not "the talking cure" but rather the "communicating cure" (Schore, 2005, p. 841). In fact language has been wrongfully thought to involve only rational discourse, concepts, and thinking (left hemisphere functioning). Actually, certain components of language—parts that are central to the therapeutic endeavor—are embedded with affect and require that the right hemisphere of the brain be dominant. These components include emotional words, humor, laughter, social discourse, metaphor, the organization of information at the pragmatic-communicative level, and voice prosody (Schore, 2005, p. 840).

COREGULATION OF AFFECT

In family treatment the therapist continuously tracks the nonverbal expressions of the members of the family in order to be aware of the intersubjective meanings—affect, awareness, and intentions—of those present. She is often likely to give verbal expression to what she observes and experiences in the other's nonverbal communications, and she encourages the other to also give them a verbal expression. By tracking the nonverbal, the therapist is insuring that the dialogue will not drift outside the intersubjective matrix. She is also insuring that the client's affective state will remain regulated while they jointly explore any stressful themes. Indeed, the essential role of intersubjectivity in regulating affect cannot be overstated (Schore, 2005):

> The essential biological purpose of intersubjective communications in all human interactions, including those embedded in the psychobiological core of the therapeutic alliance, is the regulation of right-brain/mind/body states. (p. 844)

The therapist's first intention in tracking the nonverbal experiences of all present is to be able to coregulate whatever affective states are emerging within the dialogues. If anyone in the session becomes affectively dysregulated, none of those present is likely to feel safe enough to proceed with the intersubjective exploration that represents the broader therapeutic goal.

As she resonates with the nonverbal expressions, the therapist is aware of each family member's gaze, facial expressions, gestures, and posture. She is aware of qualities of their voices—the inflections, latencies, rhythm, responsiveness, and vitality—as they tell their stories. She is aware of the presence or absence of touch and eye contact at various points as the story's themes emerge.

The therapist is aware that by far the best means of coregulating emerging affect is to match the vitality affect manifested by the other. All affective states have a nonverbal, bodily expression which, when matched by a similar nonverbal expression by the therapist, will make them more likely to be regulated by those involved in the dialogue. When the family member gives expression to a categorical affect such as anger, fear, sadness, or shame, the intensity of these affects may rapidly lead the person toward rage, terror, despair, or pervasive shame if she is left to manage the affective state alone. She is much less likely to feel alone in that state if the therapist is able to match the nonverbal, vitality of the expression of the affect. This occurs by matching the rhythm, intensity, beat, contour, shape, or duration expressed nonverbally by the person (Stern, 1985, p. 146). Through such matching, the person experiencing the intense affect feels the empathic presence of the therapist. By resonating with the vitality of the affect—and not being detached from it—the therapist is likely to be able to coregulate the affective state. When a person is joined with another who remains regulated affectively, that person is much less likely to become dysregulated.

An adolescent in family treatment may complain loudly, "What a waste of time! This isn't going anywhere!" Imagine if the therapist replies to his loud and quick beat with a soft and slow, "You don't sound very confident that this is going to help at all." The adolescent is likely to reply, even more loudly, "That's what I just said!" But if she matches the vitality of the affective expression while using the identical words, "You don't sound very confident that this is going to help at all!" The words are not nearly as important as her voice tone, inflections, rhythm, and intensity. If the voice prosody matches the adolescent's, he is much more likely to feel that he is understood and then continue in the dialogue.

Too often it is the categorical affect that is matched, along with the vitality. When the adolescent complains about therapy being a waste of time, his parents may become annoyed with him and complain in turn, "If you would approach this with a better attitude maybe we would get somewhere!" Or even the therapist may respond defensively, "I can't be much help to you if you don't tell us what you think about the situation" (though he just did tell them about the current treatment situation).

A similar matching needs also be present when the therapist is speaking with a parent. The parent may say, with exasperation: "It always seems to be me that has to change! Why isn't he being expected to change too?" A rational response might be, "But you're the parent and it will help your son the most if you model for him the best way to respond." Such a response is likely to leave the parent feeling isolated, judged, and possibly blamed for being "immature." An intersubjective response, given with matched vitality affect, would be something like this, "So you're feeling like you're the only one here that I'm asking to work at this! I'm sorry if that's the message that I've been giving you! Thanks for making that clear!" After a pause, the therapist might add, with less energy in her voice, "I think that you will find that I will be asking your son to do some pretty hard things here too. You both will, if I am to be able to have an impact on your relationship for the better." She might then communicate her acceptance of the parent's experience and invite further disclosures by adding in a relaxed and matter-of-fact tone, "If you still have that feeling over the next few sessions with your son, please tell me again. If you do, you won't feel comfortable here and I won't be being helpful to you or to him."

The therapist resonates with the overall bodily expressions of the family members as frightening or shameful stories emerge. She may then address these bodily expressions within the safety of their relationship, so that the parent or child may begin to achieve some integration of the theme which had lay hidden within this aspect of the body. I believe that when such bodily, affective, expressions emerge within attachment security and intersubjectivity, these core expressions of nonverbal (and possibly verbal) communication allow for true resolution and integration to occur.

If the therapist restricts her expression to a "professional" and detached tone, the person will feel less safe, more alone within the affect, and more likely to become dysregulated. By resonating with the bodily expression of affect—much like a parent does with a distressed infant—the client is likely to be able to remain affectively regulated and to begin to safely explore and reorganize the experiences, while then cocreating new meanings that are likely to be therapeutic. By fully expressing her own nonverbal responses that are emerging in response to the person's expressions of vitality affect, she is both creating the safety that comes from clarity but also facilitating, as well as deepening, the intersubjective experience.

These matched, nonverbal communications are necessarily here-and-now and enable the dialogue to remain experiential rather than drifting into an abstraction. They enable the therapist to safely anchor the dialogue in the present experience of the past memory that is being explored. They also enable the therapist to remain grounded in the client's response about the meaning of an event, rather than drifting into her own theory or projection.

THE COCREATION OF NEW MEANINGS THROUGH PRIMARY AND SECONDARY INTERSUBJECTIVITY

Providing experiences of primary and secondary intersubjectivity is a central way that parents influence the direction and quality of their children's development. Their child discovers who she is and how she exists in the mind and heart of her parents through the ways that she is having an impact on them. In turn, her parents discover themselves as parents through the impact that they are having on their child. Many qualities that emerge and are experienced together, intersubjectively, would often not be experienced alone. These include pride, vitality, hope, gratitude, joy, empathy, contentment, confidence, and affection. When their child experiences her parents expressing these affective states in her presence, she becomes aware that they are responding to qualities within her. They are not pretending, nor are they engaged in the "job" of being a parent. They experience deep positive states when with her, because of who she is, just as she experiences similar states with them because of who they are.

When families come to family therapy, not enough of the ideal meaning-making activities just described are likely to be present. More often the self-meanings that the child takes from his interactions with his parents include some of the following: bad, lazy, stupid, selfish, unlovable, boring, burdensome, mean, sneaky, and infantile. I am not suggesting that most parents tell their children that they have those characteristics. I am rather suggesting that after months or years of unresolved family conflict, many children come to those conclusions about themselves, and believe that their parents have those perceptions about them.

The children in treatment may hold a comparable list of adjectives to describe their parents: stupid, selfish, mean, unfair, not caring, not interested, and not involved. At times the children's perception of their parents has a quality of: "If you don't like me, I don't like you either." More often, the child's experience of his parents and self reflects his efforts to understand the meaning of their ongoing conflicts and joint unhappiness. It may also reflect his efforts to reduce the shame experienced within the self by blaming his parents.

Parents too, often develop a list of self-and-other perceptions regarding themselves and their child which are very negative and convey a sense of hopelessness. They fear that the child's symptoms or the family conflicts represent an external reality that is not likely to change. The meaning-making qualities of the parent–child relationship in a secure attachment are barely present. The meanings that are generated come from failures to understand the breaks so that repairs can be created. Often in family therapy, both parent and child are at risk for giving negative attributions to the intentions of the other. As they become vulnerable in family treatment, they also are likely to become aware of shame associated with these reciprocally perceived negative intentions.

Too often within families, stresses, conflicts, trauma, failures, or separations are not able to be adequately given intersubjective meaning that would enable these events to be integrated into the narratives of the family members. Without the cocreation of intersubjective meaning, the event remains at least partially outside of subjective experience. The memory of it elicits as much shame or fear as the event itself. The psychological reality, that the event may be experienced differently by different people, and that the experience of the event within one person can change over time, is now lost. The event has been banned from the intersubjective matrix. Within the mind, the event is neither receptive to development in the individual's narrative nor to how significant attachment figures experience that event. What meaning it has is a rigid copy of past events that also were not given comprehensive intersubjective meaning.

In family treatment, the therapist's task is to continually search under the presenting symptoms of the child, the parent, or their way of relating, and find new meaning for these symptoms. The therapist needs to create a sufficient degree of safety among all present so that they can enter into an intersubjective presence that coregulates the affect and cocreates meaning, while still being focused on the nature of the breaks and the lack of repair. The meaning that the family has given to the symptoms most likely is permeated with shame and associated anger, fear, and discouragement. The therapist needs to provide a context that will generate new meanings. The therapist will work to uncover deeper affective states, motives, and qualities in their relationship which lie under the shame. These qualities have long since been forgotten but reflect their reciprocal desire for love, support, safety, affirmation, mutual joy, sharing, and their fear of loss, rejection, and abandonment. When the therapist is able to uncover and facilitate communication about these meanings, transforming family development can occur. There is now hope that the dreams that were present when the parents and infant first gazed into each other's eyes, may actually be realized.

The active process of cocreating meaning that I am recommending would require that the therapist constantly fine tune her contribution to this process, just as the parent repeatedly repairs the intersubjective stance with her baby. The therapist continually observes the nonverbal and verbal response of the family to her meaning-making expressions, and then either modifies her expressions when they are not congruent with the family's response or else addresses the incongruent response. The therapist frequently asks a family member for his or her response to the therapist's expression, to assess to what extent the family member was perceiving qualities in the therapist that were not intended. The therapist clarifies the implications about her and about the relationship, and then offers empathy for the client if these implications elicit fear or shame or other stressful emotions.

The content of these intersubjective experiences, which are central to the meaning-making activity of therapy, are varied, unplanned, and often one-of-a-kind. The content involves a spontaneous, direct communication among the subjective selves of the child, his parent, and the therapist. In such communications, what makes the parent, child, and therapist unique individuals emerges, and what makes the therapeutic relationship a genuine relationship among such individuals also becomes clear. Within the context of such intersubjective experiences, the therapeutic relationship becomes its most transformative.

Central to the deepening of the intersubjective experience is the therapist's active curiosity about the family members' experience of the events of their lives. As she explores these experiences, frequently, what she discovers has a positive impact on her—an impact that she makes quite clear in her nonverbal and possibly verbal expressions. Often she discovers qualities in the parent's and child's experience that they seldom experienced toward the self or the other. These qualities include honesty, compassion, resilience, competence, courage, hope, trust, openness, and gentleness. At the same time, the therapist is experiencing herself experiencing the other. She often experiences herself as being accepting, curious, empathic, committed, confident, hopeful, and open to the intersubjective experience. When the therapist gives expression to these newly discovered qualities in herself and the others, the child and parent begin to discover them as well. This then often leads to hope, confidence, pride, joy, empathy, acceptance, and a renewed commitment to one another. The negative attitude present at the onset of the treatment is now often replaced by evidence of a developing positive one.

Throughout the course of the family treatment, the parents will be asked to take their cue from the therapist as they learn the art of intersubjective dialogue that will serve as the central activity of the treatment. They will learn, implicitly and explicitly, the nonjudgmental acceptance and curiosity that permeates all dialogue. They will note the nonverbal component to all dialogue. The therapist's face, voice, gestures, touch, timing, and rhythm communicate the accepting and curious stance in a way that words will never do. They will also experience the efforts to communicate empathy for their own and their child's affective experience of the dialogue. The therapist's empathy is coregulating the emerging affect. It enables the child and parent to stay in the experience much longer than if he or she were experiencing the associated affect alone or within a critical atmosphere.

The following example of affective/reflective dialogue demonstrates the dual intentions of both coregulating affect and cocreating meaning for the experiences being explored:

Therapist: (in a relaxed tone, flowing naturally from the previous dialogue about a less stressful theme) Susan (child), I was wondering what you think that conflict yesterday between you and your mom was about . . . when you both did some yelling and then seemed to just not talk to each other.

Susan: Why do we have to talk about that? It's over! (Affect of annoyance and reluctance to continue within the intersubjective dialogue, now that it is focused on that event.)

Therapist: I didn't think you'd want to, Susan! It is hard to think about! (with similar intensity and rhythm to Susan's expression of annoyance at this topic being introduced). Well, I was wondering about it because you two seem to get angry with each other in that way fairly often, and my guess is that you would both like to either not do it so much or figure out a way to handle it better. (There is no judgment about the cause of the "yelling," or that it is "wrong"; just that it might be making both of them somewhat unhappy.)

Susan: I wouldn't get mad if she didn't always let Rachel (her sister) do what she wants after saying no to me!

Therapist: Ah, I get it! No wonder you got upset! (matched vitality affect) I'm getting a sense already why you get so angry with your mom at times. It seems to you that your mom favors your sister over you! That would be so difficult for you if your mom does that! So difficult! If your mom does favor your sister, how come, do you think? How come she would do that?

(The therapist must now resist the temptation to get mom's side of the story, nor should she gather data on the "validity" of Susan's concern. This may be tempting to do but it quickly moves the therapist into the role of judge as to who was "right" or into problem solving about behavior without first understanding the subjective experience that led to the behavior and coregulating the associated affect. Such rational problem solving is often unsatisfactory to one or both members of the dyad. Instead, the therapist focuses on maintaining the flow of the dialogue, experiencing Susan's experience [joint attention], matching the vitality of the expressed affect, and following Susan's clear intention to be understood about why she is so distressed in these situations involving her mother. Shared intention: Susan's anger now has a broader framework for reflection, probably with better regulated—and less—fear and shame.)

Susan: I don't know! She just does! Why don't you ask her?

Therapist: But what is your guess, Susan? If she favors your sister . . . why does she?

Susan: She thinks that she's so good! She's so perfect! She never thinks that she does anything wrong and she always blames me.

Therapist: Ah! It seems to you that your mom thinks that your sister is never at fault and that you always are! That *would* be hard! If your mom does that I can see why you would be mad about it! Has it always seemed that way to you? Even when you were both much younger? (Therapist remains in Susan's experience, conveying empathy for the distress generated by her experience and trying to help to organize it more fully. Notice that the word *if* is used frequently.)

Susan: It seems that way to me. Ever since she was born it seems that those two have been really close and I've been left out. (Susan is going more deeply into the experience both affectively and reflectively. There is less intensity in her vitality affect and the rhythm of her speech is slower.)

Therapist: Oh, Susan, (clear expression of empathy for Susan's distress), how hard it has been for you, for so long . . . you say you've felt less close to your mom ever since your sister was born! So long . . . So that now if your mom says yes to your sister and no to you . . . it seems to you to be more proof of her spot in your mom's heart and your place outside of her heart. How hard that must be, Susan!

(Throughout this dialogue the therapist is joining Susan in her experience affectively, she is focused on the experience itself with increasing understanding about its associated meanings, with the clear intent of understanding Susan and supporting her efforts to be understood. These are intersubjective moments that will enable Susan to feel "felt" and feel understood, while understanding herself better and being more able to accept the emerging affects, even though they are more intense than they were before. She is now also more reflective about her experience and more ready to communicate it. The therapist has made it clear by her voice tone and facial expression that this new awareness is having an impact on her.)

Susan: You get used to it. (more quiet and resigned)

Therapist: I'm glad that you do, Susan, if you have to. (more quiet as well) Otherwise it would hurt so much! I wish you didn't have to . . . didn't have to get used to it . . . Have you ever shared this with your mom, Susan, have you ever told her what you just told me?

Susan: No.

Therapist: Would you be willing to take a chance and tell her? I think that I know what she would say, but I'm not sure, and anyway, it's important for you to hear her experience of what you just told us.

(The therapist has confidence in mom's readiness and ability to remain intersubjectively present for Susan or she would not make this suggestion. The therapist had previously spoken with her mother about the nature of intersubjective dialogue and given her some ideas about types of empathic responses she might make to such expressions by Susan.)

Susan: Mom, sometimes it does seem that way. Sometimes it just seems that you love Rachel so much that there is little left for me. That you are disappointed in me!

Mom: Oh, Susan, I am so sorry! (tears) If you feel that I love Rachel more than you. If you feel outside of my heart! Oh, honey! If that's what you feel I've done a poor job showing my love for you! I'm so sorry!

Susan: Maybe you love me, but I just don't feel it very much!

Mom: Then my love isn't doing you very much good, Susan. You need to feel it and I need to express it so clearly that you won't doubt it's there!

Susan: But why do you say no to me and yes to her?

Mom: I guess, when I do, I think that I'm doing what is best for each of you . . . that you are separate individuals. But if it seems that most of the no's are going to you I could see where you would think that most of the love is going to Rachel.

Susan: That's what it seems to me.

Mom: Thanks for having the courage to tell me honey! Can we work at this together? Can we find ways that I can show I love you when I'm saying no? Can we work to find ways to show you that you have a place in my heart too, that is as big as the place that your sister has?

Susan: Yeah, I'd like that.

Readers may think that it unrealistic to expect that parents will speak with such empathy and understanding. I hope to make it clear throughout the remainder of this book that parents can, and do, often speak in similar ways when they feel safe, when various obstacles to such communications are addressed, and when the therapist serves as a model for the parents in such expressions.

Once the therapist is able to get the intersubjective quality of the dialogue going, it often is much easier for the family members to continue it. This a/r dialogue relates to whatever experiences are being presented, meandering through the routine, to the unusual, to the humorous, and to the stressful. When the dialogue wanders into experiences that are associated with fear or shame, the rhythm and momentum that is present often carries the dyad into these experiences with a felt sense of safety that is sufficient to welcome them into the narratives of those present. When they wander off, the therapist just returns the focus to the experiences, clearly communicating that they are never "right" or "wrong." When we can have empathy and nonjudgmental curiosity about the experiences of the other, the resulting "being-together-within-the-experience" becomes a safe place for all. Whatever problem solving may still be needed is often now easy to achieve.

Chapter 3

DEVELOPING PLAYFULNESS, ACCEPTANCE, CURIOSITY, AND EMPATHY (PACE): THE CENTRAL THERAPEUTIC STANCE

Compassion, at least, allows a little distance from the pain. Empathy is a far more dangerous personal experience. Empathy requires that we vicariously experience *the trauma that our patients have survived. —Sandra Bloom,* Creating Sanctuary

The therapeutic stance, representing the therapist's overriding attitude in attachment-focused family therapy, is central in facilitating transformative intersubjective experiences. It is characterized by the four traits of playfulness, acceptance, curiosity, and empathy (PACE). Within this stance, "moments of meeting" are still spontaneous and unpredictable, but they are likely to occur more frequently. This stance activates the intersubjective experiences which can enable the members of the dyad or triad to have a transformative impact on one another. This stance enables those present to discover qualities in self, other, and the relationship which are likely to be not only welcomed but prized.

This stance requires that the therapist's affect is regulated. By "regulated" I do not mean "neutral" or "well-controlled." By "regulated"

I am referring to how when the therapist is resonating with whatever affect is being experienced and expressed by her clients, she remains able to respond in an organized and flexible manner, integrating all of her affective, reflective, and behavioral states. The affect may be exuberant and dramatically expressed. It may convey deep sadness for the distress of the family members. It may range from deep laughter to quiet tears, containing various expressions of joy or grief, as she joins the experiences of the family members. As she meets her client(s) and takes her seat, her intention is to assist the family. This intention soon fades away to the distant horizon because her emerging intention is to meet her client(s) in the present, and to be available for the intersubjective acts of coregulation of affect and cocreation of meaning.

Playfulness, acceptance, curiosity, and empathy are central in the early dance of affect and meaning that we experience with an infant, and in the similar dance that emerges within this form of treatment.

PLAYFULNESS

Playfulness may seem to some to be inappropriately placed within the core therapeutic stance that is being presented. When families come with memories of events associated with shame, fear, and conflict at the forefront of their attention and are motivated to reduce these states, they are not likely to initiate or even be very receptive to experiences of joint playfulness. Yet this attitude of playfulness leads infants into states of companionship with their parents from which they cocreate the meaning of their world. A playful stance is invariably associated with a sense of safety from which children are ready to reach out to the world again, affectively resonating with it, and coming to understand it within joint experiences of playful understanding with their parents. If the therapist is able to integrate a playful attitude into the treatment session it will often provide a way to realize that the stressful experiences are only one aspect of the ongoing relationship. They are able to take their place within a coherent family narrative. Playfulness may not be congruent with the a/r state of the family when they begin a session, in which case its expression would certainly be inappropriate. But over the course of the session(s), if treatment is effective, it is likely to become very evident.

Playfulness is not often spoken of in discussions of the therapeutic stance. Allan Schore (1994) stresses the need for therapy to facilitate positive affective experiences as well as addressing negative affective experiences. Trevarthen (2001) stresses the role of "dialogic joy" as being a central intersubjective experience that is crucial in the child's psychological growth.

Within the a/r dialogue about an aspect of the client's narrative, the therapist often experiences deep empathy for her client. Paradoxically, along with the empathy, the therapist and family may also experience the affective tone of playfulness within the dialogue. Playfulness enables all to step back from the primary affect associated with an event and to experience it from a somewhat different perspective and different affective state. The following represent various dimensions of the value of playfulness in the treatment session:

1. A playful stance shifts the a/r experience of the event to one that is lighter, bringing some helpful relief to the intensity of the primary stance.

2. Combining a playful stance with the primary a/r stance, both the therapist and client are able to sense that they are focused on experience—not any "objective fact"—and as a result become aware that there is more than one way to experience an event (Fonagy, Gergely, Jurist, & Target, 2002). Experiences are more open to being cocreated.

3. Within a playful stance, the therapist is able to convey an awareness that while a certain activity may be difficult for a client, the active presence of the therapist or parent will manage it. One would not be playful if there was a likelihood of failure.

4. An openness to playfulness enables the therapist and client to focus on other events as well as the "difficult" ones. While experiencing other events that are more likely to be experienced as humorous, casual, and light, the therapist and client are able to take a break from the harder work. The therapist is also conveying the belief that all experiences of the family members— not just the "problems"—are of interest to the therapist. Those present are unique, complex, individuals within a unique, complex family, they are not "cases."

5. Playfulness represents a move into positive affect which is then able to be coregulated. It is often forgotten that the child (and possibly parent as well) needs to develop her regulation abilities for positive affective states just as much as she does for negative affective states (Schore, 1994). The ability to autoregulate all affective states is a skill that emerges first within coregulation experiences.

6. For many clients playfulness is safer than are expressions of affection and caring. It also often has a place in early stages of the development of a relationship, before affection feels appropriate.

7. Within a playful stance, there is often less room for the affective states of shame or fear. It is a valuable means of coregulating these negative affective states.

Often playfulness is overlooked as being an important component of a comprehensive treatment stance. Its functions of regulating affect, facilitating the relationship, and providing another perspective on troubling events, are not well known. Playfulness should not be confused with anxious laughter or with humor that distracts from or minimizes the primary affective states because they are too difficult to bear. Such defensive humor may be used by the client or therapist when the intensity of the negative affect is too great for the therapeutic relationship to contain. Laughter then enables both to avoid the negative affective states. But playfulness, as defined here, does not avoid that state. Rather, it represents mindfully stepping back from it to take a rest from the difficult work or to experience an event in a different way.

This stance regarding playfulness is similar to that taken by narrative therapists focusing on childhood problems (Freeman, Epston, & Lobowitz, 1997):

> The price of choosing seriousness for us as therapists may be the dampening of our own resources, such as the ability to think laterally, remain curious, be lighthearted enough to engage playfully with the child, and have faith that the situation is resolvable. (p. 3)

They speak further about the benefits to the child of a playful approach: "When the adult enters into a playful interaction with a child, the child's competency and creativity expand" (p. 4).

As mentioned earlier, Colwyn Trevarthen (2001) has described intersubjectivity as reflective of the infant's innate need for "joyful dialogic companionship." He speaks of how the infant and mother engage in increasingly animated and lively, contingent, playful interactions that carry the infant's interest and create meaning in his developing world. Without the rhythmic positive affective tone, the infant's active participation in the dialogue begins to weaken. Seeing his mother's joyful face and hearing the music of her voice, the infant easily becomes engaged in a reciprocal manner, and takes a part in cocreating their joyful "moments of meeting."

In a similar manner in treatment, even when much of the focus is on negative affective states, when the child and parent are able to experience mutual enjoyment with the therapist, their sense of self-efficacy is enhanced. The therapist truly enjoys them, is responsive to their expressions, and resonates with the positive qualities within them that lie under behavioral problems or symptoms. The therapist resonates with her experience of the child or parent's courage, honesty, willingness to be vulnerable, desire for connection with child/parent, hopefulness, willingness to laugh at oneself, desire to understand, and also a wish to create a more reciprocally meaningful family. When the therapist asks the child or parent to "jump into" a vulnerable state with her, she may smile with a "whatever happens, we'll get through it together" attitude that often has a light, even playful tone. From a playful affective state, one often moves more easily into an affect of sadness and vulnerability.

In the following example, the therapist employs playfulness in response to a child's comment that might have been motivated by anxiety or anger in the 10-year-old boy, Sam. The therapist was sitting on the couch, with the boy sitting between the therapist and his mother. The therapist had introduced a dialogue with Sam about some of his difficulties:

Sam: You have bad breath. (with some annoyance and a small smile)
Therapist: What are you saying?
Sam: You have bad breath.
Therapist: (with a smile and a hint of indignation) What's your point?
Sam: Don't sit so close to me (and probably also, "Don't talk about this").

Therapist: I need to so I can understand you better . . . get to know you better (with some playful suggestion that there was nothing else that she could do).
Sam: Well you have bad breath. Sit further away.
Therapist: I can't Sam! I got to get to know you better! But tell you what . . .
Sam: What?
Therapist: You make it a bit easier for me to get to know you and I'll put a mint in my mouth! (big smile)
Sam: Yuk!
Therapist: And one for you too.
Sam: OK. (smiles)

The therapist goes back to the dialogue about the difficulties and Sam becomes more engaged than he had been before. After about 10 minutes the therapist went to her desk and returned with a mint for both Sam and herself. They both smiled.

At the onset of the next session, Sam sat on the couch closer to the therapist than he usually did. He then leaned over and said, "Hi!" with a big smile. In the car on the way to the session, Sam had chewed on a piece of garlic. The therapist laughed and screamed, jumped up, and ran out of the room to the restroom. When she returned, Sam was having difficulty controlling his laughter. His use of playfulness demonstrated that he had thought about the therapist between sessions and that he was more willing to enter into other affective states with the therapist as well.

By utilizing playfulness the therapist is not avoiding discussions about difficult themes. Rather, she is helping the client to regulate his anxiety, she is taking a break from the stressful work, and she is adding a bit of shared positive affect to their intersubjective experience. From her playful stance, she is perceiving core aspects of the selves of the parent and child and she is responding to her experiences of them. Her responses elicit self-states from the parent and child that are characterized by a sense of being valued, along with shared joy and hope. All three sense that their intersubjective experience will prove to be sufficient to resolve whatever problems are addressed.

At times progress is first evident when members of the family begin to express a playful attitude during the process of treatment. One 8-year-old girl had been participating in the treatment with some quiet compliance in response to the gentle, but persistent, questions about her inner life. She gradually moved from a position of compliance to one of mild resistance to the dialogue. At one point she directly expressed annoyance to the therapist over the continuing requests that she reflect on her motives. The therapist smiled and said, "How can you talk to me that way? I'm your therapist!"

She smiled in turn and replied with animation, "You're *not* my therapist. You're my *thera-pest!*" She, the family, and therapist all burst into laughter, after which she became more fully engaged in the treatment.

ACCEPTANCE

When the therapist first engages the family, she finds the rhythm of their presence and joins it. Affectively, she is congruent with their affective states (vitality, not categorical affect). She is attuned with them. When there are disharmonious rhythms within the family, she becomes aware of each, and when necessary joins each rhythm in turn, using the rhythm that is emerging within her to facilitate a harmony within the family members. This is all accomplished primarily through acceptance. She does not try to change any member of the family. She accepts the affective state of each. As each person experiences this degree of acceptance, his or her affective state begins to change. It becomes more regulated and then more able to remain present in the proximity of the states of the other family members.

With acceptance, the therapist is able to join the affective rhythms and bring some regulation to them. With curiosity, the therapist then, while maintaining the rhythm, begins to explore and develop the theme or themes that are running through the narratives of the family members at that time. The themes are clarified, elaborated, and any implications or associations are better understood.

The crucial stance of acceptance is implied or acknowledged in the work of Carl Rogers (1951), Les Greenberg (2002a), and Diana Fosha (2000), among many others. Marsha Linehan (1993) places it in a central role in her well-received cognitive-behavioral therapy for adults and adolescents with borderline personality disorder. It is central as well in acceptance and commitment therapy (Hayes, Strosahl, & Wilson, 1999).

Most of us, within our developing attachment relationships, hope deeply that we will be accepted as we are. Marital vows often include the phrase "for better or for worse." Until the quality of acceptance enters the intersubjective presence, the relationships maintain a distance and formality with an understanding that certain aspects of our narrative and certain intersubjective states are not ready to be expressed to each other. Acceptance communicates a commitment to the person and a confidence in who that person is. Without a sense of acceptance, fears of rejection and abandonment are not too far from awareness. Acceptance sees under the behavior and communicates that the relationship will remain regardless of the conflicts and separations. When there are breaks in the relationship, there is always a commitment to repair the break.

If a therapist expects her client to begin to give expression to, and allow exposure of aspects of his experience that are terrifying or shameful, she must repeatedly communicate her acceptance of the client, without conditions. Does that mean that she accepts every behavior that emerges in the treatment? Does she accept her client hitting her, breaking her lamp, threatening her, or swearing at her? No. Does it mean that she accepts her client's wish to hit her or break her lamp? Yes.

As a therapist, I believe, it is crucial to accept every aspect of the client's subjective experience that emerges during the treatment, apart from behaviors that are violations of the safety and integrity of the therapist or others. Certain behaviors may not be accepted, but the thoughts, feelings, wishes, fantasies, and intentions that led to these behaviors are always accepted.

Why is the experience of acceptance so crucial in therapy, as well as in attachment relationships in general? By communicating acceptance of the other's subjective experience, we are welcoming that experience into the intersubjective matrix. We are inviting clients to become aware of their experience and to share it with us. Clients' subjective experience is an aspect of their subjectivity, and thus is an aspect of their self. Each experience, by being accepted, is not being evaluated or judged, but is simply an aspect of the continuity of the client's self. The more the individual's experience is accepted, the more easily it can be integrated into his or her narrative. It will become one aspect of the uniqueness of the client's self. Because it is accepted by the therapist, it is in a position where it can lose its qualities of shame and terror. It can be understood for the experience that it was, without compromising the integrity of the self. It no longer needs to be defended against in the client's consciousness and affect. If it contained terror, it now may contain realistic fear, or no fear at all. If it contained shame, it now may contain realistic guilt, or no guilt at all.

By the therapist accepting the client's subjective experience, the way is now open for the client to also accept the presence of that experience in her narrative. It need not be distorted, minimized, or denied. Its meaning is now open to being cocreated. It is simply one aspect of the client's self, now open to becoming integrated into the narrative. Acceptance within the intersubjective experience greatly facilitates the individual's acceptance of her subjective experience. This is true in infancy and remains true throughout life.

All therapists recall times when the client's expressions of her subjective experiences were difficult to accept. Parents and children, too, often struggle to accept the subjective experiences of each other. The following statements may well fall into that category:

You're not helping me at all.
I don't care what you think.
You don't care at all about me.
This is such a waste of time.
You are clueless!
I don't want to live anymore no matter what you say.
I am just a waste of your time.
You can't help me.
You just want your money.
I'm not going to try anymore.
This is stupid.
I think I'm bad!
I don't care!
I don't want to talk about it!
You/she never lets me!
You just want me to be unhappy!
You/he is mean to me.
I don't know.
You/she thinks I'm bad.
Just leave me alone.
You/he make me so mad!

What makes the above statements difficult to accept? There are likely to be a variety of reasons. A central reason is that the above comments call into question the therapist's own sense of personal competence. The above statements suggest that the speaker is either describing a person and that person is incompetent, selfish, and worthless, or she is describing herself who is hopeless and beyond help, suggesting that the therapist is still incompetent because she cannot help the client. The person's statements, thus, may elicit shame in the therapist. If the client expresses herself with anger, the statements may also elicit anxiety or anger in turn, as the angry expression may elicit a response in the therapist similar to her response when other figures to whom she was attached, such as her parents, or who were attached to her, such as her children, were angry with her.

To reduce this response of shame, anger, discouragement, or anxiety, it may be helpful for the therapist to remember that statements such as those listed above, are not descriptions of fact. They do not define either the client or the therapist. They rather represent the client's subjective experience of herself, the therapist, or the therapy process itself. Being subjective experiences, and more than likely being quite relevant to difficulties in the client's narrative organization and affect regulation, they are opportunities for a quite valuable intersubjective exploration. After recalling that the client's expression represents a subjective experience, the therapist is in a better position to accept it. It is the client's experience of the therapist, it is not a fact about the therapist. It is then easier for the therapist to accept it and respond to it as she would any other subjective experience that the client expresses in verbal or nonverbal terms. The therapist needs to remember that parents are likely to have similar difficulties accepting the subjective experiences of their children. Parents may need assistance in remembering that their child's subjective experience may also not be objective fact.

The following dialogue presents an example of the communication of acceptance and its value in opening the way for curiosity and empathy or playfulness.

Client: You're not helping me at all.
Therapist: Thanks for telling me that. That must be hard for you . . . thinking that. How does that feel—if therapy is not doing any good?

Client: How do you think it feels—it's a waste of my time and money.
Therapist: Yeah, that's bad enough to waste your time and money . . . and you also are still left dealing with your problems . . . alone.
Client: That's nothing new.
Therapist: Yeah . . . what's that like for you, always feeling alone with everything bothering you?
Client: How do you think it is?
Therapist: I think it must be very hard to carry it all alone. Month after month, year after year.
Client: It is. But you get used to it.
Therapist: I wish you hadn't had to learn to "get used to it." What would it be like . . . do you think . . . if someday someone was able to help you with it . . . carry it with you.
Client: I don't have a clue.
Therapist: Would you wish that you could find out?
Client: If only.
Therapist: If only.

Such an a/r dialogue would be providing the client with the very experience that he was saying that he never had. Through accepting the original expression that she was not helpful, the therapist was able to provide an intersubjective experience that might be.

When the therapist clearly communicates empathy for a member of the family, at times the response is one of skepticism: "You really don't care!" To respond defensively is not likely to be of benefit to the treatment. To be effective, the therapist needs to convey a completely nonjudgmental acceptance of the person's communication. The focus is always on the experience being conveyed, not whether or not the therapist has the same experience. In these examples the therapist attempts to clarify and assist the client in reorganizing the experience by exploring various associated experiences from the past and present and by encouraging further elaboration on the original experience. The implied message is:

"You told me your experience that I don't care for you. Wonderful! That's what therapy is about and I cannot be of help if I don't understand your experiences, especially your experiences of therapy. Now would you help me to understand more fully your experience that I don't care?"

The following phrases represent a series of possible responses:

If you think that I don't care, that must be hard for you!
I feel sad that you experience me as not caring.
How does it feel to be with someone you don't think cares?
If I don't care for you, why do you think I don't?
What does it mean if I don't care?
How do you handle it, talking with someone you think doesn't care?
What do you do when you think someone doesn't care for you?
Do you have that experience with someone in your family/friend?
If you think I don't care, does it affect what you think about yourself?
Are there other times when you have the same thoughts about
  yourself?
How does it feel now talking with me when you think I don't care?
I do care for you, but am not communicating it well or you would
  sense it.
I am glad that you told me that you think that I don't care.
I worry that therapy won't be of help to you if you think that I
  don't care.

For these questions or statements to be helpful they need to reflect the therapist's experience, including his experience of vital curiosity. They cannot be memorized phrases brought out on cue or they will not be experienced by the client as being of significant value and will not facilitate an experiential response.

The therapist frequently needs to monitor the parents' readiness and ability to communicate acceptance of their child, whether or not they are correcting a given behavior. When the child does not sense acceptance, the response to the parents' behavioral challenge or discipline is likely to be much more intense and oppositional. Discipline with acceptance tends to be much more effective in reducing conflicts associated with the act of discipline. When a parent disciplines her child the degree to which she accepts his or her experience while limiting the behavior is often communicated by her tone of voice and facial expressions. If her voice and face convey strong annoyance and disappointment, the child will frequently experience the discipline as being directed at the self, rather than the behavior. If, instead, the parent conveys a more relaxed and matter-of-fact tone, separating the relationship from the act of discipline, the child often is able to regulate the affect associated with the discipline much more easily. He or she is then confident that the parent is responding to the behavior, not to the child and their relationship.

Often parental acceptance of their child breaks down when the parents want the child to behave in a certain way and the child fails to meet the expectation. When the attitude of acceptance leaves, the intersubjective dialogue quickly follows.

The following case presents that situation well:

A 14-year-old girl, Linda, had been adopted at age 4. From birth she had experienced significant neglect while living with her biological parents. Finally, at age 3, she was placed in a foster home and within a year she was adopted. She was a passive child, with little initiative, as well as few interests, and scant self-expression. She engaged in periodic indirect expressions of anger and more rare expressions of rage and threats primarily directed toward her adoptive mother. Linda's therapist had requested a consultation regarding ways to engage the child and her parents. The following exchange was central in the consultation and the recommended directions for further interventions.

Consultant: (After having explored her history to some extent and speaking very quietly about how hard things had been for her, Linda became tearful. The therapist continued to speak about her neglect and loss.) How difficult that must have been, your mom not knowing at all how to care for you . . . so sad . . . and confused . . . and lonely. And then moving to live with strangers . . . and you were just 3!

(The child has tears in her eyes and shows much sadness in her facial expression. She stares into the therapist's eyes, experiences her sadness, and maintains this reciprocal gaze for 15 seconds. She suddenly then laughs, seemingly from anxiety. With no judgment about her reasons for laughing the consultant gently asks her why she thought that she had laughed. Her adoptive mother then whispered something to the therapist and the child turned to her mother to see what had been said. Therefore the consultant asked her mother to tell them both what she had said.)

Mother: She always does that when it is getting too hard for her. (The tone in her voice, and probably the word *always* suggested a critical quality to the mother's subjective experience of her child.

Linda's mother was somewhat disappointed with her for not staying with the "hard" feeling. Linda immediately showed fear and then shame as she averted her eyes.)

Consultant: (Takes Linda's hand, trying to communicate acceptance of both Linda's laugh and her mother's experience of it. She then speaks quietly and with confidence.) Oh, Linda! I made a mistake and did not realize how hard it was for you! You needed a bit of a break and I did not notice. So you laughed, giving yourself a break. I am so glad that you did that. You were thinking and talking about some very hard things and you needed a break and I didn't notice. (Linda's tears are becoming more pronounced again.)

Consultant: (Now looking at Linda's mother, speaking more quietly while continuing to hold Linda's hand.) We don't know how hard Linda's life has been . . . and how hard it still is . . . we don't know . . . only Linda does . . . so, so hard . . . And we must never forget . . . how hard . . . and . . . how she is doing the best that she can. (Linda continues to stare into the therapist's eyes, tears rolling down her face, her body beginning to shake, noting the therapist's tears. After 10 to 15 seconds, the therapist smiles first and Linda smiles in return. Then Linda's mother, now able to accept that "she is doing the best that she can" hugs and comforts her.)

This example is a clear demonstration that the child's experience of past events needs to be understood and accepted before attending to the event itself. In this case, some of Linda's current resistance as well as her avoidant attachment style with her adoptive parents, was due in part to a sense of a lack of acceptance. Her initial years of neglect may well have made her very sensitive to experiences that she was a disappointment to others, and especially to her new parents. She needed to have it be acknowledged, again and again, that her life as a child was very difficult and that she was, in fact, doing the best that she could. When she needed a break from the distress associated with exploring her "hard times" she needed our understanding and acceptance. Once that was experienced intersubjectively, she would be more able and willing to continue her hard work toward making a coherent narrative and a more satisfying life for herself. At the same time she would be more able to turn to her parents for the comfort that she needed.

CURIOSITY

With curiosity the presenting and emerging themes are explored. The themes themselves then have an affective impact on the therapist. She experiences empathy or playfulness when encountering the family's narrative themes. The felt sense of the therapist's empathy often enables the family member to stay with a theme that is eliciting intense affect. With empathy, the person does not feel alone. He or she is able to go even further into the theme, cocreating new, more integrative meanings. With deeper understanding about the other's motives, family members are also likely to experience greater empathy for one another.

Curiosity most likely is assumed to be important in any school of therapy if only in its role in determining a working diagnosis and developing a treatment plan. Proponents of narrative therapy stress the importance of curiosity in coming to know the other's individual story. As described here, curiosity is a very affective act of joint discovery among those present that welcomes the introduction of new meanings into the narrative. Proponents of "mindfulness" are often describing a stance that combines qualities of both acceptance and curiosity.

Philosophers have wondered for centuries about the relationship between love and knowledge. They ask: "Is it possible to love a person without knowing that person? Is it possible to know a person without loving that person?" If knowledge and love are interwoven in our relationships, is it necessary for one to precede the other? Is it possible for one to precede the other, and if so, which one?

While the above questions may be an alternative to charades at a psychotherapists' party, they are a bit broad for the purposes of this work. For now, I wish to increasingly narrow our focus from cognition/affect to knowledge/love to curiosity/empathy. In this discussion, I hope to demonstrate that both curiosity and empathy are grounded in the intersubjective present. The therapist is attuned with and responsive to the emerging subjectivity of the child or parent. As the client gives expression to his or her subjective experience, the therapist is receptive to this experience in both cognitive and affective terms. She is curious about the experience and she experiences empathy for the client in the experience. As she explores the experience further with the client, she understands it more and more deeply. The deeper understanding makes way for a deeper capacity to experience empathy for the client. This deepening empathy, in turn, opens a window to understanding the experience even more fully. Curiosity is the cutting edge of empathy, while empathy leads curiosity into new depths.

The magic of intersubjectivity involves its ability to develop new subjective experiences for the past, present, and future events of our lives. With the deepening experience of the therapist's curiosity and empathy, the client is able to experience the past event in a different way. Intersubjectively, the therapist has traveled back in time, is able to experience the past event itself as well as the client's subjective experience of it, all of which enables the client to reexperience the event as if the therapist were actually present with him or her in the past, experiencing it together. The therapeutic process itself—a present event—also is experienced intersubjectively and becomes organized in a manner that includes the therapist's experience. Often the therapist is experiencing the family or individual member's courage, honesty, resilience, or competency. The therapist's experience of family members helps them to experience themselves in a similar manner.

Curiosity—radical curiosity—opens the way for the therapist to understand the client's subjectivity much more fully. Taking this understanding—in the context of radical empathy—the therapist may now enable the client to reexperience the event by the therapist coregulating the associated affect, and cocreating the new meanings that are developing. The child is no longer alone in trying to make the event—whether it had been stressful or shameful—a part of his autobiographical narrative. And now with both radical curiosity and empathy the therapeutic process comes to also include radical acceptance. The self, with all of the subjective experiences that have been intersubjectively welcomed into the narrative, is now able to find an acceptance that is more fully comprehensive and coherent.

Through curiosity the therapist is able to help make the incoherent, coherent, the inconsistent, consistent, and the discontinuous, continuous. Within curiosity, the therapist is asking to know more about the shameful or frightening experience of an event. She asks how that experience feels, what sense it makes, how it has changed the client, and what conclusions he or she has come to because of it. She further wants to know the implications emerging from the client's subjective experiences. How does the event affect the client now? Has it changed the experience of self? Has it made it more difficult for the self to participate in certain affective states, new experiences, or particular memories? Are there gaps in her subsequent experiences due to a particular past experience? Are her present experiences modified in certain ways? Does she minimize certain experiences and avoid others? Does she remain hypervigilant during other experiences? Again, what are the implications for the developing self? With curiosity, the therapist is able to assist the client in knowing more about himself. She can assist the client in discovering aspects of subjective experiences hidden in past events that were not accessible before. The child or parent may have had only a few limited subjective experiences in relationship to a given event. Now he has others—that are much less likely (due to the therapist's active presence) to be covered by fear and hidden behind shame. The past events now provide an opportunity to discover aspects of self that are more complex, congruent, continuous, and consistent.

To provide an example of curiosity I wish to present a composite case to demonstrate how curiosity is well suited to follow the lead of the client to greater depths and cocreate meaning with the client. Let us begin with an event—a 10-year-old boy who cried when he was hurt and who was told by his father to stop crying and grow up. Knowing that event does not tell the therapist the nature of the child's subjective experience of it. The therapist cannot experience empathy for the boy in a manner that is likely to be meaningful for him until she first knows the nature of his subjective experience. Thus, she expresses curiosity about it.

Therapist: What was it like for you—your father telling you to grow up?
Boy: I felt upset when he said that. I thought that he hated me. (The therapist's curiosity—embedded in empathy—can now go further, with the direction given to her by his account of the first experience of the event.)
Therapist: Upset, yes, and thinking that he hated you, that must have been so hard for you. What did you do then?
Boy: I stopped crying.
Therapist: You actually found a way to not cry after you experienced your dad's response to it. That sure makes sense if you

thought that your father hated you when you cried. How do you think that you managed to do that—not cry?

Boy: I just noticed something else. I stopped feeling sad or scared, and I even was able to make the pain go away by not noticing it.

Therapist: Not even notice the pain! Wow! That was so important to you to not cry, to not be scared, to "grow up." You said that you thought that your father hated you when you cried. Do you think that you hated yourself too?

Boy: Yeah.

Therapist: Maybe whenever you were scared or felt small and weak?

Boy: Yeah, anytime I felt that.

Therapist: So there were parts of yourself that you stopped noticing, parts that you hated that you even stopped being aware of having.

Boy: Yeah, I never thought about myself those ways and if someone said that I was scared or little I got mad.

Therapist: So you found a way to try to make others not remind you of those parts of yourself—you would fight them if they did.

Boy: Yeah, I fought all the time.

Therapist: And by fighting that would make you more sure that you were not small and weak.

Boy: Yeah, no one would call me weak!

Therapist: No one! I am so sad that you had to be so strong. So sad that you couldn't just be able to feel scared or sad or even small and weak once in awhile. Just a kid who has all kinds of thoughts and feelings and does not have to hate parts of himself for being himself. What does it feel like that I feel sad for you about this?

Boy: OK, I guess.

Therapist: What makes it OK, do you think?

Boy: I don't know.

Therapist: Do you think maybe because it's OK with me that you have those feelings and thoughts about yourself sometimes?

Boy: I guess.

Therapist: Great, I'm glad that you're OK about that.

This dialogue is only one of many that could have been made. Each response of the child is accepted and leads to further curiosity, with a possible new direction. If his response to my first question was not "I felt upset and thought that he hated me," but rather, "I didn't care!" the dialogue may have sounded something like this:

Therapist: You didn't care what your father said. Oh, I see. How do you think that you were able to do that?

Boy: I just didn't think about him or what he thought.

Therapist: Not think about him . . . or what he thought. Was that hard to do?

Boy: No, I just didn't pay attention to him when he talked to me.

Therapist: So in some ways your dad and what he thought seemed to become less important to you.

Boy: Yeah, I just didn't think about him.

Therapist: That makes sense. What he said hurt a lot, so you stopped noticing what he said and it didn't hurt as much.

Boy: Yeah.

Therapist: I'm glad that you found a way to protect yourself when you felt hurt when your dad said some things. But I'm sad that you had to do that. I'm sad that you had to make your dad less important to you so you would not feel so hurt.

Boy: Yeah.

Therapist: Why do you think that makes me sad that you had to do that?

Boy: I don't know.

Therapist: Because I was thinking that as he became less important, he began to be seem less special to you, less close.

Boy: Yeah. But I didn't care.

Therapist: Yeah, that's sorta what I mean. You had to stop caring about your dad—in a way. You had to find a way to have a life without having your dad play an important part in it. And that makes me sad. That in some ways you had to find a life where your dad became less special to you and you seemed to become less special to him.

Boy: I guess so.

Therapist: Your dad missed discovering parts of who you really are, and you missed having a dad who discovered those parts of who you are.

Boy: Yeah.

Therapist: And that's what I'm sad about . . . and glad that I'm discovering who you are. And glad that you're OK about this, with me, and with your dad discovering these parts too.

Again, such a dialogue would be helpful to a child or teenager only if it did not stray from his subjective experience of the event explored. The dialogue's value is in its ability to maintain this connection to his experience, while elaborating on it, developing implications that arise from it, exploring associated affects, thoughts, and intentions. It will also only be helpful if the parents, especially the father, are able to hear their child's description of his subjective experience with acceptance and curiosity as well, in spite of any distress that is being caused. In this example, the therapist would have to continuously monitor the father's response to insure that the child was safe to continue to express his narrative.

At no time during this dialogue is there any judgment by the therapist being made about the child's or the dad's responses. The child does not have to justify or conceal his inner life from the therapist's mind. The nonjudgmental tone communicates an attitude that the child's mind contains thoughts and feelings, wishes and intentions that represent aspects of his narrative. His story is being explored and developed, not judged and criticized. His story represents his sense of self over time, the accumulation of his subjective experiences, which one hopes are becoming more integrated through this dialogue.

A similar dialogue, permeated with curiosity, empathy, and acceptance would need to occur for the therapist to help the boy's dad to reorganize his experience of that event with his son as well as his present experience of therapy with his son.

Therapist: Hearing your son say that he recalled that you told him to grow up when he cried—and then hearing how he says that affected him—what was that like for you?
Father: Well, it doesn't seem to me to be such a big thing. My father used to call me that. It's just something that you deal with.
Therapist: So you were thinking that you had the same experience when you were a boy with your father, and you found a way to deal with it.
Father: Yeah.
Therapist: What did you do to deal with it?
Father: I just never let it bother me.
Therapist: How did you do that?
Father: Well, I didn't really cry much, but if I did I just made sure that he never saw me.
Therapist: So you kept your crying hidden from your dad, and you might have found ways to cry less than you otherwise would have.

Father: Yeah.

Therapist: Do you think that if you hid parts of yourself from your dad, you were not as close as you would otherwise be?

Father: Probably, but we never were that close. He worked all the time.

Therapist: So it sounds like if he criticized you for crying that was just one reason that you and your dad were not close. What was that like, not being close to him?

Father: I didn't think about it, that's just the way it was.

Therapist: So in some ways you're like you son—not thinking about things that might be hard to think about . . . What was it like hearing your son say that in some ways he did not feel that close to you?

Father: I didn't like hearing it.

Therapist: Because . . .

Father: He's my son.

Therapist: And . . .

Father: Well he is, and I always thought that I'd be closer to my son than my dad was to me.

Therapist: Ah, you thought that it would be different. And you're thinking that in some ways, it's the same. What's that like?

Father: Like I said, I don't like it.

Therapist: Is it that you're not being the dad that you had hoped that you would be?

Father: Yeah, I'm not. I don't want to be like my father was, but I just have a hard time being different.

Therapist: So you want to be closer to your son than your dad was to you. And you don't think that you are that often. And that's really hard.

Father: Yeah. I guess it does bother me more than I thought. And I've wanted him to be able to be closer to me than I was to my dad.

Therapist: Have you told him that.

Father: No.

Therapist: Why don't you tell him now.

Father: Son, I do want you and me to have a closer relationship than we seem to have. I'm sorry that I haven't done a better job being your dad.

Boy: That's OK, dad.

Therapist: John, are you glad that your dad told you that he wants a closer relationship?

Boy: Yeah.

Therapist: Do you want that, too?

Boy: Yeah.
Therapist: Would you tell your dad that?
Boy: I want a closer relationship with you too, dad.
Father: I'm glad, son.

It is important to describe curiosity further because I have noted that it is often trivialized as simply consisting of "asking questions." That's a good start, but it misses something crucial about the questions that we ask. We do not know the answers! Curiosity flows out of a strong stance of "not-knowing." The therapist may know the person's diagnosis, symptoms, history, career, and current relationships. The therapist may know how other clients have experienced similar events. But the therapist does not know this client's subjective experience of the event until the client gives expression to the experience. But that too, is not enough. The therapist does not know the client's subjective experience of the event until the client expresses it *and* she experiences the client's experience intersubjectively. Thus, knowing and loving are interwoven. To really know what a person is telling us, we need to empathically place ourselves within the client's experience, feel it, and assist in creating new meanings, while being there, in the past or present, with the client.

Still, we are not finished with this process. For our curiosity to be a transformative experience for our client, the client must experience our experience of his or her experience of the event. The client must experience our curiosity—and its related understanding and empathy—intersubjectively, or the understanding that is generated will have less value. It may enter the client's ego state, but will not touch the client's soul.

To reach the soul, the therapist openly expresses the experience of wonder at the person she is *discovering*, at the narrative she is experiencing. If her curiosity had come from a mind that was "not-knowing" the wonder is easily shown nonverbally in expressions of surprise, awe, delight, and radical empathy. The process truly involves moment-to-moment acts of discovery, with related expressions of deep satisfaction from the process of experiencing the uniqueness of the other.

A woman from Japan, whom I have had the privilege to come to know, stated that in her culture, the person strives to "see the soul" of the other person when they meet. She also stated that in her culture individuals do not know often enough how to "speak to the soul." She stated, quite simply, and with tears, that this model of psychotherapy seemed to her to be able to do that.

The questions that reflect curiosity are open-ended efforts to make the original experiences of events more acceptable and clear, coherent and comprehensive, consistent and continuous. The following represent common sentence-stems that may lead to a deepening and elaboration of the original experience.

How do you feel when . . . ?
Why do you think he said . . . ?
What does it mean that you (he) . . . ?
How do you manage . . . ?
What do you do when you think . . . ?
Has that happened with anyone else, too . . . ?
How did you handle that . . . ?
Does that affect what you think/feel/want about yourself?
Are there other times when you think/feel/want that?
How do you feel talking with me about . . . ?
What do you think I feel about your telling me . . . ?
Do you ever think/feel differently about . . . ?
What enables you to have different thoughts/feelings/wishes about . . . ?
Do you recall when you first thought/felt/wanted . . . ?
What do you think you would think/feel/want if . . . ?

The therapist's voice tone is crucial while asking such questions. The therapist is communicating that she is truly curious, that she has no preconceived views about what the client does—or should—feel or think. *It is the client's experience.* We help it to become organized and expressed. We join our experience with it so that it has an opportunity to develop further, to become more differentiated or integrated. But we do not work to modify it. It must always remain the client's experience. Empathy and further curiosity helps the client to believe that he or she will be truly accepted regardless of where the joint exploration leads. Older experiences are being reorganized into new experiences; but they are still the client's experiences.

When the above questions lead family members into an a/r dialogue, the therapist begins to understand the individual's experience at a deeper level. As she understands and experiences the individual's experience it begins to reorganize itself, incorporating the therapist's a/r presence within. At these times it is often helpful to the dialogue if the therapist conveys her increasing excitement about jointly discovering the intentions, feelings, ideas, or perceptions that were central to the person's experience. The therapist becomes more animated, carrying the dialogue in this process of exploration that has an air of anticipation about what is being discovered.

At these times nonverbal expressions of deep interest about the process of joint discovery are important. The therapist might speak more rapidly, raise the pitch of her voice, stare into the distance thinking out loud while she searches for just the right words, moving her hands, patting her legs rapidly while speaking repetitively. Her eyes may get big, her mouth may open as she seems to be absorbed by the dialogue and the act of discovery. She conveys nonverbally her heightened sense of the importance of the exploration. While these nonverbal communications were originally expressed in relationship to providing psychotherapy with children, they are equally effective—though possibly toned down somewhat—in communicating curiosity with adults.

These nonverbal expressions are often complemented with words, given in an animated, quick, repetitive manner, or sudden movements from loud to quiet, fast to slow. Examples include:

> You know what I'm thinking! . . . You know what I'm thinking!
> I'm thinking . . . I'm thinking that maybe . . . *maybe* . . .
> Wait a second, wait a second . . . I wonder if . . .
> Do you think, do you think . . . that maybe . . . maybe you were thinking . . .
> (quietly, after long pause, staring out the window) . . . I . . . wonder . . . if . . .
> (slowly, then building momentum) Maybe, just maybe, *maybe,* this might *mean* . . . !

Then at the act of discovery the therapist might exclaim:

> That's it . . . *that's it!!* Yes . . . *I think you got it!!*
> Yes! *Yes! I think we figured it out! I think we did!*
> *Wait* . . . *wait* . . . What you said . . . What *you* said seems *so important!*

These phrases and nonverbal expressions may seem a bit overdone, and may actually be "overdone" at times in certain situations. However, often, the family member gets absorbed in the therapist's nonverbal vitality affective state and is focused entirely on the exploration process that is unfolding, without any sense of self-consciousness. At the end of the a/r dialogue, the entire family has often experienced the dialogue with their minds and hearts, rather than as an intellectual exercise. At times adults or adolescents will laugh about the therapist's animation, but they nevertheless most often become engaged in the process without annoyance or without any sense of being manipulated. Of course, I am assuming that the therapist is deeply involved in the exploration. She truly is deeply curious, and is simply giving full expression to it and not being manipulative.

To demonstrate the value of the nonverbal component of an expression, imagine a therapist saying "that's right": She might say "That's right" in a manner that conveys that she already knew what the client just said and she evaluates his statement to be correct. Or she might say "That's right!" in a manner that conveys that she is just discovering what the client first discovered and communicated to her, so her comment reflected an act of joint discovery rather than a professional evaluation.

I recall an experience with a 15-year-old adolescent who was exploring features of her recent experiences with her family. As she uncovered some new understandings, I exclaimed, "Wonderful! Wonderful!" She laughed and repeated the words sarcastically in a manner that tended to minimize my experience of what she had done, and thus, her experience of what she had done. I conveyed mock distress over her making fun of my enthusiasm for what she had done: "How come I'm not allowed to say 'Wonderful!' when it was 'Wonderful!'? Am I supposed to say wonderful and pretend that it wasn't 'Wonderful!'?" On three more occasions in that session, I made the same "Wonderful!" expression in response to her statements and by the third time she smiled and quite willingly continued in the dialogue.

Curiosity as described here is similar to that state when we are with our baby—suspending all preconceptions, we enjoy the variety of nonverbal expressions that the infant is making and we cocreate meaning from our experiences together. We take our infant's lead in our open responsiveness to her and we assist the child in developing and telling her story. And we do that each time, again and again, being open to new variations and returning to the emerging themes.

It is within our parental socialization role that we often lose or diminish our curiosity. During discipline we often focus on our desire for certain behaviors, forgetting to wonder in response to the behaviors that are emerging. We lose sight of the fact that our child's behaviors, at least in part, are reflective of his efforts to develop a coherent narrative. Rather than join him in these efforts, we often impose our own narrative on him. His obedience becomes necessary for the coherence of the "parent" chapter in our narrative. If, at times, it *is* necessary for the child to follow our directives, it would be so helpful to remember that if we can coregulate the affect associated with integrating this function of compliance within his or her narrative (cocreating its meaning), we are functioning as a parent in facilitating the coherence of the child's narrative. There need not be a choice between my coherence as a parent and our child's coherence as a child. Within my chapter as "parent" lies the function of being the steward of my child's narrative. Following my directives need not compromise the child's narrative coherence if I engage him with acceptance, curiosity, and empathy.

The connection has been made between curiosity and empathy. As a final thought about curiosity, I would like to speak of its relationship with acceptance. It was noted earlier that at times it may be difficult to maintain acceptance when a client makes a statement such as, "You don't care about me, you just want your money." The difficulty arises from the therapist forgetting that the experience is not necessarily the fact. Or, the therapist may know that the client is speaking about an experience, but does not like it that she is being experienced in that manner. Such distress within the therapist would often not occur if the therapist were curious about what led the client to that experience. If the therapist maintains an intense curiosity about why the client has that experience, not knowing the basis for the experience, it is much easier to accept the experience. Within such not knowing, there is nothing, at least yet, to be upset about. When the meaning of the experience finally emerges through curiosity, it most often elicits empathy. If the meaning elicits anger, anxiety, or shame in the therapist, most often it is because the understanding about the experience is not deep enough. If the meaning elicits guilt in the therapist, most likely it is because the therapist's experience of her own behavior is similar to the client's experience of it. Through accepting and understanding the client's experience of her behavior, the therapist is able to respond without becoming defensive and can then modify her behavior, and repair the relationship.

When the treatment is family centered, much of the curiosity is focused on characteristics of the family itself and the intersubjective experiences of the members of the family with one another. Believing strongly that the most central value of the family is to provide each member with a secure base from which to safely explore the world, the therapist will focus on whether intrafamilial experiences support or hinder this function. The therapist will also be focusing on the quality of a/r dialogue among the members of the family. Family roles and secrets will be made more explicit. Habits and routines, traditions and rituals will be explored. The therapist's curiosity will continuously explore to what extent the family is able to develop and maintain a coherent and relaxed family atmosphere while at the same time facilitating the individuation of each family member.

EMPATHY

Empathy has now been accepted by most therapists as an "active ingredient" in effective therapy (Kirschenbaum & Jordan 2005). I believe, as does Diana Fosha and others, that empathy needs to be communicated fully, clearly, openly, and "radically" for it to be put to best use. Empathy has various functions, all of which come together, develop, and are developed by the intersubjective matrix (Greenberg, Watson, Elliott, & Bohart, 2001; Omer, 1997).

Within the context of an enveloping state of acceptance, along the path of nonjudgmental curiosity, the therapist is led to where she is now standing with her client. She is experiencing an event that her client had previously experienced without her. She is experiencing her client's experience of the event. Her experience is affective and reflective (a/r). Together with her client, she is coregulating the affect associated with the event and cocreating its meaning. This is empathy.

Empathy here described is an active mental (a/r) process that exists between two or more minds and hearts. It involves the experience of each member of the dyad (or triad) as well as the experience of each other's experience. It is intersubjective. To say that a therapist has empathy *for* her client's experience is to note that the mind's focus is on the client's world. To focus on another aspect of empathy, it might be better to say that the therapist experiences empathy *with* her client. "Empathy with" stresses two key components of empathy: First, the therapist's empathy is barren unless experienced by the client. Second, when the therapist's empathy for the client's experience is experienced by the client, he now is likely to experience empathy toward himself. The therapist and client, together, are experiencing empathy for an aspect of the client's narrative. But it does not stop there. This joint experience of empathy for an aspect of the client's narrative, now itself becomes an experience that enters the narratives of both the client and the therapist. Both client and therapist are able to say, "I am one who experienced empathy with the other," and this intersubjective experience is now part of the "self" of each. If it fails to enter the narratives of both, it is not intersubjective. When it does enter the narratives of both, the amazing power of empathy becomes evident to all.

Curiosity is the cutting edge of empathy. Within curiosity, the reflective quality of the mind is in the foreground while the affective quality is in the background. Within empathy, affect is in the foreground, reflection is in the background. Together, there is a "meeting of the minds and hearts." With curiosity the therapist is actively leading both minds into the narrative of the other. With empathy the therapist is actively experiencing with the client emerging aspects of his or her narrative. The therapist's intention is to participate in such meetings of mind and heart with each member of the family and with the family as a whole, as well as to facilitate such meetings among the members of the family.

One example of the power of empathy involves a 12-year-old girl who was asked to say the first word that came to her mind when she said her name to herself. She replied, with little affect, *garbage.* She was not able to access the meaning of that word when associated with her name. Similarly she had much difficulty accessing basic affective responses to *discipline, loss, success,* or *affection.* In a later session, after she described something that she had done for another child that was sensitive and courageous, the therapist asked her if she still felt that the word *garbage* applied to her name. She replied that it did. The therapist then asked her if she would help both the therapist and her parents to understand what she meant by *garbage.* She did not know what to say. The therapist then asked her to close her eyes and when she felt something inside that fit the word *garbage* to open her eyes and stare into her mother's eyes. After a few seconds she did so. She quickly looked away and demonstrated acute distress. After she became calm the therapist asked her what had happened. She replied: "My mom could *see* the 'garbage' feeling, and then she began to feel it." I asked her if she would do it again, and this time let her mother *feel* the 'garbage' feeling with her. She did so, and this time she and her mother cried together and then embraced. The mother held the "garbage" feeling with her, it became less shameful, and the event was more able to find a new place, with a new meaning, within her narrative. Without words, the mother was able to coregulate the affect and cocreate new meaning for the affective state, so that the word *garbage* really no longer applied to the child's self within that state.

When a/r dialogue is the most effective, the therapist is able to get the family to focus under the symptoms at their meanings. The therapist stresses to the parents that when their child gives expression to an experience of an event, their most likely best initial response is one of empathy. Many parents are able to do that with some practice. The therapist helps the parents to see that their child's experience may or may not be their experience. The terms *right* or *wrong* do not apply. If they want their child to understand his or her experience and to develop meaning likely to be more similar to their own meaning, they must first show acceptance, curiosity, and empathy for the child's experience. Examples of this important sequence where one member of the family expresses his experience that lies under a behavior and another member responds with empathy are the following:

Son: Mom, sometimes when you won't let me be with my friends, I think that you just don't know how important it is for me and you don't even care how upset I feel.
Mother: Oh, son, thanks for telling me! I didn't realize that when I won't let you go out you might be thinking that your wishes are not important to me and that I do not care how you feel. It sounds like you might even feel that you're not important to me right then. I am so sorry. And:
Susan: John (husband), when you are late for dinner over and over again after promising each time that it won't happen again, I get so discouraged, truly believing that I have a small place in your life. My feelings are not that important to you.

John: Susan, I am very sorry that you feel unimportant to me when I come home late after promising not to be. You are so important to me. I need to demonstrate it so that you know it—and words won't do it. I'm sorry.

Such dialogues are so crucial for a family treatment to have a transformative effect on how the members of the family experience themselves and each other within the family. Such a/r dialogues often do not occur spontaneously or the family would not be in treatment. When the therapist makes it a priority to facilitate such dialogues through education, modeling, coaching, and maintaining a context of safety and intersubjective exploration, they often begin to occur with very evident results.

Empathy is at the heart of transformative therapeutic experience. "Insight" without empathy tends to be treated indifferently by each family member's narrative. "Affect expression" without empathy tends to hold no meaning that can be cocreated. Empathy is never a "thing" that must be "given to" or "done to" our client. It is an intersubjective experience, with the minds and hearts of both therapist and family members focused on a troubling aspect of each family member's narrative or their joint family narratives. Empathy is then experienced by both the therapist and family for this aspect of the individual's developing self or the family's developing identity. When the family leaves the office, this experience of joint empathy leaves with them. The family member's newfound empathy for himself and for others in the family greatly deepens his ability to autoregulate his affect, coregulate the affect of the others, and create integrative meanings from the objects and events in his life.

Empathy for the individuals in the family often precedes empathy for the family as a whole. Initially the therapist is discovering how important the family members are to each other. She feels empathy for how each of them often feels intense doubts, vulnerabilities, and shame in relationship with the others. As she experiences their interwoven narratives—how deeply meaningful they are to one another—she often experiences empathy for this unique family. Her intention becomes to enable them to assist not hinder each other in developing their coherent and congruent narratives.

In communicating empathy, the therapist often simply reflects on the affective component of an event in a person's or family's narrative. The following would be typical examples:

Looks like you're having a hard time!

It's so hard to wait!

You seem to really want to finish that now!

Kind of disappointing when you can't go to your friend's house.

You really seem to be angry about that!

You look so sad over not being able to ride your bike.

That must be so hard . . . being all alone.

It is so difficult when you try hard as a parent and it does not seem to be working.

Sometimes your anger seems to cover over your love for your child and she does not experience it. When that happens you seem to be more upset—you love your child so much and it gets hidden . . . and you both don't feel close. That is sad . . . so sad.

These sentences, and countless others, are helpful in communicating empathy when they do reflect attunement with the affect of the other person, and when they are communicated with congruent nonverbal expressions that make the words come alive to the other and resonate with their felt experience.

Often empathy is felt even more fully and powerfully by the other when the therapist directly speaks of her own affective response to the other's experience. Such responses make it very clear that the family members are having an effect on the therapist. They are not "cases" and she is not "doing her job." Rather, all are human beings, being together intersubjectively. Examples include:

I'm worried that you feel that you have to handle this all alone.

I feel sad that you do not feel close to your dad now.

I am amazed at how you are willing to do such painful work if it will help your son.

I am touched at how openly vulnerable you are now with your wife.

I am grateful that you all have revealed so much of who you are, and want to be.

Frequently with parents and other therapists I make the following statements, possibly a bit playfully, all of which reflect my overwhelming experience:

Empathy is like aspirin, it works with anything.

If you can't think of anything to say, experience and express empathy. At the very least it will buy you some time, and most likely it will also be helpful.

> When you discipline your child, add empathy not anger and it is much more likely to be effective.
>
> When she expresses shame, give empathy first, and second, and not reassurance.
>
> Once you experience empathy for her, much of the rest will take care of itself.

Empathy is not a technique where one gives "empathy words" to "make" the other feel understood. Empathy is an intersubjective experience when one is in the world of the other, experiencing their experience of an event and the event itself with them. Empathy involves "being touched by" the other and giving expression to that experience so that the other "is touched" by one's "being touched."

Taken together, playfulness, acceptance, curiosity, and empathy provide an attitude that facilitates intersubjective experiences that in turn offer safety, affect regulation, and the creation of meaning. Taken together PACE provides an interpersonal setting of rhythm and reciprocity, similar to that which exists between parent and infant. Often when family members sit with us in our offices their primary affective/reflective state is not comfortable for them. Family therapy is truly hard work for all involved in the process. PACE activates the hope that reciprocal joy and companionship is possible, while regulating the negative states of shame, fear, anger, and discouragement, and while cocreating new ways of experiencing each other in states of both autonomy and intimacy.

For example, a single parent, Sue, sought treatment for her 8-year-old son Dennis. Her son had angry outbursts, both at home and at school, and Sue was increasingly angry and frustrated that she was not able to influence him to change his behaviors. During the initial meeting with Sue it was evident that she seldom expressed empathy for her son's difficulties. It was quickly apparent that she thought that in expressing empathy she would be "giving permission" for her son to engage in those behaviors, or she would be "reinforcing" the behavior. Her reservations were understood and the role of empathy was clarified. She said that she could understand and even accept that empathy might be helpful, but she still was not comfortable with it.

Empathy was felt for Sue, for her continuing discomfort, followed by curiosity, about the source of her discomfort. A dialogue then took place about how her parents were quite critical of her and that she did not recall ever having heard statements of empathy. This awareness was also met with empathy followed by curiosity over how the lack of empathy from her parents may have affected her relationships with them. She was able to recall how lonely she often was as a child, and how she seldom told them about what she was thinking. She could see how she might have felt closer to them if she thought—through their empathy—that they understood and accepted her thoughts and feelings. Sue then said that she would be willing to try to speak with empathy to her son. She smiled and tentatively agreed to allow the therapist to "coach" her in communicating empathy during the next session with her son, if it seemed to be appropriate. The session also revealed that Sue had difficulty expressing physical affection for her son, again, due to her relationships with her own parents. She also agreed to be "coached" in this. Sue then wondered out loud what she had agreed to do and laughed that the therapist had better not be "too tough" with her or she might direct her anger at the therapist. The therapist smiled and said that she thought that they would get through whatever differences or difficulties might emerge.

During the second session, Dennis and the therapist were exploring some of his recent school difficulties involving conflicts with both his peers and teachers.

Therapist: Sounds like everybody was mad—the other kids, you, and then the teacher.
Dennis: Yeah.
Therapist: So, in a way, you're all by yourself then.
Dennis: Yeah.
Therapist: It seems to you that nobody cares, and probably you don't either.
Dennis: Yeah.
Therapist: What do you do, when you're feeling alone like that?
Dennis: Nothing.
Therapist: Ever talk to anyone about it?
Dennis: No.
Therapist: Why not tell your mom, now. Tell her "Mom, sometimes when I get into fights at school, I feel all alone." (Dennis remains silent though he looks at his mother with some anxiety.) Just give it a try. "Mom, sometimes when I get into fights at school, I feel all alone."
Dennis: Sometimes I feel all alone at school when I get into fights.

93

Sue: Yeah, but, if you . . . (therapist interrupts her by reaching over and placing her hand on Sue's and smiles)

Therapist: This might be one of those "empathy coaching" times. (Sue rolls her eyes, but smiles at the therapist.)

Therapist: (still touching her hand) Why not say, "That must be hard, son."

Sue: (looking at her son) That must be hard, son.

Therapist: I wish I was there to help you when you feel all alone.

Sue: I wish I was there to help you when you feel all alone.

Therapist: But you're my son, and I love you, and I want to help you.

Sue: (with some hesitations in speech) But you're my son . . . and I do love you . . . and I want to help you . . . And these are her (the therapist's) words (looks at therapist and smiles) . . . but I do mean them.

(Mom tears up. Dennis was not looking at her but could tell by her voice and he immediately looks at her. They stare at each other in silence for 15 seconds.)

Therapist: (squeezes Sue's hand briefly, gets eye contact and smiles) And I think this might be one of those times to practice your hugs. (Sue looks at therapist, rolls her eyes, and smiles again.)

Sue: (tentatively at first, and then with more confidence, hugs her son) And, Dennis, she told me to do this too, but I'm doing it because I want to.

This example employed a gentle, playful, stance that communicated an understanding that the therapist's request might be hard, and that the parent might be ambivalent about it, but the behavior requested would be helpful, and the therapist had confidence that the parent would and could do it. Sue twice rolled her eyes at the therapist's requests and immediately smiled, expressing a willingness to try what was being asked. The tone conveyed a meaning close to, "You probably regret saying that I could coach you toward empathy and touch, and you maybe getting somewhat impatient with me, but here we go. Let's do this together now, you can be annoyed later." Within that tone, Sue showed much courage and commitment to do whatever it took to assist her son, if she thought the recommendation had merit. Often I have noticed that parents will address personal themes if it will help their child, when they would be much less likely to address them if it were just for their own benefit.

Chapter 4

FOSTERING AFFECTIVE/REFLECTIVE DIALOGUE

This time she is heard, responded to, and engaged until the alchemy of communication works its magic again. —Diana Fosha, The Transforming Power of Affect (2000)

The ongoing, present, moment-to-moment intersubjective experience that occurs among child, parents, and therapist is the central agent of change in this model of family treatment. It is our dialogue about these experiences—our complex, meandering, stirring, surprising, painful, and moving dialogue—that enables family members to begin the process of transformation within each person and throughout the family. The content itself is not nearly as important as how those present jointly experience the process, the content, and the vitality of each other in the dialogue. It is the intersubjective experience provided in therapy that will enable past events—conflicts, separations, traumas, misattunements, and misunderstandings—to become integrated into the narratives of the members of the family. Once this process becomes a natural and central component of the family relationships, then any event, past, present, or future, can be integrated into their narratives as well. They will discover that the experience of safety that they experienced in therapy has made it possible to frequently become engaged intersubjectively with one another, and that such engagements further deepen their attachment security. The family is now able to provide a depth of intimacy that is not threatened by the autonomous subjective experiences of the unique family members.

The therapist's goal is to establish a flow of joined awareness, with shared affect and intentions, among those present. Within this safe intersubjective space, all experiences, no matter how different, are welcomed. All are accepted and then joined with the others' experience of that experience, influencing it and being influenced by it. This influence does not result from any effort to change the experience of the other. The intention rather is simply to explore and discover the fullness of that experience, to accept it, and experience empathy for the impact that it is having on each person. Within this process, the act of empathic discovery affects all who are vitally engaged in the process. Within this process, a deeper meaning of the experience emerges. This meaning literally is being cocreated by all those present who have "entered" into the experience, while insuring the safety of the individuals. When safety is reduced, the individual retreats from the intersubjective flow and returns to his defenses.

During this process the therapist continuously joins the family members within the intersubjective present. They are each having an impact on the therapist—and it is a positive one because she experiences them from a playful, accepting, curious, and empathic stance. This impact enables them to incorporate her experience into the new meanings of themselves (both individually and as members of this family) being cocreated.

During this process the therapist's awareness is primarily centered in the present. She is aware of, responsive to, and expressive of, the mind, heart, and body of both herself and those present with her. She continuously holds the experience and its expression of both her client(s) and herself. She strives to stay in balance, responding to the nonverbal/verbal manifestations of her experience and that of the other. She is aware of the rhythm of the dialogue. She also becomes aware of breaks in the rhythm and she addresses these, which then frequently restores the rhythm. She is not resisting the breaks but rather welcoming them into the dialogue with the result that very often the flow of awareness continues.

What I am describing is intersubjective mindfulness. The therapist is fully in the present moment, accepting whatever presents itself, being curious about what she is being aware of, having compassion for self and other. In contrast to the more traditional centers of awareness in mindfulness (breathing, sounds, a tree), in this situation the subjectivity of the present other is the center of awareness, along with one's own subjective response to his or her subjectivity, and the other's subjective response to one's own subjective response.

As has been mentioned above, when the parent is intersubjectively present with her infant she is focused on the child's expressions and she continuously makes sense of these expressions by allowing them to affect her. Her own nonverbal/verbal responses give expression to her sense of the meaning behind the child's expressions. The parent and infant are cocreating a common meaning of these expressions, so that her infant can increasingly begin to identify his or her inner life and convey it to others.

This same process is central in this model of family treatment. Both children and parents are engaged intersubjectively and the meaning of their experiences are being cocreated. Many children cannot identify certain features of what they want, think, or feel, and they often have little understanding of the meaning of related behaviors. As a result, they often lack the skills to communicate central aspects of their inner lives to their parents. Many parents also have difficulty finding the words necessary to integrate certain experiences into their autobiographies. The therapist's role with these children and parents is not to simply help them to feel safe enough to express their inner lives. Rather, she needs to assist them in developing their capacities to become aware of, articulate, and express their inner lives. To do that, she needs to actively create a climate of curiosity and acceptance about the meaning of each family member's expressions and behaviors. She needs to tentatively cocreate the meaning of these expressions and behaviors, at times even by speaking for the person or speaking about the person to another family member.

When focused on the experience of the child, she involves the child's parents in this process, so that they can also see and respond to what the therapist sees in their child, and then join in giving meaning to these self-states. As the process continues, with the child differentiating and integrating her views of herself at each step, a coherent understanding of the meanings of her past and present behaviors emerges.

The same intersubjective process may be necessary for the parents in treatment as well. Whatever difficulties they have in providing sufficient intersubjective experiences to coregulate affect and cocreate meaning for their child may well correspond to similar deficits in their own narratives. As these aspects of their selves become seen and responded to by the therapist, they are likely to be much more sensitive and responsive to similar features in their child. Certainly it might be wise for the child not to participate in the exploration of certain themes or experiences of their parents. But often it is appropriate and the deeper understanding of her parents' narratives may make it easier for the child to understand the parents' motives and feelings and to feel more secure in the relationships.

Ongoing verbal interchanges which communicate a deep curiosity about the family member(s), as well as acceptance of the process and content of the exchange, must be congruent with the nonverbal attuned responses. As the content moves through positive affective experiences, there is a quality of spontaneous playfulness and affirmation during the dialogue. As content associated with negative affective experience is discussed, there is a greater communication of empathy and comforting. When focusing on both positive and negative affective experiences, the therapist is adopting a stance that is similar to the nonverbal dialogues that occur between parent and infant. These interchanges are referred to as *affective/reflective (a/r) dialogues*. They are entirely nonjudgmental. Whatever is explored, is understood and accepted as it is.

The therapist has used her nonverbal skills to establish a context of safety, to resonate with the affective states of the client(s), and to facilitate a deepening engagement and affective communication. The therapist maintains the *same* nonverbal communications and glides into a/r dialogue about defended negative affective experiences. If the client resists this new direction of the dialogue, the therapist then enters into a dialogue about the resistance itself. Her breathing remains calm and regular, her eyes communicate interest and openness, her voice is relaxed, matter-of-fact, and accepting, her touch offers reassurance and understanding, and her movements are rhythmic and flowing. She is careful *not* to change her nonverbal expressions when she introduces shameful or frightening topics. She does not adopt the serious, flat voice, nor the slightly tense, nonexpressive facial expressions and posture that so often characterize adults who are talking with children about "problems." Rather, she continues to communicate in a very expressive, nonverbal manner, her acceptance, curiosity, empathy, and (when appropriate) playfulness in response to whatever is expressed by the client.

For a/r dialogue to facilitate therapeutic change it is crucial that the affective tone of the dialogue be congruent with what is being expressed and received. However, nonverbal congruence around frightening or shameful themes refers to expressions of empathy and comfort, not serious rationality. The therapist is actively communicating nonverbally and affectively that she is being impacted by the dialogue. Her affective response provides a significant part of the momentum needed to maintain the flow and meaning of the conversation. Any reflective dialogue that hopes to convey personal meaning and be brought into the intersubjective realm must have an affective component to it.

In a/r dialogue the therapist focuses on the inner life of the client. She is active in making sense of the client's statements, nonverbal expressions, and behaviors that occur during the session as well as in his or her daily life. She frequently expresses curiosity about the meaning of these expressions in order to help the client to begin to understand that his or her behaviors, as well as the thoughts and feelings that underlie them, can be understood as natural efforts to manage, regulate, and organize the experiences of the person's life. When many clients do not have the skills needed to understand the meaning of their behaviors, and when they have long stopped trying to develop these skills, the therapist needs to actively lead them into becoming engaged in the process of understanding themselves. They need to understand the thoughts, feelings, and intentions that are associated with their behaviors, and then begin to comprehend the past and present experiences that generate them. Understanding a specific example is generally not important in itself. Developing interest in the process of self-exploration, followed by skills to make sense of what the client thinks, feels, and plans across a wide range of experiences, are basic to the therapeutic process. Through becoming engaged in the process, the client, often for the first time, is beginning to develop a more coherent autobiography.

Many would agree that these dialogues may well be appropriate for adult clients, but believe that they do not apply to the treatment of children: But they do! Children have the capacity to enter into such dialogues with the therapist if she creates the experience of affect attunement with the child within which the nonverbal expressions and meanings carry the weight and momentum of the dialogue, while the verbal content fine tunes the focus and content. Language need not be simply a left-hemisphere activity in the brain (Schore, 2005). Children of all ages have much greater capacity to put their experience into words, and to organize their experience better through including words, than therapists have recognized. The words absorb the personal meaning conveyed by the contingent and congruent nonverbal communications and the child often develops a deep felt sense of the meaning and intent of the dialogue. Children learn how to both cocreate meaning and also experience reciprocal affect long before verbal meanings have relevance. They definitely have the ability to participate and be affected by such dialogues when the adult knows how to elicit and maintain the engagement. This chapter and Chapter 6 will focus more on having therapeutic conversations with children because these tend to be more difficult for clinicians than having similar conversations with adults. At the onset of treatment the therapist will engage in these dialogues with the parents. When the children enter the treatment sessions the parents may initially be quiet participants in the intersubjective experience between the therapist and child. The therapist then facilitates a similar experience between parents and child. One treatment goal is for the parents to become comfortable initiating and responding to similar dialogues with their child at home.

CHARACTERISTICS OF A/R DIALOGUE

1. Attitude of playfulness, acceptance, curiosity, and empathy **(PACE).**

2. **Connection-break-repair.** Maintaining the intersubjective connection with the family is the overriding therapeutic goal. Since the themes are likely to elicit frequent relationship breaks, the therapist notes them, accepts them, is curious about them, and then initiates repair. Breaks are not avoided but rather are utilized for their meaning and as an opportunity for new change opportunities in the relationship and the self.

3. **Follow-lead-follow.** The therapist follows the lead of a family member, joins the focus, is curious, and responds. The therapist leads

into related areas, elaborating, wondering about implications, and following the response that the other gives. When necessary, the therapist leads into areas that are being avoided, while again following the person's response to that lead. This is patterned after the parent–infant dance of affect and meaning making.

4. **Nonverbal communication.** For toddlers verbal communication flows naturally from nonverbal communication. For all of us, nonverbal communication is the primary means we have for giving expression to our inner lives as well as for becoming aware of the inner life of the other. The therapist needs to be sensitively aware of the nonverbal expressions of the family members, helps to make these expressions verbal when indicated, and addresses any verbal/nonverbal incongruities. The therapist is clear, not ambiguous, in her nonverbal (and verbal) expressions. The therapist is receptively open to facial expressions, eye gaze, voice tone and variations, the range and intensity of gestures, as well as postural changes.

5. **Affective/reflective balance and integration.** Meaningful dialogue contains a blend of affect and cognition, conversation and reflection, holding the interest of the participants, and cocreating the meanings of the discussions and their place in the narratives. All memories, experiences, and affective states are included. Themes that do not spontaneously enter the dialogue are invited into it by the therapist, who then has an attitude of PACE for whatever responses are given by the members of the family. The therapist strives to maintain a broad, moment-to-moment, awareness of the following:

A. Ease and quality of expression of experience of events.
B. Self/other balance in dialogue
C. Blend of specific and general.
D. Cyclical flow of past, present, and future.
E. Degree of turn taking
F. Degree of organization and focus
G. Affective/reflective balance
H. Degree in which it is coherent, comprehensive, and succinct
I. Degree to which each is open to perspectives of others

6. **Cocreation of meanings.** Throughout the dialogue experiences of primary (person-person) and secondary (person-person-event) intersubjectivity are frequent. Matched affect, joint attention, and congruent intentions are present. Intersubjective communication

within attachment relationships regulates affect, deepens understandings, and cocreates new meanings regarding the experience of each other as well as the events that are being explored.

FREQUENT SEQUENCE OF A/R DIALOGUE

A/r dialogue tends to follow a general sequence. While there are many variations on this sequence, it still may be of value to present the following as a guide to this process.

1. An *event* is described. In most sessions, events that were experienced as being positive as well as those experienced as being negative are both explored. Generally, over the course of the sessions exploration of positive events are first, then negative ones, and again positive ones. This is similar to the attachment sequence (connection-break-repair) described earlier and tends to make a/r dialogue more effective. If the client(s) enter the office in a depressed or agitated state, certainly this will be focused on first rather than trying to manufacture a positive event.

2. The event itself is separated from the *experience* of it. Often most of us assume that the event and our experience of it are the same. Such an assumption has been strongly challenged by philosophers for centuries. But in our daily lives, by assuming that the two are the same we save time and generally are able to choose the proper course of action. If I see a light turn red, it is wise to assume that my perception is the same as the "objective" light turning red so that I will choose to stop the car when approaching an intersection. In this case, "objective" refers to the fact that I now assume that everyone else looking at the light at this moment will also see it turn red, and that they will choose a course of action that is congruent with my own.

However, in social/emotional behavioral events it is much more likely that others will not have the same experience for the same event. Different individuals are likely to have different experiences of a given event. Also, I cannot even assume that I will have the same experience of the event at different times. My experience of the event is influenced both by the event itself, but also by my a/r state at the time. Thus, the experience of an event can vary greatly between individuals and within the same individual at different times.

The therapist, therefore, cannot assume that she knows the experience of the family member when she knows the nature of the event. She needs to discover what the experience was. She needs to be curious about the experience and ask her client to describe it for her. She asks her client to clarify the experience by describing the "inner life" components of the event. She asks about the client's thoughts, feelings, perceptions, and judgments about the event. She asks about his or her wishes and intentions that may have influenced the event to happen as well as the experience of it. At the same time, she explores with her client his or her thoughts and perceptions about the thoughts, feelings, and intentions of the other person in the event. What attributions did the person make about the motives of the other person? The therapist never assumes that she knows what her client's experience of the event was. She needs to be curious about it so that she can understand her client's unique experience. During this entire process she never evaluates the experience of the event. She simply accepts it and is curious about it.

At each step, understanding elicits an affective response from the therapist, whether it is empathy, enjoyment, or simply deep interest in the process of discovery.

3. The *motives* that the client attributes to self or other related to the event are now explored. The therapist wants to understand why the child thinks that she acted that way. She also wants to understand why the child thinks that her parent (or other) acted that way. When the therapist understands what the child thought were the motives of self/other that were related to the event, the therapist is able to understand a great deal of the meaning that the child created about the event. Frequently the motives given to self have an element of shame along with or under other motives. Frequently the motives given to the parent have a component of rejection, criticism, or indifference (negative attributions).

Often the client does not know why he or she responded in a certain way to an event. At this point the therapist takes an active, curious stance, assisting the person in the *organization of the experience*. From the safety of this nonjudgmental, intersubjective stance, and deep interest, the person often is able to begin to connect the dots in a way that she was not able to do alone.

4. The client's experience of the event is now having an *impact* on the therapist. Following the understanding that is emerging from the explorations of the client's thoughts/feelings/perceived motives related to the event, there is often a deepening affective

response to the dialogue that elicits empathy within the therapist. The therapist is fully present with the client within his experience of the event. It is this impact on the therapist—the therapist's experience of the client's experience of the event—that opens the way toward the cocreation of a new meaning of the event. The therapist's affective (empathy) and reflective (curiosity) response, resting on a foundation of unconditional acceptance of the client's experience, enables the client to safely make herself available to reexperience and reorganize the event both affectively and reflectively.

5. Through experiencing the therapist's experience of the event and their new joint creation of the meaning of the event, the shame or fear associated with the event is now much less. The behavior, in the context of the new meaning that was just cocreated, has become more *normalized*. Given the client's experience of the event (thoughts, feelings, motives of self/other), her response is now open toward more coherent self-awareness and self-empathy.

6. The child is now encouraged to *communicate* this deeper meaning that she has discovered about the event to her parent(s). Through communication the child is more likely to retain this deeper meaning and to experience intersubjectively that her parent(s) understands it as well. The same is true regarding communications between parents or from parent to child.

7. The parents are now encouraged to express *understanding and empathy* for the meaning that their child now attributes to the event. The child's new experience of the event, being communicated verbally and nonverbally now has an impact on his parents. Through their experience of this sequence they are now joining the therapist in further cocreating the meaning of the event. Again, the emerging meaning is very likely to contain less fear and shame and associated negative attributions toward self and other. It is the parent who is asked to take the lead in communicating acceptance and empathy of the experience of her child. When this occurs, the child is often encouraged to respond and very frequently he responds with similar acceptance of and empathy for his parent's experience.

The parent refrains from explaining his or her behavior or the need for consequences. If these discussions are still necessary they need to be deferred until after the child has been able to consolidate his deeper awareness about what the event means to him, as well as his new intersubjective experience of his parents' understanding and empathy. This experience is likely to lead to cocreating a new meaning for the original event.

These seven stages of a/r dialogue reflect a central component of this model of family treatment. Such dialogues between therapist and child or parent and then between parent and child often form the basis for the treatment gains. Within such dialogues affect is being coregulated and meaning is being cocreated. Such intersubjective experiences are always modified to match the developmental abilities of the child.

For a/r dialogues to be therapeutic they tend to have the following features:

1. PACE is the dominant therapeutic stance.
2. PACE is the dominant parental stance. A/r dialogue does not involve lectures.
3. Cocreating meaning serves to reduce fear, shame, and negative attributions. It does not function to find an excuse for behaviors. The child (and parent) is still accountable for her behavior.
4. Early in a/r dialogue the therapist may have to help the child to "find the words." This may involve coaching or speaking for the child, interventions that will be presented in more detail later.
5. The child/parent may resist (initiate an intersubjective break) aspects of the a/r dialogue. When this occurs, the therapist accepts the break and may initiate an a/r dialogue about it. Accepting and focusing on the break will also be explored later.
6. Communication between the child and parent in the manner suggested coregulates the affect, cocreates new meaning, and facilitates both narrative integration and attachment security.
7. The affective component of the dialogue generates safety in the foreground and exploration in the background. The reflective component facilitates exploration in the foreground, with safety in the background. However, this distinction is primarily conceptual because the two are so interwoven in the lived experience.

The following represents a frequent sequence of an a/r dialogue.

1. **EVENT**
   Therapist: Billy, your mom mentioned that you yelled at her yesterday when she turned off the TV. She said that she told you to turn it off and when you didn't, she did. Then you yelled, "You stupid old bag!"

Billy: Yeah.

2. **EXPERIENCE**

Therapist: What were you thinking and feeling when you shouted that at her?

Billy: I was mad at her because I wanted to watch TV and she wouldn't let me.

Therapist: I see. You were mad because you wanted to watch it and she said no.

Billy: Yeah.

3. **MOTIVE**

Therapist: Why do you think she said no?

Billy: Because she doesn't care what I want. It was important to me and she didn't care. She never cares what I want!

4. **IMPACT**

Therapist: So you thought that your mom didn't let you because she doesn't care what you want. That would be hard . . . so hard, if she doesn't care what you want.

5. **NORMALIZATION**

Therapist: Now I understand. If you think that your mom doesn't care about you, about what you want . . . your own mom. No wonder you were mad. If your own mom does not care what you want . . .

6. **COMMUNICATION**

Therapist: Have you told her that? Why not tell her now. Tell her that sometimes when she says no to you it makes you think that she doesn't care what you want and that's really hard for you.

Billy: Mom, sometimes when you say no to me it makes me think that you don't care what I want . . . that I'm not important to you. And that's hard.

7. **UNDERSTANDING AND EMPATHY**

Mom: Oh Billy! I didn't know that you think sometimes that I don't care for you. That what you want isn't important to me. Thanks for telling me. Now I know why you became so angry when I turned off the TV. I'm going to have to find a way to show you that what you want is important to me, even when I'm saying no to you.

This example assumes that the child was able to verbalize his thoughts about his mother's motives, that he did not avoid becoming engaged in the dialogue, and that his mother would respond with empathy. While these factors are often not present at the onset of treatment, they are skills that can be and often are learned. Variations on this a/r dialogue are many, but often follow a similar format. The above example, if it were to occur in a session, would most likely lead to further discussion about reasons why the child might assume that his mother does not care about what he wants and possibly strategies—that he and his mom might use—to assist him in the future to be able to organize his thoughts and feelings differently when his mother says no to him.

The following is an example of an intervention with a 4-year-old adopted boy, Dale, and his adopted parents (this example may be found in Hughes [2004]). Dale was placed in his adoptive home when he was 30 months of age and he quickly demonstrated aggressive outbursts directed toward his adoptive mother. He had lived alone with his biological mother, Sarah, until 12 months of age, at which time she met and married Steven. Between 12 and 30 months of age, Dale experienced physical abuse from Steven and he also observed Steven abusing his mother. Sarah refused efforts to reunify with her son after he was removed, so within months he was free for adoption and was then adopted by his foster parents.

The therapist thought that Dale had identified with his stepfather in order to attempt to establish some sense of meaning and safety. He also felt rage toward his mother for failing to keep him safe from Steven. The goal of the therapist was to help Dale to understand his story in a manner that would assist him in seeing other meanings for his aggressive behaviors. His clinging behaviors and his repetitive statements of loving his adoptive mother were suggestive of his shame and his fear that he might lose her.

After speaking with his adoptive parents about his history and his current life and functioning, within his presence, the therapist asked Dale to sit between his parents. He readily did so. She then entered into conversation with him about the successes and fun that his parents had told her about his current life experiences. Gently, she then introduced the theme of his aggression toward his mother into the conversation. Dale immediately demonstrated shame by briefly averting his eyes and then raising his eyes to look at the therapist while his face was still lowered. He also sat quiet and motionless.

The following is considered to be a dialogue, not because Dale spoke—he said nothing to the therapist. It is a dialogue because Dale sat and stared into her eyes, not breaking eye contact for a moment.

Following some of her statements, he whispered to his mother what she had just said, while still staring at her. His story took almost 15 minutes to tell, but not once did Dale lose his focus.

The dialogue proceeded as follows:

And Dale, your mom and dad told me that sometimes you hit your mom. Ah, yes, you wish they hadn't told me. (His facial expression and eyes immediately manifest shame.) You probably want to say, "Mom, dad, why did you tell Allison. I didn't want her to know. She might not like me now."

Oh, Dale, I know you don't want to hit your mom. You try to stop. You try and you try. And mom and dad try to help you and they try. And they want me to help. They want me to try. And I think you want me to help too. I know you want to stop; if only we can find a way to help you to stop. We have to find a way.

We can do it!! I know we can! OK, Dale? Let's do it! OK? (Nods assent.) Yes! Yes! I knew you wanted to! I know we can do it! Yes! Yes! Yes we can!

Let's figure it out! Let's do it! Let's see. Let's see . . .

You started hitting your mom when you were just 2. You were just 2 (high-pitched voice while holding her hand only two feet above the floor.) Just 2! And now you are 4! (lower pitch voice, raising her hand higher above the floor). You were just 2 (higher pitch, lower hand) And you started hitting your mom when you were just 2, when you first met her!

How could that be, how could a 2-year-old boy (higher pitch, hand low over floor), just 2, even know about hitting moms? How could he, just 2, know about hitting moms?

Wait! Wait! I think somebody (large voice, large eyes) *big—a big person*—told you it was OK to hit moms! Some *big person* said it was OK to hit moms. And you believed him! You were just 2! (high pitch, hand low over floor). Two-year-olds don't know that big people can lie. You didn't know!

A big person lied to you!! That's what happened! When you were 2, a *big person lied* and said that it was OK to hit moms! You didn't know it was a lie, you didn't know. You were just 2 . . . (high pitch, but quieter, with hand moving slower and still low above floor).

Now the therapist sat quietly, with eyes resting on Dale's, communicating sadness and some sense of being tired at working to discover that someone had lied to him about hitting his mother.

I think Dale. (Starting to speak again, slowly and quietly, while building the momentum and force of the communication.) I think Dale. That we have to know . . .

We have to know. *We have to know who lied to* you!!! Yes we do! *We have to know! Yes! Yes! We do!*

Let's think, let's think. (Quieter again, almost a whisper, while bringing her hands up to her face and staring up to the ceiling.) We have to know. Let's think. Who could it be? . . . Who lied to you? . . . We have to know . . . We have to figure it out . . .

(Suddenly breaking the quiet, thinking-out-loud tone with a loud, excited voice, with large eyes again.) *I think I know! I think I know!*

Wait! Wait! Wait. Have to be sure. Have to be sure. (Quiet again, covering her face and talking to herself, followed by 10 seconds of silence and then another verbal explosion).

Yes, I know the big person who lied to you! I know! I know! (During which time Dale is frantically whispering to his mother, pulling on her sleeve, while still staring at Allison.)

It was Steven! Steven lied to you! And that wasn't right!!

Dale suddenly sat backwards in his chair as if the therapist had pushed him. He continued to stare at her for 10 seconds and then he climbed into his mother's arms and buried his head against her chest. Then his hand reached down to her stomach and he began to kneed her stomach as is frequent with nursing babies.

Dale's father moved over to embrace his wife and son and the three of them sat together without speaking for a number of minutes. The therapist then quietly told Dale's parents that he had realized something very important and that he just needed to be close to them for the rest of the day.

Dale stopped hitting his mother immediately. He frequently told his mother that he was no longer hitting her. He frequently asked his father to never lie to him. He also often said to his father, "It's not OK to hit moms, is it dad?"

The therapist's vitality affective expressions, each congruent with the stage of the story—of Dale's story—enabled him to experience his story affectively and then to open his mind to a possible new meaning for his story that she was presenting to him. The affect and meaning resonated with his inner life, and he was able to immediately shift his joint experience of self and other with respect to his relationships with both of his adoptive parents as well as his relationships with his birth mother and stepfather. It was the interwoven blend of vitality affect and meaning which drew Dale into his narrative and enabled them to jointly cocreate it.

FINDING THE WORDS FOR THE EXPERIENCE OF THE EVENT

Early in the treatment process the therapist may frequently have to make guesses about what the child or parent may have been thinking, feeling, or planning during certain events or prior to certain behaviors. If, at any time, the client says that she is not thinking or feeling what the therapist had guessed, the therapist immediately accepts her statement and expresses curiosity about what other meaning to give to the behavior. Making guesses is often beneficial for children—and adults too—who do not often reflect on their experience of the events in their lives or on their own behaviors. Playfulness, acceptance, curiosity, and empathy about their inner worlds of subjective experience may have been much too infrequent. They may have come to adopt an attitude that what they thought and felt and what their motives were for their actions were not important. They may have been taught that only their behavior mattered; everything else was an excuse. Or when they did express their thoughts, feelings, and motives to others they may have met with indifference, ridicule, rejection, or rage. They seldom expressed their inner world to others. They did not need to develop words to speak about their experience since they seldom spoke about it. Having no need for words, they often did not develop the ability to use words for inner dialogues. They gradually had an impaired ability to connect words to their experiences of the events in their lives. Their inner world took on a vague and nameless quality. Subjective experiences continued to occur but they were difficult to understand and communicate. When a child or adult says that she does not know what she thinks or feels about an event or why she did what she did, she often is describing a basic truth about her life. It is easy to then understand why that person has a sense of self that lacks coherence, continuity, and comprehensiveness. The ability to reflect on one's subjective experience by being able to utilize words, is crucial for the coherence of one's narrative.

Often the therapist leads the child into understanding his own behaviors by commenting on possible reasons for the behavior. (If the

child, or adult, disagrees with the reason, the guess is always set aside.)
Examples include:

> I know how important that was for you . . . no wonder you're upset!
> You probably don't know why I said no . . . That probably
> makes it harder for you, especially if you think that I don't care
> that it bothered you.
> I wonder if you got mad at him because he's allowed to go and
> you're not.
> Maybe you broke it . . . because right then . . . you just didn't care.
> After what I said, maybe you don't like me very much right now.
> Looks like you're not going to talk right now. Maybe you don't
> know what to say . . . Maybe you do but don't want to say it . . .
> Maybe you don't want me to know what you're thinking . . .
> Maybe you want me to just leave you alone.

Many children have sparse or fragmented experiences of engaging in
these a/r dialogues with their attachment figures. Often, when shown
how to do so, with the therapist taking the lead in the expressions, the
child feels a much deeper degree of affective resonance with the events
being explored and also a much deeper level of emotional connection
with the therapist. When the parent is also engaged in the dialogue, a
similar connection is experienced with his attachment figure. With rep-
etition the child is both more aware of his inner life and more able and
motivated to communicate it to his attachment figures.

Therapists have expressed concern that such an active therapeutic
stance will cause the client to fear that the therapist can "read her
mind." My experience has been just the opposite. Clients frequently
express relief that someone finally understands what they think, feel,
and want. This often leads to further relief that they now have words
with which to understand the impact that fear or shame-related behaviors have on their self-concept. Words, offered to a client so that she can
now use them to express a greater range and depth of her inner life,
help her to develop a sense of efficacy over her past and present experiences. Also, she is developing the capacity to "speak the truth" about
her experiences. At the same time she is finally experiencing what it is
like to be understood and to feel felt. With the therapist's active participation in the developing affective/reflective process, the client is experiencing a new meaning for past trauma, stress, and shame-related
behaviors. This meaning transforms the experience so that it can now
be regulated and integrated into a more coherent sense of self.

Another concern often expressed by therapists is that children need to process trauma or distress through nonverbal, play-based, expressive therapies, rather than through verbal dialogue. I concur with such reservations expressed about verbal discourse when they refer to verbal communication that is done primarily in a rational, evaluative, and problem solving manner. However, the a/r dialogue occurs within the context of attunement as expressed above, and the child is much more likely to remain present in the exploration and to experience it with a deep level of affective meaning. All a/r dialogue contains a nonverbal core with congruent verbal communications resting upon it. The dialogue occurs within the context of the therapist's very expressive facial expressions, rich voice tonality and inflections, gestures, eye contact, posture and touch, all congruent with the narrative. Storytellers have utilized these nonverbal communications for centuries in maintaining interest, building empathy for the characters, and eliciting affect congruent with the themes of the story. Narrative therapy is based on creating stories congruent with a child's own history. The act of telling the story may well be at least as important as the story itself (Schore, 1994, pp. 452–453). Emotional communication occurs primarily through the nonverbal expressions of face, voice, gestures, timing, and movements. The words themselves begin to resonate when they emerge within such expressions. Because the story being created is from the child's own life, the dyadic telling and witnessing serve to create a common meaning that is integrative and transforming.

When the therapist is taking the lead in the a/r dialogue, the client's nonverbal cues are crucial signals as to whether or not he is affectively present with the therapist during the dialogue. Any communication by the therapist is irrelevant if the client is not engaged in it. The therapist actively attends to the nonverbal cues, accepts them, and tries to integrate them into the ongoing interaction. By doing so, the client is much more likely to feel that his inner life—as manifested by his nonverbal expressions—is noticed and valued. He senses that what he thinks and feels is both important and also understood. In such a setting he will begin to feel safe at a sensory-affective level of experience, which is much more crucial than thinking that he is safe rationally. At a preverbal level of experience, he knows that he is being heard, understood, and validated. A/r dialogue now has a context in which its meaning-finding power impacts and transforms his fragmented self, thus beginning its integrative functioning.

The themes and content of a/r dialogue need to be varied. There needs to be movement back and forth between the dyadic regulation of positive and negative experiences. As members of the family need to develop their ability to lower the affective intensity of negative affect, they often also need to learn how to raise the intensity of positive affect. Often they live in a world with insufficient positive affective experiences. While this originally may have resulted from lack of opportunity, over time this fact may be due more to their own avoidance of or inability to make use of such experiences. A child may hear a supportive comment from her teacher, but the comment never enters her narrative because there is no place for it to rest. The comment does not fit within her definition of self. Similarly, a parent may have responded in a sensitive manner to a child but did not experience herself as being a sensitive parent.

For example, one father was speaking about his son who had just left for college. He spoke of his significant worries about how he had raised him and how this was likely to make his son's life more difficult now. As I listened to him I was struck by how little confidence he had in his child rearing. I was convinced that he had given his son much more than his father ever had given to him. I commented quietly, "I am so sad that it is hard for you to experience all the good that I know you have done for your son." He immediately became tearful and began to more fully experience the quality of the relationship which he had with his son.

In a/r dialogue the therapist is clearly focusing on experience— her experience, each family member's experience, their past experience together, and the current intersubjective experiences. It is often very helpful for the therapist to directly communicate her experience and possibly compare her experience with that of another in the session. She might wonder about the similarities and differences. She might wonder about the other's experience after sharing her own. What is often clearly implied by her comments is that there is no right or wrong. Also there is hope for the cocreation of new experience if that is desired by the other. It also makes it easier for the family member to hold the therapist's experience of him, while also holding someone else's experience of him, and then making sense of these differences in being experienced by different people in his life.

Examples of such a/r dialogues include:

It seems like when you think about your dad scolding you, you often think about it as proof that he just does not care for you . . .

When I talk with you and your dad about it, I experience it more as his worrying about you and not knowing what else he can do to help you handle that responsibility. What do you think about how we experience your dad's scolding differently?

I experience you as being persistent and courageous . . . just not giving up on your hopes to have a good life . . . and you seem to see yourself as being someone who just does not do anything right. We—you and I—seem to see you differently. What do you think that might mean?

I really enjoyed meeting with you today. It was great talking with you. Did you enjoy it too? I hope so because my impression is that you have not had that much fun in your life lately. Is that so? What was this like now? Enjoying our time together?

It seems to me that you both are struggling over the same important reality in your life together—whether you still love each other. My sense is that you each want to believe that the other does, but that you also believe that is possible that he or she doesn't—which is so frightening. Now you both seem to be tense that I am talking about this.

The therapist might initiate the following a/r dialogue with an adolescent who is being seen individually and who is alienated from his parents:

I see such strength and hope and honesty in how your are . . . in so much of your life . . . Did your mom ever show that she saw those parts in you? No? Then I'm sad that she never did . . . that must have made it hard for you to be able to see those parts in yourself . . . maybe you still don't . . . is it confusing then that I see those parts in you . . . and your mom didn't . . . and maybe you don't?

SPEAKING FOR

The child is more likely to be transformed by the a/r dialogue of a shame-related event, conflict, or fear if she can explore it while at the same time speaking about it with her parent. The act of communicating and being understood by someone who is deeply committed to her, will, in itself, facilitate a deepening sense of mastery over the memory of the event. The therapist might initiate the discussion and ask the child to describe and elaborate about the event with her caregiver, with the therapist facilitating the focus on the experience of the event rather than the event itself.

However, frequently the child—and possibly the parent as well—will have difficulty and be unable or unwilling to give expression to the experience. If the child does not speak, the therapist should accept her inability or unwillingness to put the experience into words and offer to tell the child's caregiver for her. *With his consent,* the therapist should then tell the caregiver the child's experience of an event. The therapist tells the child that she will guess what the child might have thought or felt or wished at the time. She will add that if she guesses wrong, the child can correct the therapist at any time or even tell the therapist to stop guessing if she does not like the flow of the conversation. The dialogue is likely to have more emotional meaning for the child if the therapist *speaks for the child* in the first person. The child might be encouraged to look into the caregiver's eyes while the therapist speaks for him or her. If the child will not look into the caregiver's eyes, the therapist could suggest that the caregiver and child hold hands, and further add that the child might feel the caregiver's understanding and love through the touch of the hand. The caregiver will have been instructed before the sessions on the nature of these dialogues. The caregiver is told that her primary stance should be similar to the therapist's; that is, communicating acceptance, curiosity, and empathy about the event, rather than focusing on questions, suggestions, differing experiences, or evaluations.

The therapist briefly describes the event. She then guesses about some of the thoughts and feelings that the child may have had, and she communicates them to the parent. At the end of the communication, the therapist—again representing the child—might ask for help from the caregiver in dealing with the stressful thoughts and feelings associated with the event. For example, the therapist might say for the child, to the caregiver:

Mom, sometimes when you say no to me . . . when you won't let me do what I want . . . I think that you just don't care what I want . . . that I'm just not that important to you anymore . . . and that's why I get mad mom . . . and that's why I threw the book . . . that's why mom . . .

To which the boy's mom might reply:

Oh, son, so that's it! That's why you got so mad! You thought that you weren't important to me! Oh, my! If you thought that, you

115

would certainly get upset with me! Now I can understand why you were so mad.

The therapist continues for the boy:

Mom, telling you about that was really hard. Part of me was feeling scared that you might think that I'm bad because of what happened. Or that you'll never be able to love me as much as you used to. I hope that you don't think that, mom, but I'm worried that you do. (pause) Please tell me what you think, mom.

The boy's mother would then reply in words similar to the following:

Oh, Johnny, that took such courage to tell me that! And how hard for you to think that I think you're bad and won't love you as much as I always have. No wonder you didn't want to tell me if you thought that! Son, I don't think that you are bad for what you did, though I can see that you might still think that. And I still love you as much as I always have . . . and I always will. You're my *son!*

The therapist, still speaking for the boy: "I'm so confused mom. I do think that I'm bad for what I did. I don't know why you don't and I don't know how you can still love me."

Mom replies:

I love you because you are you, and you are my son and always will be! I don't just love you when you are doing what I'd like you to do, and then stop loving you when you're not! No, right or wrong, like what you do or not, I still love you. I might be angry at what you do and maybe I need to work harder at understanding why you do some things that I don't like. I need to know your reasons, and then I might not be so angry, though I still may not want you to do it. But I know that you are always going to be lovable to me.

Many therapists may believe that such dialogues between a parent and child are not realistic goals for most of their families in treatment. I believe that it is realistic for many more families than one might think if the therapist is willing to take an active role in speaking for the child, as well as teaching, coaching, and modeling for the parent such emotional communications. Once the parent feels safe with the therapist, she is often quite willing to follow the lead of the therapist in finding new ways to speak from her heart and mind to the heart and mind of her child.

Other examples of a therapist speaking for the child include:

Dad, I just don't know why I don't get my homework done. I really don't. I wish I knew. All I can do sometimes is think about ways to avoid doing it. I'd rather do just about anything else. I feel trapped with a big weight on me and I do anything I can think of to get it off!

I hate coming here and talking about this shit! It's none of her business! She's probably sitting there thinking that we're a pathetic bunch of losers! Why do you make me do this? I hate it!

Don't you think that I would stop if I could! I don't want to pee in my bed! I hate the smell! Don't you know that I feel like a jerk when I do it! I'm not doing it on purpose to make you mad! It's disgusting to me too!

Sometimes when we're mad at each other, I just hate it! I don't want to make you mad. I want us to get along. I like it when we're close. Sometimes I feel real sad when we're not close like we used to be.

Sometimes I feel that no one . . . no one . . . will ever get it!

No one will ever know what's going on inside me! I don't know! Sometimes I think that I'm all screwed up! That no one will ever be able to help me.

Numerous times children have taken what the therapist initiated in the dialogue and continued on their own, totally claiming the therapist's words as their own. Often the child will intently look to his parent for a response to "his" words. At times the child will correct a few words, wanting the therapist to speak again for him, incorporating the changes given. Frequently the child will express wonder and gratitude over the therapist knowing what he thought and felt, even though he often did not know himself what he thought and felt until the therapist spoke the words.

The therapist also may speak for the parent—with permission—when the parent is struggling to find the words to say to her child. For example:

Bob, I know at times I yell more than I should. I know that I do. And I don't want to. I try not to, but find myself yelling again. I find myself yelling at you just like my dad used to yell at me, and

I always swore that I'd never treat you like he treated me! I'm sorry, son. I'm going to keep working on that.

Marilyn, I really want us to work this out better. I love you so much and I know that it probably doesn't feel like it to you. I juggle so many responsibilities that I take from you. And when you get mad about it, I react as if you don't have a right to get mad! I'm sorry about that! I've got to find ways to discuss these things with you first. I've got to get your side before just taking something from you, no matter what my reason is. You deserve that.

I'm so proud of you! You were able to figure out what was bothering you, and you came right out and told me! You trusted me with that! Thanks so much for the trust! I think that we can work this out now! Thanks so much!

When the therapist speaks for a member of the family it often increases the person's affect while enabling him to remain regulated. If the person has said the comments himself it may have evoked a level of fear, rage, or shame that was dysregulating. Speaking for the person often enables him to feel safe, remaining in the background. If he wishes, he can deny that those are his thoughts and feelings. If his parent does not respond in an empathic and understanding manner, he can more easily pretend that it does not matter because those were not his words.

SPEAKING ABOUT

While speaking for a person tends to increase his affect and reflection, speaking about him tends to decrease his affect and increase his reflection. Again, the child is able to remain in the background, not being expected to talk or to respond. It enables the child to better tolerate any distress associated with the a/r dialogue than if he were being expected to more actively participate. Often the therapist might speak about a child when she thinks that he needs a break from the dialogue, the affect is becoming too intense for him to regulate, or she wants to reflect upon the dialogue before continuing on.

When the therapist speaks about a child to his parents she is certain to say positive things, bringing out his strengths, and speaking with hope. By doing so she is conveying her intersubjective experience of the child to both the child and his parents. The impact that the child is having on her will begin to have a congruent impact on both the child and his parents. When he does not have to respond because the therapist is not speaking to him, the child is often more receptive to what is being said about him. The child is more likely to experience the therapist's motive as being to share her impression of him with his parents, rather than to convince him of something. Also the child is in a safer position to observe his parents for their response to what the therapist is saying about him. They are looking at the therapist not at him. He can openly observe them as to whether or not they seem to be experiencing him in a manner similar to how the therapist is experiencing him. Examples of speaking about a child are the following:

> Susan and Tim, I think that your son has said some very important things now. It took courage to say that he took the money and because he was able to do that he began to figure out why he might have done it. And then he came right out and told you! Not as an excuse! But he seemed to be showing some new understanding . . . and some hope . . . yeah, hope that this is going to go a long way in helping him to get on top of this problem that he's been struggling with.

> Becky and Mike, I noticed something there while your daughter was talking. I noticed that she wanted you two to be proud of her for what she is doing. This is hard what I'm asking her to do and she's doing it. I think that she really wants to make this work with you two. She wants it to go back to how it used to be with you.

> Your son is making it clear now that he is really mad at this. He's mad at me for not leaving this issue alone and I think he's mad at you for telling me about it. I think that we have to understand where his anger is coming from. He's working hard to make a life for himself, to figure out what he wants, what is right for him, all of that. And we're sitting here telling him what we want for him, what we think is right for him. And I think he needs to make the point now real clear. He doesn't like what we're doing!

> Jackie hasn't agreed with you. And I think you were really hoping that she would. But I'm glad that she was honest and did not pretend that she would do it when she really had no intention of doing so. Maybe right now she is saying, "Don't rush me. I need some time to think about this." If she is, I think that we should give her the time and not push for now. We're asking lot of her. So please be patient. Maybe next week we can explore this further.

Talking about a child to his parents is a wonderful opportunity to convey acceptance and empathy, to bring out the positive, to reduce the affect, and increase the reflective function, and to share the impact that he or she is having on the therapist with the parents. Similarly, the therapist may talk about the parents to the child:

> I think that your mom and dad are really trying to work this out with you. Your dad admitted that he should not have gotten angry and he really seemed to feel bad about that . . . like he's going to keep working on how he talks with you when you disagree. But what I felt the best about when your parents were talking . . . the looks on their faces . . . they seemed to just be sad . . . really sad . . . that you guys have drifted apart from how close you used to be . . . they seem to want to find a way to get that back . . . a way that you would feel OK about.

> Sam, when I watched your mom talk about you she seemed to love you so much . . . but it seemed to come out in a way that you might experience as being disappointed. She seems to want so much for you, it's like, if you are struggling with something, she might want to fix it too much. Cause she loves you so much, it's so hard for her to let you struggle with it . . . to let you decide when to ask her for help or not . . . to show her confidence in you . . . and maybe to try to hide her worry more.

These examples of the therapist talking for and talking about members of the family demonstrate the active stance that the therapist takes in helping the family to organize, reorganize, and express their experiences. Often members of the family repeat the same patterns of experience in well-worn tracks that extend far back into their attachment histories. By participating in the cocreation of new meanings of experience through a/r dialogue, the therapist is often successful in activating new patterns. In maintaining this active stance the therapist is assuming responsibility for insuring the momentum of the a/r dialogue and the treatment as a whole. If she is maintaining the family's sense of safety, including her readiness to facilitate the repair of any relationship breaks, the family members are often willing participants in the intersubjective journey.

Chapter 5

TREATMENT ONSET:
MEETINGS WITH PARENTS

Cooperative communication involving the parent's capacity to perceive and respond to the mental state of the child is the hallmark of the securely attached dyad. These mutually attuned experiences allow the infant to develop a reflective capacity that helps to create a sense of cohesion and interpersonal connection. The other's mental state is a positive element in the infant's life. —Dan Siegel, The Developing Mind *(1999)*

Prior to the onset of treatment sessions that involve the whole family, it is most often necessary to have between a few and several sessions with the parents. The primary assumption in this attachment-focused family therapy is that the parents need to become the source of attachment security for their children. Once the parents discover that they can feel safe themselves and also address whatever problems exist within the family—while at the same time helping their children to feel safe within the dialogue and within their relationship—they often manifest a level of confidence and commitment to treatment that enables rapid progress to be achieved. The purposes of this initial stage of treatment involve:

1. Developing an alliance with the parents. This will include providing them with a safe setting for their thoughts and feelings regarding their child to be expressed and be heard,

without concern that they will be hurt by the therapist's expressions or that their children will be hurt by their parents' expressions. The therapist needs to establish that she will serve as an attachment figure for the parents and that the parents and therapist will, together, serve as attachment figures for the children. This exploration will also include the awareness that neither they nor their children will be blamed for the child/family difficulties.

2. Exploring the parents' own attachment histories in order to assess the transmission of their own history into the attachment patterns that exist with their child.
3. Presenting the attachment-focused parenting and treatment models.
4. Inviting the parents to actively participate in this model of treatment.

In this chapter I will present these four features of the initial parent sessions. The emphasis placed on each issue varies greatly depending upon the family

DEVELOPING AN ALLIANCE WITH THE PARENTS

It is crucial at the onset to communicate with the parents in a manner that conveys respect for their caregiving and authoritative role within the family. The parents have the responsibility for deciding what is best for all members of the family. They have the responsibility for deciding how and what they want to accomplish as a family in providing for the best interests of their children and themselves. Parents may value highly the function of the family in insuring that their children will have strong moral values and a commitment to contribute to society. They need to be assured that the therapist's efforts to address whatever led them to her office will not jeopardize their basic values. They need to have confidence that her interventions will facilitate and not compromise the central goals that they hold for their family.

If the parents are to develop an alliance with the therapist, they need to develop a sense of safety within the therapeutic relationship. If they are to openly acknowledge the difficulties that brought them into therapy they need to experience the therapist's acceptance of their subjective experiences as parents. For adults who choose to be parents, the parental role is a central feature of their identities. To acknowledge that they have problems within this role places them in a state of heightened vulnerability. If they feel judged and criticized as parents they are likely to react with shame, defensiveness, and resentment. They may respond with increased efforts to convince the therapist of the severity of their child's problems. They may also place obstacles in front of the therapist's recommendations. They are at risk to develop a stance in therapy that leaves them competing with the therapist over who best knows their child. If their child's progress would prove them to be wrong, they may be ambivalent about this progress. They certainly are at risk to withdraw from treatment.

If the parents are to feel safe, they need to experience the same degree of playfulness, acceptance, curiosity, and empathy from the therapist that is being provided for their child when he or she is present later in the treatment. They need to experience the mind and the heart of the therapist in intersubjective terms. The therapist needs to be communicating that she experiences their commitment to their child, that she knows that they want what is best for him or her, and that they are doing their best. If they have made mistakes, it is not from a lack of trying or from poor motives. The therapist is communicating that she sees and responds to their motives and goals for their child. She experiences them as being good people who love their kids and who work hard to give them the best life that they can. If the therapist is successful in creating a sense of safety for the parents, she will have assisted them in experiencing realistic guilt over any mistakes that they may have made in their parenting behaviors, rather than experiencing shame.

If the parents are able to feel safe with the therapist they are likely to be able to become aware of and express their deeper thoughts and feelings about their child. These feelings may include rage, despair, and pervasive anxiety. They may be increasingly aware that they do not "like" their child. They may be beginning to experience their child as being "bad," "lazy," "selfish," or "dumb." When parents are free to express themselves fully about their child to the therapist, they are giving the therapist an early insight into the child's experiences of primary intersubjectivity that are developing in response to her parents' experience of her. The parents will not feel safe to express these negative experiences of their child unless their experiences are responded to with acceptance, curiosity, and empathy. Only after the parents believe that the therapist understands their concerns over

123

"the problems" will the therapist begin to attempt to broaden and deepen their perspectives.

Once parents have expressed their concerns and perceptions about their child's functioning to the therapist it is often helpful for the therapist to step back in time with the parents to recall other, earlier, perceptions that they have had about their child.

Hopes and Dreams

First, the therapist might well inquire about the parents' hopes and dreams before they had their child. Most likely the parents' inner lives at that time involved a very caring stance with a passion to be a good parent, to protect, love, and guide their child so that she would have a good life. As the parents express these original parenting thoughts and feelings, they are brought into contact with the early positive wishes and feelings that they had. They may well have forgotten those times, and by remembering them, they are able to move closer to an increase in hope and commitment.

When the therapist is able to hear and respond to those early hopes and dreams, it is much easier for her to develop a core state of acceptance, curiosity, and empathy for the parents. She is able to see under the possibly angry and punitive stance that the parents are taking in the present, and relate to the parents' best intentions and affective states as they existed in the past. By having the therapist hear and respond to those early experiences and wishes, the parents are gaining confidence that she does truly experience how much they love and want what is best for their child. Also, as they recall those positive experiences from the past, they are more likely to be able to reexperience those qualities that they had experienced in the past.

Doubts

Second, the therapist might explore when the parents first developed doubts about how well their child was functioning, as well as their ability to help their child and to maintain a positive relationship with him or her. The parents will be describing early difficulties manifested by their child or in their relationship with their child. This may represent the first times that they began to doubt whether or not their hopes and dreams would come true. In exploring these past experiences, ideally the parents will show a readiness to enter into a state of vulnerability. This will provide the therapist with the opportunity to communicate empathy for their distress. It will enable the parents to feel safe that they will not be judged poorly when they express any failings or doubts.

Grief

Third, the therapist then needs to explore if the parents have experienced grief over the loss of their hopes and dreams for their child, as well as for the end of the intensely positive affective experiences that they may have had with their child in past years. Were the doubts and failings so pervasive that the parents became convinced that their family life would never improve? Did they begin to see the behaviors—either their child's or their own—as representing some basic character or relationship flaws that could not be changed? Were the parents demonstrating ongoing anger and despair that represented unresolved grief?

Shame

Fourth, the therapist needs to explore if the parents, following an ongoing pattern of failures in relationship with their child, reacted with shame to their inability to improve their relationships or the child's functioning. Such shame in the parents, if not recognized and resolved, will lead to denial, defensiveness, blame, and excuses, followed by resentment and rage. If the therapist is able to assist the parents in reducing the shame, then she is likely to be able to assist the parents in feeling guilt over whatever errors they may have made as parents. With guilt, the parents are then able to address and repair these features of their relationship with their child.

Resentment

Fifth, the therapist will now have the context in which the patterns of any resentment toward their child developed. It will now be easier for the therapist to experience empathy for the parents and for the parents to feel safe that the therapist will know that they truly love their child and are committed to his best interests.

Acceptance

Sixth, the parents may well now be more accepting of their parental narratives. They are then likely to be more open and less defensive in exploring their strengths and weaknesses as parents.

Commitment

Seventh, through experiencing empathy and a reduction in any shame that resulted from the family difficulties, the parents are more likely to develop a new sense of commitment to try again to be a more successful parent.

Realistic Hopes and Dreams

Eighth, the parents are now able to create more realistic hopes and dreams—with the active participation of their children and the therapist. The intersubjective experiences of self and other will enable them to reflect more deeply on who they are as a family and who they want to be.

Attachment Security

Ninth, having successfully journeyed through their parenting history, and looked back at their original attachment histories, the parents are able to provide attachment security for their children while they all explore the various chapters of their family narrative in the present.

Pride and Joy

Tenth, as progress becomes evident, the entire family becomes aware of an increase in pride and joy over the increase in successes and decrease in failures. Guilt begins to occur without shame. A parenting history that may be different from the original attachment history begins to develop. A coherent autobiographical narrative emerges that includes being a parent. Any continuing difficulties are met with PACE rather than shame and resentment among the members of the family.

While hearing the parents' concerns about their child's functioning and their relationship with the child, the therapist will be communicating acceptance, curiosity, and empathy over the difficulties that they are experiencing. No judgments are being made about the source of the problems. The therapist's motive is to experience the family from the perspective of the parent, not to evaluate whether or not that perspective is problematic. However, in this process, the therapist is also working to deepen the parents' perspectives. This is done through an attitude of persistent curiosity about the situation. The therapist is continuously seeking to understand more about the inner lives of the child and parent. In doing so, she is encouraging the same open, curious, and nonjudgmental stance by the parent.

126

For example, a parent may report that her child argues with her over everything that he is told to do. She adds that she thinks that her child does this because he always has to be right, or he just wants the attention, or he always has to have his own way. Without judging the parent's perception, the therapist questions it, asking for elaborations, implications, or the history of such a motive. The therapist might ask:

What makes him seek attention that way?

What do you think makes it so hard for him if he does not get what he wants?

How does he seem to respond when you begin to argue with him?

What happens if you do not argue back?

Why is making a mistake so difficult for him? Is it for you?

Were/are there times when he does not argue, but rather accepts your decision?

What do you think is the reason why he does that sometimes and not others?

Is it easy for him to initiate plans or discuss what he thinks first?

Do you and he not feel close after those arguments? What's that like for you? For him? Is it hard to feel close again? What's that like for you? For him?

Do you think there may be other motives that might explain those behaviors?

Such questions are not expressed with the assumption that the parent is able to provide a clear response. Rather, they are asked in an effort to facilitate an open, not-knowing, joint parent–therapist stance about their child's motives, thoughts, and feelings. Such a stance will reduce any negative judgments that are current and facilitate a receptive stance of getting to know their child once again.

At the onset parents are encouraged to describe their child's behaviors for which they are seeking treatment. It is important that the therapist not dismiss these concerns as unimportant. It is equally important that the therapist not suggest that these behaviors will be addressed eventually, possibly in a few months, after the more important issues are first resolved. To develop an effective alliance with the parents, the therapist needs to communicate a desire to understand the parents' concerns about their child and an agreement that their concerns warrant their joint attention. At the same time, the therapist will take advantage of this initial focus on symptoms to begin to demonstrate the core of the treatment model. The therapist is communicating the point that, in understanding the symptoms, it is crucial to understand what lies under the symptoms. The therapist communicates acceptance, curiosity, and empathy for the symptoms and their effects on both the child and the parents.

The first words of Table 5.1 represent a sampling of frequent symptoms that children may manifest that bring them and their parents to treatment. The following phrases represent possible reasons for the behaviors. At this beginning stage of treatment the therapist is not suggesting that she knows the "right" motives for the child's behaviors. Rather, she is communicating the need for an open and curious attitude to understanding better what the child's motives might be for his or her behaviors. The therapist is deeply interested in what lies under the behavior, communicating to the parents that such understanding is likely to hold the key to change.

In arriving at an understanding about possible reasons for the child's behavior, the therapist is facilitating the parents' ability to experience empathy for their child. The therapist may need to stress that reasons are not excuses, in order for the parents to be willing to try to understand their child, with acceptance, not judgment. The therapist may suggest that a reason becomes an excuse only when the reason removes accountability for the behavior. Reasons guide interventions; they are part of the assessment that is needed before treatment, and any appropriate parental discipline, can begin.

While this dialogue is occurring between the therapist and parents the therapist is also likely to be noticing parental behavior that the therapist may believe is possibly contributing to the child's behavior. Table 5.2 shows a sampling of such parental behaviors. Just as it is important to understand the reasons for the child's behavior in order to facilitate parental empathy toward the child, it is equally important for the therapist to understand the reasons for the parent's behavior in order to facilitate the therapist's empathy toward the parents. Sensing the therapist's empathy toward self, the parents are likely to be more able to acknowledge and have empathy for themselves when they manifest behaviors that they are not comfortable with. Feeling empathy from the therapist, they are likely to feel less shame for self and be more able to experience guilt when appropriate and repair any problems that may be present. Feeling empathy from the therapist, they are equally likely to be more able to feel empathy for their child.

TABLE 5.1. CHILD'S BEHAVIOR/UNDER THE BEHAVIOR

Child's behavior

Argue, complain, control, cling, withdraw, not ask for help, not show affection, bang head to sleep, scream over routine frustrations, constant attention seeking, poor eye contact, lie, steal, gorge food, peer relationship problems, educational underachievement, school refusal, general anxiety, compulsions, social withdrawal

Under the behavior

Sense that only self can/will meet own needs

Not feeling safe

Frequent sense of shame

Sense of hopelessness and helplessness

Fear of being vulnerable/dependent

Fear of rejection

Feeling "invisible"

Inability to self-regulate intense affect—positive or negative

Inability to engage in the coregulation of affect—positive or negative

Felt sense that life is too hard

Assumptions that parents' motives/intentions are negative

Lack of confidence in own abilities

Lack of confidence that parent will comfort/assist during hard times

Inability to understand why self does things

Need to deny inner life because of overwhelming affect that exists there

Inability to express inner life even if he or she wanted to

Fear of failure

Fear of trusting happiness

Discipline is experienced as harsh and unfair

Inability to be comforted when disciplined/hurt

Inability to ask for help

In "noticing" the parents' behaviors it is best to do so in a direct and natural manner, without a serious, judgmental, tone. The therapist might simply ask the parents about what areas of themselves—with regard to their parenting—they tend to be the most critical. Which of their behaviors would they like to change? Which behavioral changes would be likely to help their child with his or her problems? While being just as direct, the therapist then could become curious about why the parents think they engage in those behaviors. Understanding the roots of the behaviors, the therapist—and parents—are more likely to have empathy for the

TABLE 5.2. PARENTS' BEHAVIOR/UNDER THE BEHAVIOR

Parent's behavior

Chronic anger, harsh discipline, power struggles, not asking for help, not showing affection, difficulty sleeping, appetite problems, ignoring child, remaining isolated from child, reacting with rage and impulsiveness, lack of empathy for child, marital conflicts, withdrawal from relatives and friends, anxiety and depression.

Under the behavior

Desire to help child to develop well

Love and commitment for child

Desire to be a good parent

Uncertainty about how to best meet child's needs

Lack of confidence in ability to meet child's needs

Specific failures with child associated with more pervasive doubts about self

Pervasive sense of shame as a parent

Conviction of helplessness and hopelessness

Fear of being vulnerable/being hurt by child

Fear of rejection by child as a parent

Fear of failure as a parent

Inability to understand why child does things

Inability to understand why self reacts to child

Association of child's functioning with aspects of own attachment history

Feeling lack of support and understanding from partner and other adults

Difficulties addressing relationship problems with partner

Felt sense that life is too hard

Assumptions that child's motives/intentions are negative

Belief that there are no other options besides the behavior tried

parent for the behaviors and the parents will be more willing to work to modify them if necessary. This entire discussion is done with PACE (playfulness, acceptance, curiosity, and empathy) and serves to become the foundation for all subsequent efforts to address parental behaviors that seem to be contributing to the family difficulties.

Understanding that their motives as shown in Table 5.2 are similar to those presented in Table 5.1 will begin the process whereby the parents are slower to make negative judgments about their child's motives. Through establishing an intersubjective context of acceptance, curiosity, and empathy with regard to the parents' concerns about their child, the therapist is laying a foundation so that she—and the parents—are able to establish a similar context for exploring these themes with the parents and child together. The phrases as presented in Table 5.2 will begin the process whereby the parents are slower to judge the motives for their own behaviors. As any underlying shame dissipates, the parents will be more likely to experience greater empathy for themselves which will facilitate many possibilities for change.

After successfully initiating a working alliance with the parent the therapist may or may not ask to have a similar meeting alone with the child. This would be necessary if the therapist believes that by not seeing the child, the parent will not be confident that the therapist understands the situation enough to make a treatment plan. It would also be necessary if the therapist believes that the child will not be willing to engage in joint treatment if he or she knows that the therapist has heard the parents' perspective but has not heard the child's perspective. It would also be necessary if the therapist had significant questions or concerns that she wanted to address before presenting her model of treatment and parenting to the parent.

However, often such a separate meeting with the child is not necessary. The therapist believes that the attachment perspective is appropriate for addressing the full range of child/family problems. If the therapist's goal is to have the parents provide attachment security for their children, then their presence is crucial. If, as the sessions proceed, other approaches are indicated, they can easily be incorporated into the treatment. Also, the child is often a reluctant participant early in the family sessions, regardless of whether or not she saw the therapist alone at the onset. The child's participation will be insured only after she experiences, intersubjectively, the therapist's attitude (PACE) toward her and discovers that the sessions are helpful. The child will respond more quickly when she experiences safety while being with the parents in the joint sessions.

EXPLORING THE PARENTS' OWN ATTACHMENT HISTORIES

If the above areas of focus have proceeded well, the therapist is able to now explore relevant factors from the parents' own attachment histories. At this point, the therapist will have created a working alliance built upon safety, characterized by playfulness, acceptance, curiosity, and empathy. The parent will also understand the relevance of their attachment histories in understanding the current family interaction patterns. The therapist summarizes our increasing knowledge that the attachment patterns that are transformable in adulthood are central to the parent–child relationship and to the related qualities of safety, affect regulation, and meaning-making, tend to be patterns that are similar to what existed in prior generations. She will state clearly that the greatest predictor of an infant's attachment patterns are the attachment patterns of his or her primary caregivers. Given this, the parents will be asked to explore briefly their own attachment histories and associated attachment behavioral patterns. (Some of this exploration may well have been begun when the therapist explored the parenting history at the onset of the sessions.) Comparisons will then be made between the parents' patterns in their families of origin and those manifested by their child. Parents will also be asked to note whether or not certain behaviors of the child serve to activate certain patterns from their own histories.

In describing the central ways that parents influence children from the perspective of attachment and intersubjectivity, this work has focused on the joint processes of coregulating affect and cocreating meaning. Coregulating and cocreating refers to the *mutual* regulation of affect and the *mutual* creation of meaning. It needs to be stressed that the influence is proceeding in both directions. If a parent is to have an influence on her child, she will be influenced by her child. While generally more of the influence may move from parent to child rather than vice versa, it nevertheless moves in both directions. When the parent is unresolved with regard to a particular memory or affective state associated with her own attachment history, this mutual movement becomes very evident. Her child's affective state or experience of meaning may well create an intense reaction of a similar nature within her. Her reaction may become quickly dysregulated, possibly leading to intense affect, rigid thought, and impulsive behavior. She is not able to assist her child through coregulation and cocreation because she is struggling to autoregulate and to remain coherent herself. If her child needs her at that time, she is not available. In fact, if she is becoming dysregulated and reactive, her presence is likely to increase her child's dysregulation rather than contain it.

The cycle just described is not uncommon. The child is struggling with the affect and meaning associated with an event and his struggles elicit a parental reaction. Because the child's struggles become associated with similar, unresolved struggles that the parent had in her own attachment history the parent's response is not helpful, but rather hurtful. The parent is often left thinking that her child "wanted to hurt me." She may be left feeling overwhelmed, angry, frightened, or shameful, not unlike feelings that she had in similar situations in her family of origin.

The therapist addresses this pattern directly. She describes the intergenerational nature of attachment behaviors. She asks to understand the parents' own attachment history in order to have a better understanding of the current family attachment patterns. Her attitude is based on PACE. It is clear that she is not searching for reasons to blame the parents for the current difficulties. She is not judgmental. She simply wants to understand their experiences as children, to better understand their experiences as parents, parenting their child.

In asking about the parents' attachment history, the therapist is focusing on their relationships with their attachment figures, their traumas, losses, and other significant events in their childhood. The 10 questions listed in Table 5.3 are taken from *Parenting from the Inside Out* (2003), by Dan Siegel and Mary Hartzell. This book is an excellent resource for parents who are willing to make the effort to understand themselves, especially with regard to how their own attachment histories have an impact on their relationships with their own children.

As parents begin to share their own histories they often become aware of various similarities between their past experiences and those in the present that involve themselves or their child. This awareness is facilitated by the therapist's acceptance, curiosity, and empathy about whatever they are recalling. This awareness often will immediately increase the parents' abilities to reflect upon and respond to their child's behavior rather than simply react to it.

One example of this pattern involves Melodie, a mother of a young adolescent boy who often became angry with her. His anger would trigger an intense reaction of rage on her part, leading to screaming matches, threats, consequences, and then angry withdrawal from each other. As we explored her own history, she could not recall anyone in her childhood who would become angry with her the way that her son now did. Nor could she recall ever having been traumatized in any way by an attachment figure or by any other adult. As we puzzled

TABLE 5.3. QUESTIONS FOR PARENTAL SELF-REFLECTION (FROM SIEGEL & HARTZELL, 2003, PP. 133–134)

1. What was it like growing up? Who was in your family?

2. How did you get along with your parents early in your childhood? How did the relationship evolve throughout your youth and up until the present time?

3. How did your relationship with your mother and father differ, and how were they similar? Are there ways in which you try to be like or try not to be like each of your parents?

4. Did you feel rejected or threatened by your parents? Were there other experiences you had that felt overwhelming or traumatizing in your life, during childhood, or beyond? Do any of these experiences still feel very much alive? Do they continue to influence your life?

5. How did your parents discipline you as a child? What impact did that have on your childhood, and how do you feel it affects your role as a parent now?

6. Do you recall your earliest separations from your parents? What was it like? Did you ever have prolonged separations from your parents?

7. Did anyone significant in your life die during your childhood or later in your life? What was it like for you at the time, and how does that loss affect you now?

8. How did your parents communicate with you when you were happy and excited? Did they join with you in your enthusiasm? When you were distressed or unhappy as a child, what would happen? Did your father and mother respond differently to you during these emotional times? How?

9. Was there anyone else besides your parents in your childhood who took care of you? What was that relationship like for you? What happened to those individuals? What is it like for you when you let others take care of your child now?

10. If you had difficult times during your childhood, were there positive relationships in or outside your home that you could depend on during those times? How do you feel those connections benefited you then and how might they help you now?

11. How have your childhood experiences influenced your relationships with others as an adult? Do you find yourself trying not to behave incertain ways because of what happened to you as a child? Do you have patterns of behavior that you'd like to alter but have difficulty changing?

12. What impact do you think your childhood has had on your adult lifein general, including the ways in which you think of yourself and the ways you relate to your children? What would you like to change about the way you understand yourself and relate to others?

over the intensity of her rage at her son, she suddenly recalled a person from her past who did remind her of him. Melodie recalled herself, when she was about his age! She recalled her own anger, directed at her parents. When asked if her parents responded as she now did—with rage and threats—she stated that they did not. Rather they responded with anxiety. Her mother would withdraw to her room and sometimes cry. Her father would become silent and sometimes go for a walk. She then stated that she began to hate herself for becoming angry with them and hurting them. Her anger became full of shame. She had come to reject that aspect of her early adolescent development. She also most certainly did not learn how to regulate intense anger, just as her parents had not. Now her son, relating with her as she had done with her parents, activated those shameful feelings that elicited sudden rage toward him, the felt source of her shame. This sudden awareness left Melodie feeling calm. She now understood her rage and she was immediately confident that she would be much more able to manage her son's anger. By our next session, her anger toward her son was much less. A few sessions later her son was brought into the sessions. She was able to respond to his anger in an empathic and confident manner. She and the therapist were able then to express curiosity about the sources of his anger and discovered many hidden fears that he had been struggling to manage on his own. After a few more sessions, treatment was no longer needed.

Certainly at times, the gains are not so rapid, and parents are less able to either explore their narrative or see connections with their current parenting behavior. On the Adult Attachment Interview the majority of adults are able to discuss their attachment history with an interviewer in a satisfactory manner, maintaining a fluent dialogue while recalling significant attachment-related events from their youth, and forming a coherent narrative around them (Hesse, 1999). However, a significant minority of adults are not able to manage the complex tasks of both recalling significant aspects of their past and maintaining a dialogue with the interviewer. Some adults have little to recall about their life with their parents. They speak of their relationships with their parents as if they were not that important in their lives. Other adults recall details that do not appear to be relevant to the story or which are inconsistent or which interfere with the act of telling. They appear to continue to struggle with interactions that they had with their parents years ago. Still other adults appear to dissociate while recalling/telling and appear to be lost in the past.

At times parents who seek family therapy manifest aspects of their attachment history that are not fully integrated and organized, leaving their own narrative somewhat lacking in coherence. When this is the case the therapist asks the parent to explore these themes in greater detail in order to seek a resolution that will prove to be very beneficial for the family treatment. Often this simply necessitates brief individual/couple treatment prior to the onset of the family sessions. Periodic sessions are necessary with the parents alone, sometimes continuing throughout the course of the family sessions, in order to address factors related to their attachment histories. Sometimes the parent(s) need to be referred to another therapist (or two) because the interventions are likely to need sufficient time and intensity to require the involvement of more than the family therapist.

PRESENTING THE ATTACHMENT-FOCUSED TREATMENT/PARENTING MODEL

Since many attachment concepts have not become part of our society's implicit awareness about the needs of children and families, it is helpful at the onset to present core principles of child rearing that are part of this family treatment model. This list is not exhaustive. Providing this information at the onset of treatment, however, will help the therapist to convey the assumption that part of the treatment will involve teaching the parents additional skills—affective, and reflective behaviors—that will facilitate family change. Books that I have found to be helpful in conveying these concepts to parents are *Time-In Parenting* (2002) by Otto Weininger and *Unconditional Parenting* (2005) by Alfie Kohn. An excellent reference on parenting that is very congruent with this work is *The Science of Parenting* (2006) by Margot Sunderland.

Closeness, Affect, and Its Coregulation

When a child experiences strong negative affect, such as fear, sadness, shame, or anger, the parent's presence is often very beneficial, if not crucial in regulating this affective state. Coregulation of affect often provides the safety and intersubjective skills needed for the young child's developing skills in the autoregulation of affect. By matching the rhythm of the child's expressed affective state while regulating her or his own affect, the parent enables the child to begin to identify, contain, and regulate the expression of the affect that is being experienced. A child's ability to manage strong affective states, whether they are negative or positive states, immediately increases when he or she is in the presence of an attuned attachment figure.

Certain child-rearing principles that stress isolation when a child experiences intense affect, especially anger, may be consistent with some models of development but are not congruent with attachment theory. Anger should be treated no differently from fear, sadness, or any other intense affective state in providing the child with one's affect-regulating presence. Through such presence, the parent is showing the child that such a state does not bring rejection, does not have to be faced alone, and is not something that the child needs to hide in shame. The state of anger is no different from any other affective state. It is accepted, understood, and coregulated by the parent.

Isolation from the parent is likely to be indicated only if it is the best option among those available. It might be chosen if the parent is not able to regulate her own negative affect and so may frighten the child. It might also be chosen if the parent tends to ignore the child when she is doing well, and attend to her only when the child is engaged in inappropriate behavior associated with certain affective states such as anger. Or it might be chosen if the child's shame is so intense that the parent's presence makes it more extreme. However, it must be stressed that in these examples isolation is only preferable to even worse options, and so is not to be recommended as a long-term solution to a problem. It is much better for the parent to increase her ability to regulate her own affective states, be available and responsive to the child in all of her affective/behavioral states, and assist the child in reducing her states of shame so that the parent's presence is not so dysregulating when the child is in a state of shame.

In emphasizing the benefit to the child of having parents coregulate the developing affective states, it becomes clear that parents need to accept responsibility for being able to regulate their own affective states. If parents, when present with their child, hold dysregulating feelings of rage, anxiety, or disgust toward him, their child will develop with an impaired view of self (primary intersubjectivity) and be at risk of being unable to learn to regulate his own affective states.

Parental closeness and affect regulation abilities are also necessary if a child is to learn to regulate positive affective states. Excitement and joy can quickly turn to uncertainty and anxiety if the parent is not present to share in the excitement and reassure the child (often nonverbally) that this intense affect state can be regulated and given meaning that is positive. When children have too few opportunities for such pleasurable affective states because of ongoing parental depression or conflict, they are at risk for having difficulty managing stimulating or novel situations that they encounter throughout their childhood.

Touch is central to the coregulation of affect and facilitating a sense of felt safety between parent and child. Touch permeates the child's prenatal existence and remains important throughout the individual's life span. Touch is important both in coregulating affect and in cocreating meaning between parent and child. The comforting touch helps the child to attain resolution about the most painful loss. The deep touch assists the agitated child in becoming calm. The gentle touch enables the annoyed child to accept a parent's limit on her behavior. The caressing touch enables the child to feel love when she thinks that she may be unlovable. Touch needs to be varied, finding a place in family relationships in many contexts and for many reasons. It needs to be long and short, deep and light, playful and affectionate. Within touch the parent–child relationship is felt more deeply. Good times are experienced as being even better and bad times are easier to get through.

A clear example of the power of touch in relationships occurred in a treatment session with a young adolescent boy and his mother. With some coaching the 13-year-old boy was able to tell his mother that he did want to learn to rely on her more easily and to work through their current difficulty with conflicts. Since he was looking at the floor, the therapist asked him to look at her. He did and she told him that she wanted to help him to be able to let his mom get closer to him during his hard times. As she gently said those words she reached out and placed her hand on his. At the instant that she touched him, he burst into tears, and, turning to his mother, fell into her arms.

A child needs to view his or her home as both a secure base from which the child will leave to explore the world, and a safe haven to which the child will return when he or she needs a break from the world. To serve these functions well, the parents will ensure that the individual's needs for safety, autonomy, and emotional intimacy are met. Children are likely to need "time at home" more than do adults. Therefore parents should ensure that there is plenty of "at home" unscheduled, casual time available where the child can relax, not having to compete, and not being evaluated. Periodic "holidays" from school may prevent recurring "sick" days that seem to function to give the child time at home. Time after school and on weekends where there is no homework and no organized sport or comparable activity is "valued time," not "wasted time."

Connection-Break-Repair

Attunement—the intersubjective sharing of affective states—is at the heart of the parent–child attachment. Within matched positive affective states, there is reciprocal joy, excitement, and fun. There is relaxed contentment and pleasant companionship. There is a realization, often implicit, that the pleasure being experienced is greater because it is being shared with the other. Along with these attuned affective states are shared attention and intentions. Together, the parent and child are intersubjectively present, and within such psychological states, the meanings of self, other, and world become more vibrant, understandable, acceptable, and coherent.

Within secure attachments there is a certainty and continuity in the relationship that is neither threatened nor damaged in response to conflict, separation, or misattunement. Since such conflicts and separations will most certainly occur, secure attachments always include the ability of the parents to repair the relationship with their child after such a break. Each member of the family is confident that no matter what happens, the relationships will be maintained. This conviction is the bedrock of the ability of the family to provide safety for all. No matter how long the separation and how severe the conflict, unconditional love and readiness to care for the others in the family when they are in need will remain.

A securely attached infant experiences her parent as being available and responsive when the infant is in distress. The parent's presence helps to coregulate the distress so that it does not become dysregulating. If at times, during brief periods of mild distress, a parent is not responsive, the child gradually learns that she can manage the distress alone, and the parent will often allow or even encourage the child to do so. When the distress is too difficult for the child to manage alone, the parent will be there to assist her, and they will manage it together. Over time, the amount of stress that the child can manage alone increases, but she still knows, even in adulthood, that the parent will be available and responsive if needed.

In secure attachments, breaks in the intersubjective state are likely to cause some distress, but it is easily managed because the repair of the bond occurs quickly and fully. During acts of parental discipline, the young child is likely to feel some shame and feel separate from the parent. For example, a mother raises her voice to her toddler to tell him that he is playing too roughly with the kitten. She may quickly take some action to stop the play if her voice is not sufficient. The toddler looks down, becomes passive and forlorn. The mother quickly reattunes with her toddler, speaking with a nurturing voice, directly him how to play with the kitten appropriately or redirecting him to another activity. The shame state ceases and the relationship is repaired. The parent coregulated the distress caused by her discipline and then cocreated the meaning of the discipline. Her limit was neither a threat to self nor to the relationship. Her limit referred to her toddler's behavior involving a specific type of play with the kitten.

With young children, states of shame associated with parental discipline are not likely to be autoregulated well. They require active repair through coregulation with the parent. In secure attachments, as the child develops with the certainty of interactive repair, parental discipline elicits guilt rather than shame. The discipline is experienced as being associated with the behavior, not with the child's self nor with the relationship. This child is often able to autoregulate the guilt and it takes little on the part of either child or parent to repair the relationship and for both to be available for intersubjective experiences.

However, in many families certain childrearing practices and ways of relating lead to conflict that is less easily resolved and which trigger shame within both parent and child because they are failing to negotiate a conflict and move toward resolution. The conflict now represents more than a behavior and becomes a threat to both the relationship as well as to the sense of self in both members of the dyad. This sequence can be at the root of much family discord and leads many families to treatment.

The therapist may directly address this problem in family treatment with recommendations for dealing with this sequence at home. She speaks openly of the fact that all secure attachments involve countless times when the usual state of feeling close and safe is followed by a break, which requires a repair. The therapist strives to help the family to maintain a commitment to identifying the break and need for repair and then doing it. Breaks that are repaired are very beneficial to secure attachments as they insure the continuing balance between autonomy and intimacy that is present in well-functioning families. At times such information and recommendations are not sufficient. A history of unrepaired breaks may cause the parent or child to have much difficulty regulating their affect and creating positive meaning sufficient to repair the current break.

The therapist leads an exploration with the parents into reasons why relationship breaks and their subsequent repair are likely to be difficult for the parents. Examples include the following:

1. Breaks are perceived as representing a failure or weakness in the relationship.
2. Breaks, as failures, are "wrong" and someone needs to be "blamed" for their presence.
3. Breaks are perceived as representing a major problem because each member of the dyad is likely to attribute negative motives to the behavior of the other.
4. Breaks, as differences, are perceived as being a threat to the stability of the relationship.
5. Breaks are poorly understood because family members do not commonly communicate their thoughts, feelings, motives, and desires to each other.
6. Breaks, as mistakes, are not able to be accepted as they are often associated with pervasive shame, rather than specific guilt which would motivate repair. The conflict now represents more than the original experience and it becomes a threat to both the relationship as well as to the sense of self in both members of the dyad.
7. The parents' own attachment histories manifested insecurity or unresolved features that prevent them from remaining "present" in the face of breaks.
8. The parents' sense of their authority is based on the need for compliance. Anger is seen as being "disrespectful" and not a normal aspect of relationship breaks.
9. During breaks, the parent or child is unable to manage the expression of anger leading to the emergence of hurtful verbal aggression.
10. Breaks are caused by parents employing relationship withdrawal—or the threat of it—as a discipline technique.

Not only do breaks often take on a negative and dysregulating characteristic, so too do the acts of repair often become very difficult for both the parent and child to initiate and successfully complete. This is likely to relate to a number of factors including:

1. Initiating repair is seen as "giving in" to the other.
2. Initiating repair is often experienced as an apology that neither wants to give.
3. Initiating repair places one at risk for being rejected by the other.
4. Initiating repair raises the possibility that by focusing on the break, the conflict will intensify again.
5. When parents initiate repair it is often seen by them as diminishing their authority.
6. Parents often see repair as "processing" in which the primary intention is to prevent the recurrence of the break. The need to actually repair the security of the attachment is overlooked.

Once the reasons for the difficulties in successfully repairing breaks in the parent–child relationship are understood, the therapist is in a good position to assist the parents in taking the lead in being able to initiate repair during the treatment sessions and at home.

The following guidelines are likely to serve as an outline for facilitating the attunement-break-repair sequence:

1. The habitual, interpersonal/affective atmosphere of the home is open, inclusive, and is generally comfortable to all members of the family.
2. Differences are addressed openly, with focus on how specific behaviors affect the self/family along with a proposed way to resolve the differences.
3. All members of the family who are involved in the conflict have a role in its resolution.
4. The goal of discipline is to teach, not to punish; to help the child to learn, not to feel shame. If one person hurts another, the goal is for the person to feel appropriate guilt—not shame—over his or her act and repair the relationship.
5. To facilitate effective discipline, the parent is encouraged to speak with empathy rather than anger. Empathy keeps the focus on the behavior, rather than the child, whereas anger moves the focus to the relationship and away from the behavior.

Being "sad for" a child over the difficulty that he has learning a behavior and for any related consequences tends to be much more effective than being "mad at" him.

6. The parent is committed to repairing the relationship and returning it to the original relaxed and mutually enjoyable intersubjective state as quickly as possible. The parent does not use psychological distancing over an extended period of time as a way to "teach" the child to make better choices. The attachment relationship is kept out of the discipline.

7. When the parent's discipline does involve anger directed toward the child, the anger is short and associated with the effects of the child's behavior. When the anger reflects the parent's own affective state and is not seen as being a necessary part of discipline, the parent acknowledges that and will apologize for the anger when appropriate.

8. The parent may initiate a discussion in which both reflect on particularly difficult conflicts in a manner that communicates that they both felt strongly about something and were not feeling close to each other for a while. The parent is communicating acceptance of the break as being natural to all relationships and not being something that warrants shame or fear. She adds that she is happy that they are feeling close again.

Intersubjective Perception and Influence

Parents continuously perceive the expressions and actions of their infants as representing traits that others are unlikely to see to the same extent. Parental perception may involve the discovery of a coherent meaning in expressions that represent initial tendencies toward those traits. The parent may perceive as actual traits expressions that represent potential qualities. By their parents experiencing them as actual, their infant is more able to make them actual. This is the "zone of proximal development." The parent influences her child's development by accepting what he or she expresses, perceiving the potential as emerging into the actual and expecting—without pressure—that those qualities will be manifested too.

Through their acts of perception of their child's subjective expressions—not "objective" behavior—parents are having a significant influence on their child's development. Their perceptions are both affective and reflective. When a parent experiences interest, enjoyment, delight, and love while with a child, he will experience himself as being interesting, enjoyable, delightful, and lovable. Closely observing eye gaze, body movements, and vocal expressions, the parents are "discovering" the infant's emerging, interests, skills, and talents. In fundamental ways the infant grows into these perceptions.

Too often parents overlook the profound way that they influence their child by perceiving his positive qualities and abilities that lie under his behavior. As their child begins to talk and acquire more of the skills of his family and culture, parents begin to believe that their major influence is in focusing on his or her behavior, telling the child if the behavior is "right" or "wrong," and if that does not suffice, giving him a "consequence" that is intended to motivate him to do what is "right" and refrain from what is "wrong." In focusing on behavior, the parents often lose sight of what the behavior might represent about their child's inner life. They lose sight of his underlying strengths and desires. Being uncertain about his motives, they often assume a worse motive than their child may have actually had. These parents have forgotten that the source of their influence on their child's development when he was younger involved the depth of their perceptions. Focused on the behavior, they lose sight of their child. Experiencing this focus on behavior, their child is at risk of experiencing their evaluations but not their unconditional love. Hearing the lecture and consequence, they are at risk to experience influence as based on power and external judgments and rewards rather than experiencing the more profound influence that emerges from intersubjective experiences.

When the parent communicates her intersubjective experience of her child her influence is much more congruent with her child's motives. With joined affect, awareness, and intentions, the child and her parents are likely to jointly discover the best course of action that will address the wishes and concerns of both. If they fail to achieve that agreement, they are still more likely to trust each other's motives. What conflict that emerges is likely to be mild, short-lived, and more easily repaired. The child is likely to be much more receptive to her parents' influence when it emerges intersubjectively. Discipline within such an intersubjective context is likely to be a routine aspect of family life.

In conveying the importance of the intersubjective approach to discipline, the therapist is inviting the parents to look at their child anew. She is asking the parents to assume that their child is most often doing the best she can. Their child has habits, values, and perceptions similar to their own, and does appreciate her parents' experience and perceptions as a guide for what is best for her. Too often when parents initiate family therapy their perceptions are negative and they assume negative motives under their child's behavior. What influence they have tends to be based on their positions of power within the family, rather than reciprocal influence. They tend to forget that if they do provide their child with a sense of safety and if they have confidence in their child's abilities, their child is likely to have more confidence in herself as well.

There is a profound difference between intersubjectivity and reinforcement regarding how parents influence their children's behaviors. With the act of reinforcement, parents are evaluating their child's behavior, judging it to be "correct," and providing a consequence intended to maintain the behavior. The child is expected to rely on the judgment of the parent, rather than to develop his own judgment about what is best for himself. He may come to overly depend upon his parents' judgment. Or he may begin to directly—or indirectly—oppose his parents' judgment because it is experienced as being controlling or indifferent to the child's own experience (thoughts, feelings, motives, perceptions, etc.). Within the intersubjective experience the parent is not engaged in the evaluation of her child but rather is discovering qualities within her child's experience which facilitates her child's ability to experience the same qualities within himself. Dependency or opposition are much less likely to occur because the parents are more focused on cocreating the meaning and coregulating the affect of the child's experience rather than on evaluating his behavior.

Consider the following example of the difference between intersubjectivity and reinforcement in a parent's discipline of her child.

Eleven-year-old John came home from school, quickly changed his clothes, and was in the process of running out of the house to spend time with his friends. His mother knew that the family was going to her sister's house for the evening and that John would not have time to do his homework later. She told him that he could not go outside because of his homework, but he yelled and continued toward the door.

Reinforcement Discipline

Mom: John, you get back here. You have to do your homework first!
John: No, mom, I really want to see my friends!
Mom: No. Your homework must get done now.

John: I'm not going to do it now!

Mom: (a negative reinforcement option) John, you are going to do it or you will not be allowed to play with your friends for two days.

Mom: (a positive reinforcement option) John, you have to do it now. If you get it done I'll let you spend some extra time with them tomorrow.

John: I hate this stupid homework. And I don't want to go to Aunt Jean's.

Mom: Get started now John, and stop complaining, and you'll be able to see them more tomorrow.

Intersubjective Discipline

Mom: Wait, John. You won't have time to get your homework done later because we are going to Aunt Jean's house.

John: No, mom, I really want to see my friends!

Mom: I can see that son. I know that they're important to you and you haven't seen them all day.

John: I haven't mom! I just want to see them!

Mom: I know you do, John. I know how important they are to you. And right now getting your homework done probably does not seem nearly as important. You probably would like to say, "Who cares about the dumb homework . . . and Aunt Jean's house—I don't want to go anyway."

John: I don't care mom and I don't want to go.

Mom: I can understand John. You have a great time with your friends, and not seeing them because of homework and Aunt Jean probably does not seem fair.

John: It doesn't mom!

Mom: It wouldn't have seemed fair to me either, John, when I was your age. I'm sorry that it is working out this way today.

John: Ah, mom, sometimes things suck!

Mom: And I think that this is one of those times for you.

These differences in words are likely to be reflective of what are more pervasive differences in general patterns of perception and involvement between John and his mother. When a parent focuses on reinforcement as the primary means of influencing her child, her focus is on his behavior, not his experience, and he is less likely to feel understood and less likely to believe that his thoughts and feelings matter. With her eyes on his behavior she is less likely to know how important his friends are to him, and to be less sensitive to his thoughts and feelings during the act of discipline. She is also less likely to see the need to repair any breaks in their relationship due to the act of discipline.

When a parent regards her intersubjective presence as crucial in influencing her child's behaviors, she habitually sees his behavior within a deeper context of his experience. She frequently has experienced his experience of fun and feeling liked and competent when he speaks of his friends and when she sees him with them. He probably has often shared his ambivalent feelings about homework with her as well as the boredom that he often feels when he has to go with the rest of the family to relatives' homes. He has experienced his mother's habitual sharing in his experience of his various interests and disinterests, and he also has experienced her not ignoring his thoughts and wishes when she tells him about a behavior that is expected. When she clearly states that it is a homework/relative time, not a friend time, he trusts that she knows how hard that will be for him, and he experiences her empathy for his distress. He remains confident that their relationship is unaffected by his anger over the behavioral expectation, and he is also confident that his mother truly "gets" how disappointed and angry he his. With influence through reinforcement it is easy to forget the context (thoughts, feelings, relationship) of the behavioral expectation and the conflict is at risk to overshadow the more central factors. Within intersubjectivity, the conflict maintains its limited place within the intersubjective nature of the relationship.

Certainly at times it is necessary to just focus on the immediate behavior in a manner that clearly and firmly directs (influences) it. These times might involve safety or just the pressing demands of many responsibilities. However, when the parent habitually influences through intersubjectivity, these times remain the exceptions and are easily experienced and are often accepted by the child.

In essence, the intersubjective influence emerges from the habitual times of shared affect, awareness, and intention where there is an ongoing reciprocal influence on the organization of experience of the parent and child. When these moments are habitual, their presence is assumed and felt almost as fully as one's experience of oneself. The parents' intentions to guide their child's development are interwoven with their experience of their child's intentions. Discipline and related conflicts then do not present any significant risk to either attachment security or the autonomy of parent or child.

147

Attitude of PACE

The same qualities of playfulness, acceptance, curiosity, and empathy that are the heart of the family therapy are also seen as the everyday way of interacting within the family. If the parents are able to maintain this attitude for most of the time during most days, the overall family atmosphere will be one that generates safety, comfort, sharing, and reciprocal enjoyment. When conflicts occur they are seen as routine stress that is easily managed by the overall security of the attachments. This attitude makes it likely that conflicts will not lead to dysregulated affective states but rather are able to be integrated into the intersubjective matrix.

The parents are presented with a description of these qualities along with an explanation as to their power in facilitating attachment security. They are asked to recall how these qualities were present during their early experiences with their child's infancy. They also are asked to explore how they think they may have drifted away from that attitude. (Such a drift is quite common, but neither necessary nor desirable in the ongoing socialization of children.) The therapist experiences empathy for how hard they anticipate it might be to go back to that attitude. Their fears and doubts are explored as to what that attitude would entail.

This attitude definitely does not imply that the parents need to be "permissive." The attitude has an evident place in authoritative, but not authoritarian, families. This attitude does not exclude anger as an appropriate and even necessary component of discipline at times. Anger related to certain serious behaviors (i.e., deliberately hurting the dog) may be very necessary or the seriousness of the consequences of the child's behavior will be minimized. However, in those cases, anger should be brief and clear in its focus. The parents should then be encouraged to repair their relationship through reconnecting with PACE fairly quickly. Appropriate consequences may well necessarily follow, but there is little value—and only risk to attachment security—in extended relationship withdrawal. Difficulties in implementing the attitude will be explored openly, often relating these difficulties to aspects of the parents' own attachment histories.

Other Parenting Characteristics to Facilitate Attachment Security

Parents are able to facilitate the forming of a secure attachment by their children through a variety of ways of interacting with them. It is valuable for the therapist at the onset of treatment to explore these interactions with the parents. She is able to alert the parents to those features that she believes are important in facilitating attachment security. She is able to explore with the parents their strengths and weaknesses with regard to those qualities. She can then focus on building on the strengths and addressing the weaknesses. She is able to explore how the parents may be able to complement each other in responding to their child's various needs. She is able to elicit information about how the parents perceive each other's interactions with their child. She is able to connect their own early childhood experiences in these areas of functioning with regard to their current child rearing. This will enable her to open for discussion the parents' own attachment histories. Finally, she will be developing a guide for treatment planning and goals.

A summary of interaction patterns that influence the development of attachment security can be found in Table 5.4. Parents are asked to complete the profile for themselves and for their partner. Their respective responses will then be explored, focusing on their perception of their strengths and weaknesses as well as those of their partner. Special notice will be given to areas of discrepancy in their perceptions as well as differences in their child rearing. These differences may uncover ongoing conflicts. Parents will be encouraged to reflect on the sources of their interaction patterns, whether or not they see value in changing these patterns, and how they might begin to change them if they choose to do so.

ELICITING THE PARENTS' COMMITMENT TO THE TREATMENT MODEL

Prior to the onset of the joint sessions involving the parents and their child or children it is advantageous to elicit a commitment for a course of treatment that will address the parents' reasons for seeking family therapy. It is hoped that the parents will have confidence that they will not be blamed for their child's difficulties. The therapist will have validated their importance in their child's life. They will know that the therapist perceives them as being central to the solution of the difficulties within the family. The therapist will have conveyed that they have the skills or they have the ability to develop the skills necessary to resolve the family problems. They will have a basic understanding of attachment principles and interventions congruent

TABLE 5.4. PARENTING PROFILE FOR DEVELOPING ATTACHMENT

Respond from 1 to 5 (1 represents very little; 5 a great deal of the characteristic/skill). Focus on adults' abilities, not whether or not the child is receptive to the interaction.

(1 = very little, 5 = very much)	My Perception Of Self	My Perception of Partner
1. Comfortable with giving physical affection	———	———
2. Comfortable receiving physical affection	———	———
3. Comfortable expressing love for child	———	———
4. Ready to comfort child in distress	———	———
5. Able to be playful with child	———	———
6. Able to be calm and relaxed much of the time	———	———
7. Able to maintain a sense of humor	———	———
8. Ready to listen to child's thoughts and feelings	———	———
9. Patient with child's mistakes	———	———
10. Patient with child's misbehaviors	———	———
11. Patient with child's anger and defiance	———	———
12. Patient with child's primary problems	———	———
13. Able to show empathy for child's distress	———	———
14. Able to show empathy for child's anger	———	———
15. Able to set limits, with empathy, not anger	———	———
16. Able to give appropriate consequence and remain firm	———	———
17. Able to allow child to accept consequence of choice	———	———
18. Able and willing to give child necessary supervision	———	———
19. Able and willing to give child much attention	———	———

TABLE 5.4. (*continued*)

20. Able to express anger in a quick, to the point manner	———	———
21. Able to "get over it" quickly after conflict with child	———	———
22. Able to accept, though not necessarily agree with, the thoughts and feelings of your child	———	———
23. Able to face, address, and discipline when appropriate, the behavior of your child	———	———
24. Able to encourage and enjoy your child's interests and explorations that are separate from you	———	———
25. Able to acknowledge failings and mistakes in raising your child	———	———
26. Able to be ready to support your child's independence	———	———
27. Able to remain emotionally regulated when your child is dysregulated	———	———
28. Able to value and respect your child's needs for autonomy and his differences from you	———	———
29. Able to avoid experiencing shame and rage over your mistakes in raising your child	———	———
30. Able to remain focused on the long-term family goals	———	———

with these principles. They will know how the sessions will be structured and the likely course of treatment. Their roles and the role of the therapist in the sessions will be explored. In certain ways during the sessions the parents function as assistant therapists. In certain ways during the sessions the therapist functions as an assistant parent. The therapist provides attachment security to the parents and the parents and therapist provide attachment security to the children.

In developing the working alliance between therapist and parents, the therapist clarifies their respective strengths. The therapist is the "expert" regarding issues of attachment and therapy, whereas the parents are the "experts" with regard to their unique family and the individuals within it. The therapist will emphasize that differences between their perspectives are certain to occur. She will not avoid these differences, but rather address them directly when they occur. Her "expert" perspective has less value than does their "expert" perspective insofar as it determines family interaction patterns and long-term goals. The therapist is guide and consultant; the parents make the final decisions.

When there are differences that are not resolved, these too need to be explored with acceptance, curiosity, and empathy for all. If the focus can remain on the long-term goals for the family, and if the therapist and parents perceive similar goals, then differences regarding present interventions can simply be seen as different pathways to achieve the same goal. However, if the goals differ significantly, or if the therapist or parents believe that differences regarding interventions are likely to interfere with maintaining a basic trust and confidence in each other's "expert" status, then the therapist needs to initiate discussion about possible termination and referral to another therapist.

It is often helpful for the therapist to develop a "waving" relationship with the parent(s) before beginning the family sessions. During the initial sessions with the parent, at some point the therapist says:

> Do I have your permission to wave to you during the session with your son when I think that you are saying or doing something that might be hurting your relationship with him? After I wave, I'll give you a suggestion about what you could say or do that might help your relationship with him.

Such a statement, when made with a tone of respect and empathy for the parent(s) is often agreed to, and then the "wave" is often able to be used quite effectively, with the parent feeling little shame or discomfort. If it does elicit a negative response, the therapist simply addresses that response, either with the child remaining present or separately, depending upon the circumstances. Parents are aided in this intervention when their willingness to be "coached" in front of their child is acknowledged to their child as a sign of their commitment and love for him. The therapist might also suggest that the parents "wave" to her if they think that she is saying or doing something that is hurting the family relationships.

When, due to time constraints or the wish to manage an immediate crisis, the initial phase of meeting with the parents is not done adequately, there is a risk that the subsequent treatment process will be compromised. The parents and therapist may not have developed the open communication, confidence in each other, and sense of safety necessary to adequately explore and resolve the many issues likely to lie ahead. The therapist will not be able to clarify the nature of the treatment, both during the interactions within the sessions as well as with regard to the interventions that are likely to be recommended for the home. The parents' "ghosts" from their own attachment histories will not have been understood, and are likely to create havoc with the intersubjective presence during the sessions as well as with the attachment-focused parenting recommendations. The therapist is responsible for insuring that the parents feel safe during the sessions. The therapist is also responsible for insuring that the children feel safe during the sessions. In planning for the children's safety, the therapist builds confidence in the parents' ability to facilitate their child's sense of safety while the stressful themes are being addressed in treatment. The initial meetings with the parents alone are often crucial in efforts to build this confidence.

When the children are brought into the sessions, they too are given a brief description of the nature of the sessions and the goals that have been developed with their parents. Their perceptions of these goals, as well as the function of family treatment, are then explored in an effort to elicit their engagement in the treatment process at the onset. During this exploration, the nonjudgmental tone of the therapist as well as the explicit statement that all of the family members' contributions to the family strengths and difficulties will be addressed, will make it easier for the children to become engaged in the treatment.

A family therapy that focuses on facilitating secure attachments and states of intersubjectivity must certainly have an impact on day-to-day family relationships if it is to be effective. Such therapy, when the parents and children are all actively involved, models ways of facilitating safety, communication, affect regulation, and meaning making during the session so that the same interventions can easily be applied within the home. This process is implicit within the session and is often seen to generalize to the home with little explicit recommendations given. However, for various reasons, at times it is necessary to make such recommendations explicit for the parents and the children in order to achieve the greatest benefit from the sessions.

This chapter does not provide a "cookbook" for parents so that they can know what to do in a given situation. Such specific directives would fly in the face of the entire thrust of the book. The power of attachment relationships comes from their attuned, contingent quality. They work so well in facilitating psychological development because of their nonlinear nature. The sequential chain of the intersubjective experiences between parent and child is constantly being re-created, link by link. The first link in the chain—the only link that could be a clear "cookbook" directive—will be limited by the next link. The second link's response is determined by many factors, including the perceived context in which the first link was expressed. The context itself is difficult to define because the context experienced by the parent is likely to differ from the one experienced by the child.

Thus, any directive given can be taken only as a guide to help one to maintain the attuned dance between parent and child within which attachment brings safety and joy and exploration and mastery. Or the directive may be a guide regarding ways in which breaks in the attuned dance do not generate breaks in the narrative or the security of the attachment. Or the directive may be a guide regarding ways to reengage in the dance following the inevitable, and at times necessary breaks. Thus, such guides will present possible first or second links in the intersubjective chain that makes up an attachment relationship. Equally important is the necessity for such guides to focus on accepting, being curious about, and having empathy for the next link—the child's link again—in the chain, because only by so welcoming the child's step in the dance, will the parent be able to coregulate the affect and cocreate the meaning associated with this stage of the dance.

Difficulties Getting Started

The most important time to address relationship breaks, misattunement, defenses, and conflicts is at the beginning of treatment, with the parents. If they are not addressed then, the therapeutic alliance will not be stable, the parents will not feel safe, the therapist too will struggle with trying to feel safe, and certainly the children who join the sessions later will not feel safe.

In contrast, when these difficulties are successfully addressed, all feel safe and the parents have experienced—they know it from the inside out—the a/r dialogue that the therapist hopes to utilize throughout the treatment sessions. With the therapist and parents working in concert, it is much easier to become successfully engaged with the children in a similar manner.

The following are examples of the types of difficulties that are likely to emerge during the opening sessions, as well as how the therapist might address them.

"Are You Blaming Me?"

At the beginning of the first session with the parents the therapist explained that the nature of the treatment involved her first getting to know the parents, their perspectives, and concerns, before bringing the child into the sessions. As the explorations moved toward the parental responses to some of the child's behaviors, the following sequence occurred:

Father: Are you blaming me?

Therapist: Oh, my, is that what my questions seem like to you? That I'm blaming you? I'm sorry if that's what you are experiencing now. That was not my intention.

Father: Well, you keep asking about what I did. You seem to be saying that I handled it wrong.

Therapist: I may be suggesting other ways of responding to your son's defiance, but I truly am not saying that you are causing his defiance.

Father: It kinda seems like it.

Therapist: I may suggest that you might get a different response from him if you approach him differently, but I'm not blaming you. I know that you love your son and are doing the best you can.

Father: Yeah. (unconvinced)

Therapist: Now my fear is that you think that I think that you are the problem, that I might think that you're a bad dad.

Father: I'm not sure what to think.

Therapist: Well, thanks for being so honest at the beginning because if you think that I think that you are to blame for every problem that you guys are having then you're not going to feel safe with me. You're not likely to trust that I can help you and your son with what you are struggling with.

Father: (silent)

Therapist: Help me to understand. If we disagree on some of your child rearing, if I have some suggestions that I think might improve your relationship with your son will it be hard for you if I tell you?

Father: I don't know. It might depend on if I think that you just feel sorry for him and are expecting me to do all of the changing.

Therapist: Thanks, that helps. My sense is that you do worry that I'll be blaming you and saying that what you do is an excuse for your son's behavior.

Father: Well if I'm the only one you ask to change, of course I would think that.

Therapist: I get it. You're OK if I say that you're not a perfect dad. You'll be fine with my suggesting that you try something different. But you want me to know that you want to see me putting some expectations on your son too.

Father: Yeah, that's right.

Therapist: Thanks for making this clear. I think that we might have some difficulties in our relationship in the sessions ahead because I probably will be asking you to try other ways of relating more than I ask your son. I'll be doing that—not because you're "wrong" and he's "right"—but because you're the dad and I'll be able to get him to change much more easily if I can get you to try some other approaches than if I approach him directly. He's a teenager and I'm not likely to be more able than you were to get him to stop swearing at you and your wife by telling him to stop it. But that does not mean that I'm blaming you. I simply know that in the long run, what you do and how you see him is more important to him than how I see him and what I say. You are much more important to him than I am. He loves you, not me.

Father: It doesn't seem like it the way he acts.

Therapist: That's what I'm getting at. If an adult would act that way toward you it certainly would be a fair assumption that he doesn't like you, and certainly doesn't love you. So when he acts that way what does it mean?

Father: That's why we're here.

Therapist: Great! That's what I want to help you to figure out. If he loves you, as I assume he does, and you love him as I know you do—though you might not like being near him sometimes—then why do these hurting, yelling matches occur? Why does he swear? What is he feeling inside when he has all that anger outside? My guess is inside he feels as sad and worried as you do, not being close to you and his mom right then.

Father: It doesn't feel like it.

Therapist: And that is probably the hardest for you. The swearing is bad, but if your son does not want to be close to you—his dad—my guess is that feels horrible.

Father: Yeah, it does. But I'm not going to give in to him just so he likes me.

Therapist: And you're telling me loud and clear that you're going to do what is best for your son, and if you think that I'm going to suggest something that would help you to "get along," but would simply be giving in to him, you'll be out the door.

Father: That's right.

Therapist: I wouldn't want it differently. What I am assuming is that under the conflicts is your love for each other, and if I can bring that out we'll see an improvement in his behavior in a lot of ways. What is best for him is also what is best for your relationship.

Father: OK.

Therapist: You're going to be watching to see if I do what I say I'm going to do? (smiles)

Father: You can say that.

Therapist: Because the bottom line is you love him. And if I ask you to do some things that are hard, but you think that they will help your son, my guess is that you will do them.

Father: Of course.

Therapist: Of course. So to start right in, would you mind telling me what your relationship with your dad was like?

Father: What does that have to do with me and my son?

Therapist: Good question. It's none of my business unless it will help you and your son. I ask because so much of how we intuitively raise our kids is like how we were raised. Even when we might not like some of the ways our parents raised us, we still find ourselves relating with our kids the way our parents related to us.

Father: My father was OK. He had to work hard for the family. He did the best he could.

Therapist: Great. Please don't think that I'm going to find reasons to blame your dad. I just want to understand what your relationship with him was like. How did he respond when you expressed anger toward him.

Father: Are you kidding? I never would. Back then that just wasn't how you treated your parents. You did what you were told and if you didn't like it you kept it to yourself.

Therapist: What would be your guess, if you had got mad at him?

Father: I don't know. He might have smacked me I guess.

Therapist: OK. So with your dad you never really had much practice in disagreeing with him . . . in telling him you were mad about something. So now when your son does, you don't want to smack him, so you're not really sure what to do.

Father: He shouldn't be doing it.

Therapist: So if I suggest that if your son had a way to express his anger with you, be heard and hear your views, while you really listened to him, and then decided what was best . . . and then he accepted your authority while groaning a little about it, you might not want to hear my ideas.

Father: I didn't say that.

Therapist: So is there a way for your son really to be allowed to be angry with you, and he can tell you that, and it would not be disrespectful?

Father: I guess.

Therapist: Great. Maybe we won't have so many arguments after all. How about if we get back to you and your dad. Did you two share much? If you were upset, could you tell him and would he comfort you?

Father: You don't let up do you? (laughs)

Therapist: (smiles) No. Because you love your son. And I want to help you to raise him so you're proud—of him, of yourself, and of your relationship.

"I'm Doing It For Her!"

It was the second session with the parents of an 11-year-old girl, Annie, who had been underachieving at school for several months. When her parents, Rita and Kevin, and especially Rita, would talk with her about her homework and a letter of concern from her teacher, she would not talk and would often cry and become withdrawn. She wanted to be with her friends, and in desperation, her parents restricted her playing with her friends until her schoolwork improved. She withdrew further and would often sit for hours at her desk, getting little done. When her mother tried to help her, she would become irritable and resistant.

Therapist: What do you think this means? Her almost continuous refusal to do her schoolwork?

Mother: I don't know. We're not asking her to do too much. Just what she's capable of.

Therapist: And she has friends and other interests. And she never had this problem before. And you mentioned that there really are no other stresses in the family now.

Mother: That's right. It makes no sense.

Therapist: How is this affecting you, Rita?

Mother: I worry about it all the time. I've tried everything and I don't know what else to do.

Therapist: This is hard on you.

Mother: Of course it is! I'm her mother! I want what is best for her!

Therapist: I'm sorry. Did you think that I thought that you did not want what was best?

Mother: You seemed surprised that I'm worried about her.

Therapist: And you thought that I think that you might be worrying too much? That maybe you're worry is causing her to stop working?

Mother: Well it's not! I'm doing this for her, not for me!

Therapist: Ah! You do seem to be sensing that I'm blaming you somehow for your daughter's difficulties. My questions are hard for you.

Mother: How could you think that I'm causing her to be this way?

Therapist: Thank you for asking these questions and telling me what you sense in my attitude toward you. You don't seem comfortable with how our conversation is going.

Mother: (tearful) How could you think that I have anything to do with this?

Therapist: Again, I'm sorry that you are experiencing my questions this way. This must be hard for you. You love your daughter and are doing your best to give her the best and you're thinking that I'm blaming you for her problems.

Mother: Aren't you?

Therapist: I don't believe I am, but you seem to feel that, and that is what is important right now. What's that like? Feeling that I'm blaming you?

Mother: (more tearful) It's so unfair! I do everything for her! And its always my fault!

Therapist: Always?

Mother: Yes. He (gesturing toward her husband) thinks I'm too hard on her . . . that I worry too much about her. My parents say that I should just leave her alone. But I'm not going to do it. They're wrong. I'm doing what is best for her!

Therapist: No wonder this is upsetting for you. If you think that I agree with your husband and parents if they believe that you worry too much or are too hard.

Mother: I'd just like someone someday to say I'm doing a good job.

Therapist: Being a mom—a good mom—seems to be so important to you. Rita, would you say that your mom tried as hard with you as you are doing with your daughter.

Mother: That would be the day. She never cared about anything I did. All she wanted was to please my father. Her kids could take care of themselves for all she cared.

Therapist: So you in many ways had to raise yourself. And when you became a mom you were determined to show more interest in your kids than your mom did for you.

Mother: That wouldn't take much. But yeah, that's what I want and am. I'm a better mom than she ever was!

Therapist: And it must be so hard now, when your daughter is not doing well. And you try so hard to help her to be happy and successful.

Mother: And she doesn't seem to appreciate what I'm doing for her. Like she wants me to ignore her like my mother ignored me!

Therapist: How painful that must be for you! In some ways it seems like the lack of closeness that existed between you and your mom, might now be starting to happen between you and your daughter. Oh, my, how painful!

Mother: (crying) Why is she doing this?

Therapist: That's what we need to know, isn't it! You were feeling so happy, so close to her during the first 10 years of her life. In many ways, having with her the life that you wished for but never had with your mother. And now you are afraid that you might be losing it, losing your daughter. So terrifying!

Mother: What can I do?

Therapist: What you are doing now, Rita. You are looking at what is happening, and it is so hard to do—what this feels like for you, what sense it all makes—and you are doing it now, to find a way to help your daughter. You are doing it now.

Mother: I don't see how this is helping.

Therapist: If we can begin with understanding what has made your life so hard, and still makes it hard, that might help us to begin to understand why your daughter's life might be getting hard too.

Mother: How?

Therapist: My sense, Rita, is so much of the pain that you feel now is being terrified that you are failing as a mother, and your daughter is also beginning to fail in her life.

Mother: No! I can't fail her! I can't!

Therapist: What would that mean, Rita, if you fail as a mother?

Mother: That her life will turn out like mine. That she'll hate me like I hate my mother! (begins crying intensely)

Therapist: After all you've done for her. How much you love her. That she might hate you like you sometimes hate your mother.

Mother: What did I do wrong?

Therapist: (quietly) If you made mistakes, Rita, it is not because a lack of love . . . or a lack of trying. If you made mistakes it may be that you were not shown very well how to be a mom. You're doing your best though. I know you are. And your daughter will know that someday, if she does not know it now.

Mother: Will she?

Therapist: Rita, your daughter wants a relationship with you as much as you did with your mom when you were a little girl. The difference now is that you want it too . . . and it doesn't seem to you that your mom did.

Mother: I do want it.

Therapist: Yes, you do. Yes, you do. And that is why it is so hard for you when your daughter begins to fail, and you can't help her no matter how hard you try. (turning to her husband) Kevin, would you agree with me . . . that Rita loves your daughter so much and wants so much to be a good mom for her.

Dad: There's never been any doubt about that. I just think that she loves her too much.

Therapist: I don't think that she can love her too much. Maybe she is making mistakes in how she is showing it. Maybe her relationship with her mother is getting mixed up in her love for her daughter, but she does not love her too much.

Dad: Yeah, I get what you mean.
Therapist: I think she needs you, Kevin. I think she needs to know that you see what a good person she is. How much she wants and tries to be a great mom.
Dad: I know that.
Therapist: Would you tell her now.
Dad: Rita, I know that you love, Annie. I know that she means the world to you and you'd do whatever you could to make her happy and have a good life. I do know that. (tearful)
Mother: (quietly, looking down) Thanks.
Therapist: Rita, would you look at your husband and thank him again, and let him give you a hug. (Rita and Kevin hug briefly) Rita, I admire your courage. And your commitment to your daughter. Now, if you are willing could we continue to understand more about this . . . about some of the roots of Annie's struggles now, and your's too. (Rita nods) Thank you. Would you tell me a bit about your hatred toward your mom?

The therapist needs to be persistent, addressing one area of shame and fear after the next, while always being responsive to the client's resistance and signs of dysregulation. If her intent is clear as to her motives, if she perceives and gives expression to her experience of the other's strengths, and if she is ready to experience and coregulate any affective states that emerge, the client is often increasingly ready and able to become engaged in this dialogue. Parents often show more motivation and determination to enter and proceed through these dialogues than do other adults because of their commitment to their children. They—and their children—need therapists who will expect them to do so, while being truly with them in the intersubjective experience.

Chapter 6

BEING WITH CHILDREN

If the day ever came when we were able to accept ourselves and our children exactly as we and they are, then, I believe, we would have come very close to an ultimate understanding of what "good" parenting means . . . One of the most important gifts a parent can give a child is the gift of accepting that child's uniqueness. —*Fred Rogers,* The World According to Mr. Rogers

This work differs from many works of family therapy in its emphasis on the active role of the family's children in the treatment process. This work differs from many works of child therapy in its emphasis on the direct communication with children that occurs within the treatment process as well as in the presence of their parents. Our manner of being with children is central to this treatment. Many adults, including therapists and parents, do not relate with children and youth in quite the same way that I am suggesting throughout this work. It is a manner similar to how we related with them when they were infants and toddlers. Much of what is said in this chapter regarding how the therapist "is" with the child applies similarly with how the therapist "is" with the parents as well. The joint work with parent and child is stressed throughout the other chapters. The focus of this chapter on the child is believed to be necessary because adults commonly do not communicate with children in the manner that is being suggested.

Many adults are often unaware that the primary manner whereby we can have an influence on children and facilitate their development is by being with them within states of primary and secondary intersubjectivity. Within these states we are able to assist them in regulating their affect as well as in creating the meaning that they give to the events and objects within their lives. Within these states, advice, directives, encouragement, and reassurance can also be of assistance to the child. Outside of these states, such interventions are often ignored, resented, or experienced as being out of congruence with the child's experience, including his thoughts, feelings, and intentions. Outside of these states, such interventions often create a conflict between parent and child, neither sensing that she is understood, neither experiencing empathy with the other.

The child, like her parents, is in the therapist's mind and heart, and the child, like the parents, experiences this. The intersubjective presence of the therapist is the overriding context in which the treatment occurs. The child experiences herself in the therapist's mind (through acceptance and curiosity) and in the therapist's heart (through playfulness and empathy). Experiences of primary and secondary intersubjectivity are the central change agents in the therapist's manner of being with children. Similar intersubjective experiences occur between parent and child, parent and therapist, as well as within the parent, child, and therapist triad.

Features of the intersubjective experiences that are the focus of this work are increasingly being described in models directed toward the treatment of adults (Fosha, 2000; Johnson, 2004). The same principles and similar interventions are possible—and at least as effective—with children. For this to occur we need to remember and implement knowledge that has emerged regarding child development from within theories and research regarding attachment and intersubjectivity.

Within primary intersubjective experiences infants begin to organize their sense of self. They discover what their parents are discovering—namely that they are delightful, interesting, lovable, enjoyable, and unique—qualities which are central to who infants are. Infants' affective states are coregulated—either deepened or moderated—by their parents' congruent affect. Infants are having an impact on their parents' hearts—they are moving the parents—as well as their minds. Infants hold their parents' interest and affect their understanding. The meanings of infants' inner states reflected in their actions, including their nonverbal expressions, emerge from the meanings that the parents attribute to these states as they discover and are affected by them. These experiences are inherently reciprocal. Children discover many positive traits within themselves because their parents respond in positive ways to the children's expressions of their inner life. There are qualities within children that evoke these positive responses from within their parents. At the same time, parents are discovering qualities within themselves as parents because they are having an impact on their children. They are experiencing themselves as the parents that their children are experiencing them to be.

In becoming engaged with the child in therapy, the therapist is continuously discovering and experiencing the child's inner life intersubjectively, as well as demonstrating her experience by her affective/reflective response to it. In entering the child's world, the therapist finds that she is wondering and worrying, puzzled and surprised, impressed and saddened, by the emerging story. She finds herself being deeply interested in the child's story and deeply moved by it. The child reveals how she is struggling to make a life, to develop a coherent sense of self, to make sense of her experiences of the events and objects in her life. The therapist experiences this struggle intersubjectively and she joins it. She discovers the child's courage and strengths, competencies and honesty, compassion and ability to be comforted. When she explores with the child the stresses and perceptions of rejection or indifference that he or she has faced, she discovers the child's resilience and persistence in trying to create a good life. She does not ignore the child's symptoms, but rather discovers the strengths within them. As she resonates with these qualities within the child, he or she in turn is experiencing the therapist's experience of him. The child is having a positive impact on her, which is affecting his or her sense of self. The following are examples of how the therapist shares her discoveries of the child with him or her:

> It seems to me that you're saying that when you are the most angry at your dad, you also are worried that you both might be hurting each other right then . . . and you really don't want that . . . you really want to find a way with him to work it out and be OK with each other again.

> I wonder if you're also telling us that when your mom says no to you part of you is thinking that she does not care about what is

important to you . . . and then maybe even that you're not that important to her . . . have you ever told her that?

My sense is that you're telling us that your life lately has really felt hard for you and also that it does not seem to you that we get it . . . how hard things have been . . . and how alone you have felt dealing with it all.

I admire how willing you are to discuss these hard things in your relationships with your parents—and with them right here listening. And because of your courage to do that, my sense is that they know you more deeply, and most likely are also touched by how hard you are working at this.

As the therapist discovers features of their child, the parents discover them as well. They are affected as she is affected. They are able to give meanings to their child's intentions, thoughts, feelings, and wishes that they had not been able to do before. Often lost in their child's troublesome behaviors, they have forgotten how they used to discover unique qualities about their child when he or she was an infant and toddler. They find these qualities again, lying under the symptoms or emerging from within the child's distress and withdrawal. With possible assistance from the therapist, the parents then communicate their emerging awareness to their child. Examples include the following:

That took courage to tell me that, son. Thank you. I worry about that too. I don't want our disagreement to pull us apart. Our relationship is much more important to me than any conflict . . . much more.

I'm sorry, son, I just did not know how upset you were . . . how convinced you were that I just did not care about your struggles. I just saw your anger and thought that you should stop it. I didn't know what it meant. Thanks so much for helping me to understand.

I didn't understand, honey, I didn't . . . and I'm sorry that I did not know how hard things have been for you. I so much don't want you to have to handle it all alone. I want to be able to help you . . . more than I've been doing.

Oh, Billy, I'm feeling so proud now that you were able to say how much you want to work this out! You spoke from your heart! And you touched my heart! Thank you!

This activity of primary intersubjectivity involves no judgment. The therapist is completely accepting of the story as it unfolds. Evaluations will inhibit the meaning making, intersubjective process that is occurring. The therapist is assuming that the child is doing the best he or she can to make a life that is best for that child. Inconsistencies in the story that worry or puzzle the therapist will be addressed from a stance that only tries to understand the inconsistencies, not to change the story. If the child is actively participating in this exploration of her story, she will work out the inconsistencies in a way that is true to her need for a coherent narrative. The therapist remains confident that through her active, intersubjective presence in this process, the most helpful and authentic rewrite will occur. The therapist's mind and heart, in joining those of the child within her story, opens more possibilities for the development of the child's narrative. The child remains the editor of her work in progress.

Activities of secondary intersubjectivity involve the same processes. The therapist shows genuine interest in the child's experience of the people, objects, and events in his life. There is no judgment involved, just the desire to understand the child's experience of his world. If a child says that his parents are "mean" in their care of him, there are no efforts to change his mind through arguing about parental responsibilities, rights, or motives. Rather the therapist works to deepen her own understanding of the child's experience of his parents being "mean" to him. The therapist then might have any number of questions, depending upon the flow of the dialogue that enable the child to more fully experience what he meant by "mean" with respect to his parents' care of him. The therapist might develop the following dialogue:

Therapist: Wow, you think that your parents are mean to you. That must be difficult!
Child: Of course it is!
Therapist: Are there ever times when they are not being mean?
Child: I guess.
Therapist: Why do you think they seem to be mean sometimes and not others?
Child: I don't know. Ask them.
Therapist: Maybe we'll have to find out what they think about your view, but first why do you think they would be mean to you? Why would they be?

Child: I don't know!

Therapist: This seems hard to talk about—why your parents would be mean. If it seems to you that they are that way—do you think maybe, at times, that they just don't like you as much as they used to? That you're not as special to them as you once were?

Child: (quietly) Sometimes I think that.

Therapist: (quietly too) Ahh . . . that must be hard . . . when you think that you're not so special any more . . . so hard.

Child: Yeah, it is.

Therapist: How do you handle those feelings?

Child: I just go to my room and put my music on.

Therapist: Ahh . . . I'm glad that you have a way . . . to handle them. Have you ever told them?

Child: What?

Therapist: That sometimes you don't feel that special to them.

Child: No.

Therapist: I wonder what they would say . . . would you be willing to now? I can help you to find the words if you would be willing to try it.

Child: OK.

Such a dialogue could move in many directions depending upon the child's response at each step. This is not about the "objective reality" as to whether or not the parents are being "mean." A central word in the dialogue is *if*, because it indicates that we are discussing the child's experience, not trying to establish if her experience is "true" or "false." The focus continuously remains on the child's expressed experience of her parents. If we stay with the child's experience it leads to many opportunities for elaboration. Associated experiences emerge. Implications that flow from the original experience become apparent. Possible inconsistencies emerge. We explore how they are integrated. If they cannot be integrated, we wonder how the child lives with—and makes sense of—these inconsistent parts within his story.

When the child experiences the therapist's nonjudgmental curiosity about her narrative, she is often likely to explore it with the therapist. She does not have to defend her experience that her parents are being "mean" to her. She experiences the therapist as being interested in her story and not tampering with it. She experiences the therapist's intention to understand her story. Since it is the child's own story, it is hard for her to resist such open, nonthreatening opportunities to speak about it. The therapist's nonjudgmental questions lead the child more deeply into the process of making her story more coherent. Attaining narrative coherence is deeply satisfying and when she finds that the therapist's intention is simply to aid in the process and to experience it with her, intersubjectively—not to write the script—it is hard to resist.

If we stay with the child's experience that her parents are "mean"—now explored and elaborated—she is often able to recount (with the therapist's help) to her parents a more comprehensive organization of the "mean" experience. She may say to her parents something such as: "Mom, sometimes when you say no to me I think that you are just being mean. I think that maybe you just don't care about what is important to me and that doesn't seem right. It almost doesn't feel then like I'm that special to you!" The parent—again initially with the therapist's help in understanding why and how she might assist her daughter—may respond with: "Thanks for letting me know that you think that I'm mean sometimes. You don't think I care what you want! Oh my! And you even don't feel like you're special to me right then! That must really be hard!"

With the above quality to the dialogue between parent and child, a resolution to persistent conflicts comes within sight. Both parent and child—from their unique perspectives—have been seeing the other's motives with a negative lens. Now, through a lens involving attachment vulnerabilities, both are likely to be less defensive and more receptive to repairing their relationship. The above dialogue might naturally lead to the parent then adding:

> I think that I have a better sense now of your anger. I think that I get it! It's easy to understand because I sometimes feel the same as you! Sometimes I worry that I'm not so special to you anymore either. I want so much to be a good mom for you . . . sometimes I worry that I'm not being very good at it.

The point here that must be made again and again is that when the child does not have to defend his experience he can explore it openly. As he explores his experience, and it unfolds and deepens, he discovers connections that emerge between it and other aspects of the narrative. This is the magic of intersubjectivity. When he is able to explore the experience with another who has an attitude of playfulness, acceptance, curiosity, and empathy, the meaning of the experience evolves and becomes more fully organized—it is being cocreated intersubjectively. The expressed new meaning often contains within itself the resolution of the conflict between the parent and child or between the two parents. This meaning frequently involves qualities of fear, sadness, confusion, shame, and doubt that are associated with the attachment relationship. When these qualities are expressed and responded to without judgment, but rather with PACE, resolution and reconciliation often emerge without lectures, shame, or forced compliance. When one member of the dyad begins to give open expression to his vulnerabilities, the other is often quick to follow.

As has been stated in previous chapters, the therapist needs to insure that the parents will maintain a similar attitude during the session or the child will not be safe if she does begin to openly explore her experiences. To insure this, the therapist will have had some meetings alone with the parents for the purpose of addressing their own shame through PACE and then developing confidence that when the therapist accepts the child's negative experience of them, she is not agreeing with the child, but rather is creating an opportunity for relationship repair.

Often children—and adults too—think and feel that no one knows their story. They work to create their story alone. This proves to be very difficult and produces limited results. When a child works alone in her mind to create the meanings that develop a story, she is very restricted in her perspective. The isolated child does not know what questions to ask and what places to search for a meaning that makes sense and preserves the integrity of her self-narrative. When her heart—alone—experiences the story in the making, she often meets the affect of shame and other associated states of fear, anger, or sadness. These affective states, experienced alone, are often dysregulating and may well lead toward a dissociative response that is not able to be integrated into the narrative. These states tend to lead her away from places and events that might make it easier to develop the story. Shame, for all of us, but especially for children, is often too hard to experience alone and so is strenuously avoided. When the child allows the therapist's mind and heart to enter the storymaking process, there immediately are new places to visit and new experiences to integrate. With their minds and hearts together, they are able to cocreate new, vibrant, clear, and congruent meanings. These new meanings have little of the shame and fear that were present before. Rather, they hold safety, hope, and opportunity for the future of the child's developing narrative.

CHARACTERISTICS OF BEING WITH A CHILD

There are various features of being with a child within an intersubjective, affective/reflective presence in therapy that I wish to briefly summarize.

1. The intersubjective experience precedes any self–other differentiation that occurs. The therapist's prior knowledge and empathy for the child have little meaning until the child experiences them intersubjectively, the first time, and each subsequent time.

2. The therapist's affective state is *attuned* with the *affective state* of the child. The therapist enters into the rhythm of the child's presence. A contingent, reciprocal affective process of follow-lead-follow then emerges.

3. The therapist's attuned response is with the child's vitality affect, not necessarily with the child's categorical affect. The therapist joins the rhythm and possibly the intensity of the child's nonverbal, affective expression and in so doing, assists the child to feel "felt" and understood at a deeper level.

4. The therapist's *attention* follows the child's *attention* and quickly a reciprocal process of leading/following is established. All the while, the primary focus of attention is on an aspect of the child's narrative as well as the events and objects that might be relevant to the narrative. The focus ranges over the verbal and nonverbal expressions, perceptions, affective/reflective states, memories and wishes of the past, present, and future as well as the intersubjective process itself.

5. The therapist's *intention* includes the following:
   A. To maintain a sense of safety for the child.
   B. To actively discover intersubjectively the child's various experiences of her internal and external world through persistent, nonjudgmental curiosity.
   C. To become attuned with the affective states that the process and content of the exploration elicits (frequently this involves empathy).
   D. To communicate the emerging experiences of understanding and empathy to the child, implicitly, and often, explicitly.
   E. To coregulate the affective states that are active in the intersubjective present, and to cocreate meanings for the memories, affective states, and experiences that are being experienced together.

171

However, when any of these intentions are not successful, the therapist completely accepts this intersubjective truth as well, just as she accepts everything else that is happening (certain behaviors, such as verbal or physical assaults, are the exceptions to this unconditional acceptance). Most likely she will then turn her mind and heart to what might have made it fail to occur and will explore the understanding and empathy that emerge with regard to this failure.

The following features are also frequently seen in affective/reflective dialogue with children. However, it is important to stress that they are not techniques to create an effect. Rather they often emerge naturally if the therapist does not inhibit them, and through the therapist's being aware of them, their presence is likely to make the intersubjective expressions more clear, affectively experienced, and meaningful.

1. The therapist sits close to the child, often on the edge of the child's "comfort zone." The right degree of closeness can be sensed nonverbally. If the therapist is too close, as is evident in the resulting posture, level of tension, or facial expression of the child, the therapist simply moves away a bit until the child appears to be more relaxed. When the therapist is too far away, she senses this by noting that the affective tone is not as rich, it is more difficult to hold the child's interest, and more difficult to become engaged in affective/reflective dialogue. She then moves a bit closer. There are various reasons for sitting as close as possible:

A. It establishes greater psychological safety, once the child is accustomed to the degree of closeness.
B. It makes it easier to be attuned with the child's affective state.
C. It makes it easier to hold the child's attention.
D. It makes it easier to notice the child's nonverbal expressions which might elicit the therapist's curiosity and subsequent a/r dialogue.
E. It makes it easier to clearly communicate, nonverbally, one's own affective/reflective experiences.
F. Makes it easier to touch the child when appropriate for purposes of coregulating affect with comfort, enjoyment, or affection. It also makes it easier to place extra emphasis on a particular understanding through touch. Touch also assists a child to maintain his attention to a theme.

The physical closeness recommended here is very similar to the closeness apparent when the parent and infant are engaged in their "emotional dance." Physical closeness is one variable that parents intuitively employ in order to facilitate their infant's engagement in the dance.

2. The therapist makes clear nonverbal expressions, often with emphasis. These nonverbal expressions enable the therapist to coregulate the emerging affect, hold the child's attention and interest, and establish complimentary intentions. A rhythm usually emerges fairly quickly where the nonverbal expressions of both members of the dyad are in synch. This is an obvious feature of the parent–infant dance and is crucial for the intersubjective effectiveness of this dance. The same feature has a place in the parent–child relationship throughout childhood as well as in the therapist–child relationship. The following are examples of three crucial modalities of nonverbal communication:

A. Facial expressions—clear expressions of surprise, delight, confusion, awe, enjoyment, sadness, empathy, acceptance, curiosity.
B. Voice tone/inflections. Often melodic, rhythmic. Punctuated with pauses, variations in speed, emphasis. Frequent repetitions of words and phrases.
C. Gestures/posture. Animated/quiet, quick/slow, expansive/controlled, based on the attentional focus and emerging affect. Often leaning forward. Much variability often present.

3. Verbal expressions are congruent with the nonverbal expressions. The therapist's intention in his choice of words is to remain—without judgment—focused on the inner life experiences of the child, not the "truth" of the object or events. The focus is continuously being brought "under the symptoms," to the affect and meaning associated with the events and objects that are being presented in the story. The expressed words often have these characteristics, some of which were discussed in Chapter 4, "Fostering Affective/Reflective Dialogue."

A. Frequent, nonjudgmental questions, followed by surprise, delight, "ah-hah expressions."
B. Exclamations, or quiet repetitions of what was just said.
C. Thinking out loud to communicate intentions, curiosity, empathy.
D. Empathic or playful communication of affect.
E. Talking about the child to the parent (to decrease affect and increase reflection).
F. Talking for the child to the parent or the therapist (to increase affect, reflection, and a felt sense of connection while maintaining safety).
G. Facilitating the child and parent's ability to engage in a/r dialogue with each other.

Whereas nonverbal expressions often occur without verbal content, within this model of therapy verbal expressions are almost always made with clear, congruent, nonverbal expressions. The nonverbal content carries much of the affective aspect of the dialogue, whereas the verbal component carries much of the reflective aspect. The nonverbal expressions along with curiosity often carry the momentum of the dialogue, and dialogue that is transforming is always affective/reflective. At times the nonverbal component will carry both the affective and reflective, without any need for words. The child or parent is able to indirectly read the mind of the therapist in the smile, movement, or vocal expression, while directly experiencing the therapist's heart. Sometimes making this explicit with words is helpful, while other times allowing it to be communicated nonverbally conveys a deeper meaning.

Speaking with children is seen in this model of family intervention as being very effective. By making the child's implicit knowledge explicit, the therapist is able to lead the child into a much deeper understanding of his inner life. Events, including conflicts, stress, shame, or trauma, were partially experienced as being nameless, marked by dysregulating affect and elaborate defenses. When given an experiential name, it is often much easier for them to become regulated and integrated within the narrative. Within the context of therapeutic intersubjectivity, the child is now more able to understand and communicate aspects of his experience that he had never before been able to share with anyone. He now is able to communicate with his parents in a manner that conveys his inner life more fully and also deepens his sense of connection with them.

When being with children the therapist needs to maintain the relaxed, rhythmic, voice quality that is common when we speak spontaneously with young children. This is likely to contain a soothing, almost sing-song quality, punctuated with sudden expressions of surprise or delight. This is likely to reduce the child's defensive behaviors and assist her in feeling safe. The child will then be more likely to become engaged in the dialogue in a fully reciprocal manner, rather than passively listening or "tuning out" from being "spoken to." When this tone is congruent with the child's inner life, she often feels a sense of open curiosity and respect and rarely experiences the tone as "talking-down" to her.

Some may be skeptical that words could have such transformative power for children. Words fail to do so when they are rational interpretations of the child's behavior and history. They often fail to do so when they are given within a lecture with an intention to problem solve. It is when they emerge from the intersubjective matrix, representing the therapist's discovery of the affective and meaningful aspects of the child's experience of an event/object, that the therapist's words with the child become so powerful. The therapist's discovery is made from within her own experience of the child's experience. She does not know what the words will be until she sits with the child in the event, experiencing it too, coregulating the affective states that they both are experiencing, and cocreating a new meaning for the event. These are not "rational" words! These are words that are "embodied" in the reciprocal vitality of the intersubjective present. A 10-year-old girl, after one such transformative session, sat within a state of deep contentment, staring first at her mother, then the therapist, and then looking within herself. She stated with wonder, "I never knew that I thought that. But I do. And I know that I thought that for a long time, but I never knew that I did."

Children, and adults too, often have difficulty finding the words to describe their subjective experiences. Their feelings, wishes, intentions, and associations are often nameless. As a result the therapist needs to take an active stance initially in helping the child—and adult—to find the words. The therapist may often ask them questions that will facilitate a curiosity about their feelings and intentions. She may then raise possibilities about what words might fit their experience. Initially she may stimulate this process of discovery by wondering for the child—speaking for him in the first person—what he was thinking (as described in Chapter 4).

While there may be value in maintaining an ambiguous therapeutic response in some forms of treatment with adults, I perceive little, if any, value in being ambiguous with children for more than a brief period of time. It is the clarity of his intersubjective impact on the therapist that will often lead the child into discovering aspects of self that are transformative. Intersubjectivity is at the core of how adults influence the development of a child's autobiographical narrative with its self-states laden with affect and meaning. The therapist's initiatives and responses, given with clear meanings expressed through vitality affect, create both the safety and the acts of self-discovery that we are seeking.

The above features of the therapist–child dialogue have many similarities with the therapist–parent dialogue. The following represent ways that the therapist sometimes relates differently with children from the way she relates with adults:

1. With children there is usually a greater need for taking breaks in the dialogue because of the child's greater difficulty with maintaining attention, regulating affect, or maintaining motivation.
2. When matching the child's vitality affect, the therapist is likely to show greater variation, range, and intensity.
3. There will be a greater need for the therapist to "speak for" and "speak about."
4. The therapist will more often be likely to touch the child to provide comfort and to assist in regulating affect and attention.
5. The therapist is likely to have to assume greater responsibility for maintaining the momentum of the dialogue.
6. The therapist is likely to have to lead more and follow less.
7. The therapist is likely to assume greater responsibility for deepening new understandings and cocreating new meanings.

In this model of treatment the child is first helped to find the words that are congruent with her intersubjective experience. Next the child is helped to communicate, with affect, these words to her parents. In doing so, she is offering her parents the opportunity to experience her experience with her—intersubjectively—and also to coregulate and cocreate its meaning. This step is the central reason for choosing family treatment over individual treatment for children when the parents have the motivation and ability to enter into this a/r dialogue with their child. It completes the circle. The act of communicating to the parents the meanings that are emerging from the therapist–child a/r dialogue, enables the new awareness about self and other to enter into the child's manifested story much more fully and deeply than if the parents were not part of the intersubjective experience. By entering the shared world of communication, the experience becomes more "real" to the child, as it becomes more "real" to his or her attachment figures. The family treatment's goal is to provide the parents with another opportunity to engage in primary and secondary intersubjective experiences with their child. When successful, they will be in the position to be attuned with their child's affect, joined with her in her focus, and sharing the intention to understand and be moved by each other's narrative. Within these intersubjective moments, the realities of "mom," "dad," "son," and "daughter" transform and deepen the self. The narrative of each family member is then transformed into a unique work of literature.

Chapter 7

MANAGING SHAME

Shame is an affective experience that violates both interpersonal trust and internal security. Intense shame is a sickness within the self, a disease of the spirit. —Gershen Kaufman, The Psychology of Shame (1996)

Understanding the affective state of shame is crucial if we are to understand the nature of gaps and distortions in the formation and development of our personal narratives, our attachment relationships, and the range and depth of our intersubjective experiences. Pervasive shame functions to hide the self from the anticipated negative evaluations of others. Within this state, the person experiences herself as being wrong, stupid, bad, unlovable, or worthless. Within this state the person assumes that her behavior reflects intentions, self-states, or abilities that are flawed, selfish, lacking, or evil. Shame greatly restricts the nature of the self as it emerges during the course of development. It colors certain experiences so that they reflect one's hopelessness and worthlessness. These experiences are defended against through anger, denial, excuses, or blaming others. If the shame intensifies, more extensive defenses against it involve rage or dissociation. Events associated with shame and its defenses are not experienced intersubjectively and are not successfully integrated into one's narrative. The narrative becomes fragmented, filled with gaps, distortions, and inconsistencies. Shame is likely to represent the greatest barrier to developing a coherent autobiographical narrative. Events that are full of shame do not become subjective experiences fit for inclusion into one's story of oneself.

When an event causes a reaction of intense shame, the event becomes frozen in our mind, being unintegrated with the more interactive, meaning-making structures of our mind, and rigidly seeks to avoid similar events in the future, that might elicit similar reactions of shame. The new events may have many dissimilarities with the original shameful event. The person does not notice these differences as the amygdala has already made a judgment that precludes new learning: Establishing a feeling of safety is paramount. The event is avoided and the person is left with the assumption that it was of the same nature as the original event.

The focus of this chapter is on the state of shame, rather than on fear, anger, or sadness which are also seen in family therapy. While fear, anger, or sadness may become dysregulating, they more often are routinely regulated within the safety of attachment security, present within the family. Such families often do not seek family therapy because they have their own patterns of repair within their interactions of daily living. It is when fear, anger, and sadness are infused with shame that the normal interactive repair behaviors are likely to be poorly functioning. When fear, anger, and sadness are associated with shame, they are at risk of becoming chronic states or intensifying and becoming terror, rage, and despair. Rather than being routinely regulated within the family, they become increasingly dysregulating to both the individual and the family; often, at all costs, they are avoided. Whereas fear tends to activate attachment behaviors within a child, shame tends to deactivate attachment behaviors. In fear, the child seeks her parent; in shame, the child hides from her parent. When the therapist is able to assist the family in reducing the shame that is felt by one or all of the family members, then any affective states of fear, anger, or sadness that emerge regularly are much more likely to be resolved and integrated.

When the original event that proved to be permeated with the affect of shame is associated with our relationship with our attachment figures, the implications for our subsequent development are profound. When the attachment figure elicits shame in a frequent and unpredictable manner, the child is likely to avoid contact with the attachment figure whenever possible. If physical avoidance is not possible, the child is likely to "freeze" and avoid psychological contact with this figure. When the attachment figure elicits shame in a frequent, but more predictable manner, such as when she is angry, the child is likely to avoid physical or psychological contact with this figure when she is in such states or even in circumstances which may elicit such states. When the parent elicits shame primarily as a result of the child's behavior, the child is likely to avoid physical or psychological contact whenever he thinks that he did something that his parent will not like. Thus, the child's avoidance of his parent may be restricted to situations involving his own behavior, or the parent's affective state, or the parent herself, regardless of her state. Clearly, the more limited are the areas of avoidance, the less damage is being done to the relationship. The less pervasive are the shameful events, the less restricted are moments of intersubjectivity and the more available are such moments for regulating the affective states of fear, anger, or sadness.

Gershen Kaufman (1996) summarized well the devastating effects of habitual shame:

> The binding effect of shame is central to understanding shame's impact on personality development. The binding effects of exposure, of feeling seen, acutely disturb the smooth functioning of the self. Exposure binds movement and speech, paralyzing the self. The urge to hide, to disappear, is a spontaneous reaction to the self's heightened visibility; it can overwhelm the self. To feel shame is to feel inherently bad, fundamentally flawed as a person. A consuming loneliness gradually can envelop the self in the wake of shame, and deepening self-doubt can become one's constant companion . . . (p. 18)

When the child avoids a parent due to shame, even in the most limited situations, the child is unlikely to enter into intersubjective experiences with the parent at those times. In such situations, the child's ability to learn about self/other or to develop meaning about that affective state or that type of event, is going to be impaired. This impairment is a natural result of the limitations placed on primary and secondary intersubjectivity at those times. Meaning making and affect regulation, so crucial for the development of a child's coherent narrative and integrated self, occurs and develops the best in these intersubjective experiences. Shame restricts these experiences. Pervasive shame creates the risk that intersubjective experiences will be habitually avoided and the organization of experiences into a coherent narrative will be impaired.

It is important to note that entering minor states of shame is a routine aspect of the early social/emotional development of children. When they are engaged in attunement with caregivers or, from a position of felt safety, are actively exploring the world, they quickly feel shame when their caregiver is not sensitive and responsive to their affective state or intention. They had anticipated that they would enjoy an inter-subjective experience and it failed to occur. Or they were enjoying an experience with an object and the attachment figure did not share that enjoyment, but rather limited the experience. In that circumstance the child quickly enters a parasympathetic state, triggered by the accidental misattunement or discipline from the caregiver. This is communicated by the caregiver through changes in her nonverbal communication involving eye contact, facial expression, voice tone, as well as gestures, movement, and touch. The expansive, sympathetically driven attune-ment or exploration is now restricted and moves into parasympatheti-cally driven reduction and withdrawal of affect, behavior, and cognition from the experience (Schore, 1994). Shame is a painful neg-ative affect that is difficult for the toddler to autoregulate, though he attempts to do so often by gaze avoidance, becoming motionless and speechless, and hiding psychologically, and possibly physically.

At these moments, the attuned attachment figure is sensitive to the painful negative affect that her toddler is experiencing as well as the child's difficulty regulating it. She assists the toddler by coregulating the affect through empathy and comfort. Then, through reassurance, a brief explanation about the behavioral event, or redirection, she becomes reattuned with the child as he enters into a more positive affective state. Shame is contained. It remains small and is able to be regulated, initially with the affective and behavioral interventions of the parent and eventually through the child's own increasing autoreg-ulation abilities. When the parent—after eliciting a shame response through misattunement or limit-setting—quickly repairs the relation-ship, the shame is contained and the important role of socialization is successful (Schore, 1994, p. 241). The child learns that at times when the parent misattunes to him or her, this simply reflects one temporary characteristic of a relationship and is not a threat to the continuity of the relationship. The parent inevitably will reattune and be present. The child also begins to notice that the parent seldom or ever misattunes at those times when he needs the parent the most, such as when he is ter-rified or experiencing intense pain. When the child screams the parent will be present and responsive. Those times when the parent is not attuned fall within the less important times and the child discovers that he can often manage such situations and his associated affect—at least for short periods—quite adequately without the parent's participation.

The child is also able to begin to comprehend that certain behaviors lead to his or her parents' acts of discipline and that by inhibiting the behaviors, the states of shame are avoided. This step—that discipline is directed toward the behavior, not the self—is a crucial step in the child's moral development and demonstrates one of the central features in the developmental progression from shame to guilt.

SHAME VS. GUILT

Too often clinicians and parents speak of "shame and guilt" as if these were two words for the same affective/cognitive state, or at least two aspects along a continuum, describing the same underlying moral emotion. The work of June Tangney and Ronda Dearing will help us to differentiate between "shame" and "guilt" and to become aware of the crucial importance of doing so.

According to Tangney and Dearing (2002) the following are central differences between shame and guilt:

1. Shame focuses on self, guilt focuses on behavior.
2. Shame is a much more painful affect than is guilt.
3. With shame one experiences feeling small, worthless, and powerless. With guilt, one experiences feeling tense, remorseful, and regretful.
4. With shame one is concerned with the other's evaluation of oneself. With guilt one is concerned with the effect of one's behavior on others.
5. With shame one desires to hide, escape, or attack. With guilt, one desires to confess, apologize, and repair the relationship.
6. With shame, the self is split between the observed (devalued) and observing self. With guilt, the sense of self remains unified and is not devalued.

Tangney and Dearing demonstrate clearly how shame involves an assessment of one's self, whereas guilt focuses on one's behavior and its consequences. With guilt, one does something wrong, and the self is left intact. With shame, one's behavior is a sign of an aspect of self that is damaged. One's behavior reveals to others that one is inherently "bad" or "flawed." As a result, the self attempts to achieve a distance from the behavior and hide from the eyes of others. With shame one shrinks from being exposed, whereas in guilt, one addresses one's own behavior with the other in order to repair the damage that the behavior caused to the person or the relationship with him or her.

When, under conditions of shame, one is not able to hide, but remains exposed to the other, one is likely to lash out in a state of rage. Tangney and Dearing have found that individuals of all ages in states of shame are likely to "shift the blame elsewhere," externalizing the problem and directing rage at the supposed source of the problem. An added benefit of moving from shame toward rage at others is that by becoming angry, the person is "reactivating and bolstering the self, which was previously so impaired by the shame experience" (Tangney & Dearing, 2002, p. 93). There is no such relationship between guilt and anger. Studies cited also note that whereas there is a positive correlation between measures of guilt and empathy, the correlation between shame and empathy is negative. Finally, the authors note that shame is correlated with many measures of psychopathology, whereas guilt is not. In family treatment all participants—parent, child, and therapist—are likely to be vulnerable to the effects of shame.

Shame becomes extreme in cases of child abuse or neglect or moderate in cases of habitual harsh discipline, especially when it involves emotional abuse and withdrawal from the child (Schore, 1994, p. 207). It is certainly not a surprise that in these cases experiences of shame are very poorly contained.

Shame is also not contained well when the parent consistently fails to reattune and repair the relationship following routine discipline and misattunements. At those times the child is at risk for not being able to autoregulate what would otherwise be routine experiences of shame and they therefore become more pervasive and intense. This child does not gradually move from states of shame to states of guilt, which are associated with specific behaviors or small, routine failings on the part of their caregiver. Rather, shame remains and it threatens the relationship. In these situations the shame is likely to become a felt part of the child's core self. The child concludes that he is shameful, and did not simply engage in an inappropriate act; that parts of him are flawed, unlovable, bad, and deserve harsh discipline. The child believes that at these times he does not deserve to be comforted in response to stress, whether it is the stress of shame, fear, or other dysregulating states.

Children tend to develop extensive, rigid defenses in their attempts to regulate such overwhelming and increasingly chronic states of shame. One defense is to avoid affective interactions with their caregivers. These interactions do not elicit safety, self-pride, and validation. Rather, the child anticipates being perceived with disgust, rejection, rage, and contempt in his parent's eyes and voice. These children affectively—and possibly physically—attempt to hide from attachment figures, in an attempt to feel less shame.

Attachment relationships are fragmented, fragile, and unstable when a person's subjective experience is frequently restricted by shame. Within shame states one is quick to assume that one's attachment partners perceive one as being bad or worthless or similarly lacking in vital personal characteristics. Within shame states one also perceives the behavior of one's attachment figures as being motivated by negative intentions. One assumes that the attachment figure perceives the self in a manner congruent with one's self-perception and therefore acts toward the self just as one deserves.

Given such perceptions of self and other, one can see that in states of pervasive shame one is likely to avoid discussing—and therefore exposing—any self-themes that are shameful. While in such states of shame the person is likely to avoid any and all intersubjective experiences with attachment figures because it seems inevitable that the attachment figure will perceive and respond to the person's shameful qualities. Such perceptions and responses inevitably will lead to rejection and abandonment.

Thus, the client in states of shame is likely to want to hide such states and their associated themes from their autobiographical narrative as well as from their interactions with attachment figures. The client is also likely to work to avoid recalling—to deny—any experiences, memories, or affective states that are likely to be associated with such states of shame. Such a person's life then becomes narrowly defined as to what may enter relationships, memories, awareness, and current experiences. Whenever an experience, either internal or external, crosses the restrictive boundaries, the person immediately becomes at risk for becoming disorganized and dysregulated, in affective, cognitive, behavioral, and possibly physical terms.

As a result of these defenses the child or parent is less likely to learn about what it was that he did wrong and what circumstances led to the behavior. The individual is less likely to learn from his mistake and refrain from that behavior again, less likely to notice the effect of his behavior on others, and in so doing is less likely to develop empathy for others. The person will be less likely to be motivated to "right" the "wrong" that he had done, being less willing to accept the consequences and assist the other. Rather, his motivation will be focused entirely on protecting himself from the states of pervasive shame that are likely to be felt if he engages in any of those behaviors that show sensitivity to the one that he hurt.

Individuals who suffer from shame are likely to find psychological treatment very difficult because shame activates the tendency to deny one's behavioral problems and hide from the eyes of others when these problems are exposed. In such states the person is often convinced that the attachment figure will see the "flawed self" under the behavior when the behavior is explored. In such states the person is very likely to withdraw into defensive states that attempt to avoid and prevent the exposure of the shameful self. The "secure base" that the therapist is trying to create proves to be very fragile and transient because the client often believes that such security is based on the fact that the therapist or attachment figure has not yet seen the "shameful" self. Once this self is exposed, all security is thought to be likely to vanish and the client expects to be rejected and abandoned.

Not only do such clients anticipate that others will see them as being "bad," but they see themselves that way. This certainly is likely to be a central factor in the fact that many individuals with histories of abuse and neglect who now manifest various psychological problems are low in measures of "reflective functioning" and lack insight. These individuals are not likely to reflect on their motives and intentions for their behaviors because they are convinced that such explorations will only lead to evidence of being worthless. They assume that "under the behavior" is something that is worse than the behavior itself. They are likely to resist the therapist's efforts to explore the subjective meaning of particular behaviors because they dread what will be uncovered.

This suggests two core reasons why shame is such a central factor in both the development of psychopathology and in the resistance to treatment. First, shame places one in a fog, hidden from potentially significant others, actively avoiding the exposure to another who could provide—through intersubjective experiences of acceptance, understanding, and empathy—a pathway toward both affective regulation as well as self-awareness. Second, shame prevents the development of the ability to reflect on, understand, and make sense of one's behaviors and subjective experiences. This reduces the ability to develop a coherent and continuous narrative that includes attachments as well as affective meaning and purpose to one's life.

All participants in family therapy are at risk for experiencing shame during the treatment session. This affective state will make the process of entering into an intersubjective state with others much more difficult. A 10-year-old girl in a family session may express the conviction that her aggression toward her younger brother makes it clear that she is "bad" and he is "good." She may lash out at her parents for being "unfair" and favoring him over her. She will resist exploring her aggression openly due to her terror that others will conclude that she really is a "bad" girl.

Her brother may be aware that his sister is "in trouble" more than he is and that his mother tends to take his side during conflicts, because he may be more successful in controlling his anger than is his sister. At the same time he is aware that he is not as "good" as his mother may believe and he may fear that the therapist may uncover his deceptions. His need to present himself as "good" has become associated with his worth and he may dread the possibility that the therapist will discover that he is "bad."

This child's mother may be convinced that her daughter's aggression is a sign that she is failing as a mother. She may lash out at her daughter, saying that she should stop blaming her or her brother and instead ignore him rather than hitting him. She may resist exploring her relationship with her daughter out of fear that the therapist will make excuses for her daughter and find fault with her, the mother. A deep terror lurks: she is a "bad" mother.

This child's father may also experience shame when he is not able to "fix the problem." No matter what he does, he is not able to stop the conflicts between his daughter and son, as well as the conflicts developing between his wife and daughter. He is most comfortable "solving problems" and he is not able to solve one in his own home. In his mind and heart, he is a "bad" father.

The therapist is not immune from shame. She may feel the parents' pressure to get their daughter to stop her aggression. If the child continues to be aggressive, the therapist will have failed, and they, and she, may develop doubts about her competency as a therapist. She may well choose to blame either the mother, father, daughter, or—if she is creative—the brother, for the lack of progress, thus leaving herself free from shame. Or if she concludes that another therapist would get better results; she is a "bad" therapist.

The intersubjective experiences that serve as the foundation of this model of family treatment are especially vulnerable to states of shame and secondary dysregulated states of chronic fear, anger, or sadness. These states breed defensiveness, avoidance, and distancing behaviors. The therapist needs to be aware of these states and address them with empathy whenever they are present. To protect the members of the family against shame the therapist needs to remind all of them in word and deed that the dialogue being sought is the expression of subjective experience, not any effort to "prove" that something is "objectively" present. The child may say that she feels that her mother is being unfair to her. This does not mean that the mother is "objectively" being unfair. Rather than entering a debate as to whether or not mom is unfair, the therapist makes it clear that what is most important is helping the girl to understand—and experience empathy for—her experience that her mother is unfair. Questions regarding what that feels like, how she manages those feelings, why, if she is correct, her mother would treat her unfairly, will be at the forefront of their attention, not efforts to resolve a behavioral conflict. Once these underlying thoughts and feelings are coregulated and clarified, the therapist is in a position to facilitate a dialogue about the deeper meaning of the conflict or the symptom. Within such an intersubjective exploration, new meaning is being cocreated. Often then the therapist will ask the child to say to the parent a statement such as: "Mom, sometimes when you say no to me it seems that you are being unfair to me. Then I don't feel close to you and I don't like it when that happens." Such comments are made within an expression of vulnerability, conveying an experience without blaming anyone, and are likely to be responded to with understanding and empathy rather than defensive justifications.

At other times the therapeutic focus will be on the experience of shame itself. The mother may be able to intersubjectively experience herself briefly as failing her son who is stealing from a store. She fears that she is helpless to prevent his behavior and she doubts herself as a parent. She becomes aware of how much she doubts herself as a parent and how frightened she is that she will cause harm to her son's future. At this point she is likely to enter a very painful affective state of shame that the therapist will have to coregulate through her empathy and unconditional presence. As this affective state lifts, the mother is likely to arrive at a deeper understanding of the effect that her son's behavior has on her, on him, and on their relationship. With the reduction of her shame, and through reflecting on her own behavior, she may become aware of certain behaviors that now elicit guilt. She is likely to want to repair whatever damage those behaviors caused to the relationship. This is then likely to help her to be aware of options in her responses to his behavior in the future. If the shame is not contained, such intersubjective meaning making will fail to occur.

Often both parents and children attempt to avoid the experience of shame through defensiveness or feigned indifference to a dialogue. When expressions of shame finally emerge, this represents an opportunity for a therapeutic transformation of the person who is now vulnerable to the experience of shame and receptive to empathy and comfort. Often the opportunity is lost when the attachment figure or the therapist quickly responds to a person who says that he is worthless by reassuring him: "You're not worthless, you just made a mistake!" Such reassurance covers over the emerging sense of shame so that it is unlikely to become integrated into the narrative. The message to the person who is finally finding the courage to acknowledge to self and others that he experiences himself as being "worthless" is not being met with an accepting, intersubjective matrix. Rather he is left thinking that the other does not understand how he experiences himself, does not want to be exposed to that "disgusting" trait, is lying about her experience of him, or is not strong enough to experience the shame with him.

Expressing empathy for a child's state of shame is more likely to reduce his experience of shame than will reassurance. The therapist, or parent, might say:

> Oh, John! So when you do something wrong you often think that it is because you are "bad"! Now I understand better what makes it so hard for you when you do something that you should not do. Wow! No wonder you tend to get angry when we talk about your behavior that gets you into trouble. To you it's a sign that you're "bad!"

Empathy easily leads into curiosity about the shame state. Given the natural tendency to avoid thinking about events that are associated with shame, curiosity is likely to be very beneficial if the therapist is able to regulate the affect with empathy. For example, the therapist might ask some of the following:

> Are there times when you do something wrong when you don't feel that you're "bad"?
>
> Have you felt that about yourself for a long time? Do you recall the first time that you thought that you were bad when you did something wrong?
>
> How do you manage that feeling of being "bad"?
>
> Do you think that others see you as "bad"? Is there anyone who does not see you as "bad"? Why do you think that person does not do so?

Those questions lead to related ones, all of which also lead to empathic comments, in order for the child to begin to reorganize his or her experience of shame. It is intersubjectivity—not a lecture or reason—that will facilitate a new exploration of the child's narrative

As the shame decreases, each member is more likely to be able to participate intersubjectively with the other family members in an effort to understand, affectively and reflectively, the story that is emerging. They will be less likely to hear the story with a defensive and critical ear. In a similar manner, with a decrease in shame, the other family members will be more likely to respond with appropriate guilt if something is said that does reflect a mistake that he or she made in the past. Guilt, then, will motivate the person to fix the problem and begin to repair and heal the relationship. It is crucial to remember that there will be room for realistic guilt and motivation for corrective behavioral change only when the states of shame are diminished.

An example of opportunity/crisis involving the initial expression of shame is the following. An 11-year-old girl, Melinda, had stolen some money from her mother, Denise, in order to buy things for her friends at school. When she was confronted about it she lied to her mother and ran to her room. Both mother and daughter had been experiencing ongoing distress for the past several months due to the unexpected decision of her father to leave the family and obtain a divorce. During the session Melinda had entered into an a/r dialogue about how hard her life had been, including the recent event in which her mother expressed the belief that she had stolen some money from her and then had lied to her about it.

Therapist: How difficult it must be now for you! Your dad left, you don't see him much, and you aren't sure what is happening. And I don't imagine that you feel very close to your mom now either—with her being annoyed over what she thinks you did.

Melinda: Nothing ever goes right! I can't help it!

Therapist: You can't help it?

Melinda: Yeah! I can't! I didn't want to steal her money! I couldn't stop myself! (Silence follows with Melinda crying quietly and avoiding her mother's gaze. Denise suddenly looks sad. Her daughter's acknowledgment of stealing and her very clear distress left her with no anger, but only empathy for her daughter's pain.)

Therapist: Oh how hard that is for you to think about! You didn't want to steal the money, but you did and your mom was mad . . . and you felt so alone . . . and still do.

Melinda: I can't . . . ! I'm stupid! . . . I'm *not worth anything!!!* (Melinda's crying intensifies.)

Denise: Oh, baby! You're not stupid. You're worth everything . . . (Denise embraces her but Melinda becomes rigid and tries to pull away.) You just made a mistake, that's all. Just a mistake.

Therapist: (quietly and gently to Denise) I think that Melinda is not ready for your comfort yet. Could you just pull back for a bit . . . (making eye contact with Denise) Your daughter has some strong feelings now . . . and . . . they are scary and painful for her. Would you be willing to help her to feel those feelings . . . and not try to talk her out of them? (Denise looks puzzled as to what she was being asked to say.) Would you say quietly to you daughter, and maybe gently touch her hand. Could you say, "Oh, Melinda, that must be so hard for you if you think that you're not worth anything. I am sad at how much pain you seem to be feeling now."

Denise: Melinda, it must be hard. I am sad for you . . . You seem to be feeling so much pain. (Denise is becoming tearful and there is much pain in her voice.)

Therapist: Now would you say, "Thanks for letting me know, honey . . . Thanks for letting me know how much you are hurting."

Denise: Thank you for telling me, honey. (Denise begins to cry as she squeezes Melinda's hand. Melinda then suddenly flings herself into her mother's arms and they both cry together.)

Therapist: (after waiting until they become quieter). You daughter is feeling that it is all her fault. Everything! That she's not worth anything to anyone! That must be so painful to think and feel that about yourself. And she has such courage to be honest with those feelings. And to let you comfort her . . . To let you love her . . . even if she does not feel very lovable.

Melinda: I'm not lovable! I'm not!

Denise: Oh, baby . . .

Therapist: (Speaking quickly, trying to help Denise to stay with the shame.) Tell your daughter how sorry you are for her that she does not feel lovable. How hard *that* must be for her.

Denise: Oh, honey, it must be so hard . . . if you don't think that you're lovable. I am so sorry for you now! And I love you so much! To me, you've always been lovable, and you'll always be lovable to me.

Melinda: (looks into her mother's eyes) But I stole from you, mom!

Denise: Yes, you did . . . you did . . . and I love you . . . and you are still lovable to me. (Melinda leans into her mother again. She seems sad and exhausted. Denise rocks her slowly in her arms. She strokes her back and hair and kisses her hair.)

This session proved to open deepening intersubjective dialogues between Denise and her daughter. Another session followed in which Melinda expressed the conviction that she was responsible for her father's decision to divorce. Again, the therapist asked Denise to respond first with empathy for Melinda's expression before providing her with reassurance and information. The affective state of shame needs to be accepted before the individual is receptive to exploring its origins, affective/cognitive associations, and alternative ways of experiencing an event. Later, her father refused to participate in the treatment, and did not remain active in Melinda's life. Rather than moving into heightened shame over this, Melinda was able to express her anger and then sadness about her father's decisions. Denise again conveyed empathy for her daughter without expressing rage at her ex-husband, which would have impaired Melinda's ability to organize her own experience of her relationship with her father.

When shame becomes exposed and expressed and is responded to with empathy, the resulting intersubjective experience is often transforming. The sense of self deepens and becomes more coherent as an aspect of the past begins to be welcomed into the narrative. A new meaning of an event is now being cocreated. Without the barrier of shame, the event can be integrated into the self. If guilt is present, it further motivates that person to repair the relationship with the other. The attachment security is enhanced and the self is transformed. Conflicts that had existed within the family for months, if not years, are now amenable to repair.

Chapter 8

BREAKS AND REPAIR

People have said, "Don't cry" to other people for years and years, and all it has ever meant is, "I'm too uncomfortable when you show your feelings. Don't cry." I'd rather have them say, "Go ahead and cry. I'm here to be with you." —Fred Rogers, The World According to Mr. Rogers

In psychotherapy, whether individual or family therapy, as in relationships among attachment figures, there are frequent moments when there are breaks in the intersubjective dance. During these times the interactions do not contain the attunement, joint attention, or shared intentions necessary for the mutual regulation of affect and cocreation of meanings. From the perspective of the therapist, such a break might represent the client(s) "resistance"; from the perspective of one or more family members, the same break might represent the therapist/parent/child's intrusive or insensitive comment or lack of response. From the perspective of the attachment theorist, the same break might represent a normal phase of all attachment relationships.

In many of the families who seek treatment, relationship breaks often are very difficult to integrate into the flow of the ongoing relationship and are very difficult to repair. Routine conflicts due to differing interests, priorities, perspectives, and desires often become increasingly intense and lead to a rupture in attachment security. The same is often the case for routine misunderstandings, moments of misattunement, and mistakes. These daily "breaks" in intersubjectivity become major problems when they are not accepted, understood, and resolved. In some families the situations that created them are often avoided and the range of intersubjective experiences becomes restricted. In other families these situations become compulsively reenacted—searching in vain for reconciliation—but lacking the interactive repair skills needed to make it possible.

The ability to repair relationship breaks is crucial in all families who hope to be able to maintain attachment security between parent and child and between parents themselves. The ongoing continuity and commitment of both the family and treatment relationships is developed through the repair of breaks in a/r dialogue whenever they occur. Within secure attachments there is a certainty and continuity in the relationship that is neither threatened nor damaged in response to separation, misattunement, discipline, or conflict. Each member of the family is confident that no matter what happens, the relationships will be repaired and maintained. Attachment security is the bedrock of the family. No matter how long the separation and how severe the conflict, the parents' unconditional love and readiness to care for their children when they are in need will remain (Kobak, 1999).

Within families who seek treatment this confidence in the unconditional continuity of the relationship is often not felt by any and certainly not by all. The family may have had—and may still have—many positive experiences of attuned, reciprocal responsiveness. However, this family may have great difficulty integrating the breaks that naturally occur within all relationships. Breaks due to separations, discipline, differing experiences, and conflicting priorities may represent a threat to one or more family member and may generate a defensive, alienating response. This response is likely to become evident through angry outbursts, anxious silence, and rigid avoidance of any activity or comment that might activate the break. In such circumstances, repair of the relationship following the break is likely to be delayed and incomplete. The relationship is not returned to its prior secure state, but rather is left vulnerable to further breaks and not flexible enough to integrate the routine breaks that are certain to reoccur.

INTERACTIVE REPAIR

Frequent use of interactive repair is crucial if an attachment-focused family therapy is to be effective. Relationship repair is necessary if all members are to experience safety while their daily family difficulties are being explored. The therapist needs to continuously repair her relationship with each family member and with the family as a whole. Without repair her efforts to explore events that are characterized by shame and fear will be met with defensiveness, anger, or withdrawal. The therapist also needs to be continuously aware when there is a need to repair the relationship between members of the family. Since this family is unlikely to be able to successfully repair these breaks, the therapist needs to initiate and guide the process. The therapist models for both parent and child the need to successfully repair relationship breaks if they are to resolve conflicts and deepen the sense of safety and meaning within their relationships.

The therapist is continuously aware of the presence of relationship breaks as manifested by nonverbal expressions (facial expressions, voice tone and inflections, gestures, and posture), incongruity between verbal and nonverbal expressions, as well as her own affective/bodily responses to the expressions of the other family members. Frequently, upon becoming aware of a break, the therapist will choose to address it, by openly identifying and discussing it with the same attitude of PACE that is present for all other therapeutic interactions.

For example, when a therapist was demonstrating a sense of empathy for a 10-year-old girl who expressed distress at not being allowed to visit her friend because she had not done her homework, she noticed that the girl's mother demonstrated annoyance in her facial expression. She turned to the mother and said:

Therapist: You seem to be upset over my discussion with your daughter.
Mother: Well, she knew what would happen if she did not do her homework! I told her!
Therapist: Did you think that I thought that you had not told her? That you were not fair?
Mother: No, but she needs to learn to do a better job with her responsibilities!
Therapist: Do you sense that I do not think that responsibilities are important?
Mother: No, but, you seemed to feel sorry for her not seeing her friend. But she knew what the rules were!
Therapist: Oh, I think I see why you were upset! Do you think that by my feeling empathy for her distress over her not seeing her friend, that I'm suggesting that maybe the rule should have been ignored—since it upset her so much?

Mother: Yeah, if she just is sad about something, then I should give in to her!

Therapist: OK, now I get it! You think that my empathy for her distress means that she should not have any consequences. That, in a way, I'm taking your daughter's side against yours and saying maybe you are being too hard.

Mother: Yeah, aren't you?

Therapist: Oh, I'm sorry if I communicated that. No wonder you looked upset with me if you thought that I was taking her side. Let me clearly say that I'm not taking any side about the need for that consequence. Rather I'm letting her know that I feel with her about her not seeing her friend—for whatever reason. By feeling her sadness with her I am hoping to help her to be able to handle her unhappy feelings better, and make it less likely that she will express her distress in some inappropriate way.

Mother: OK.

Therapist: Is it fair to say that at home you are not likely to express empathy for your daughter's distress if it results from her not doing what she should have done?

Mother: No. I guess that I'd worry that she would think that she would be able to get away with it then.

Therapist: I see. So you would focus on the rules in a rational manner, communicating that if she had followed the rules she would not feel the distress.

Mother: Yeah, I guess.

Therapist: I understand your motives, I think. I worry that your daughter may then think that you really do not care that she is in distress, that you only care for the rules and not for her unhappiness if it is caused by her not doing what she should. So in a way, she's all alone with her distress, if her choice caused it.

Mother: I hadn't thought of it that way.

Therapist: My guess is that you were not raised that way . . . the way that I'm suggesting. You were left alone with your feelings, rather than given help to regulate them. I'm suggesting that discipline does not have to exclude empathy. Indeed, empathy can make discipline more effective. The homework rule does not mean that you are indifferent to her feelings. You do feel sad with her when she is sad! So, you are showing that the homework rule must be pretty important, since you are sensitive to her distress and feel sad with her when she is in it—regardless of the reason."

By noticing the mother's nonverbal response to her empathic dialogue with the daughter, the therapist was able to first repair her break in the relationship with the mother and then help the mother to see the value in her repairing her break in her relationship with her daughter—while not having to sacrifice discipline.

In this example, the therapist might also have focused longer on her relationship with the mother, if the mother continued to express a defensive response. That would suggest that the mother was feeling shame over the possibility that the therapist was suggesting that she might respond differently with her daughter. This might then lead to an exploration of the mother's difficulty whenever anyone—including her children—questions her decisions. Such a pattern would suggest that the therapist needed to gently explore connections between her response—not expressing empathy for her daughter's distress—and her own attachment history.

The break–repair sequence is often an excellent means of exploring and understanding underlying thoughts, feelings, and intentions that are eliciting reactive or defensive behaviors on the part of either parent or child. Breaks may represent states of underlying fear or shame. Difficulties with repair may represent patterns that greatly impede the family's ability to explore and resolve conflicts while maintaining a sense of safety necessary for intersubjective discoveries and mastery.

For example, the parents of an 8-year-old boy may be angry with him because he left his bike out in the rain and also because he is angry at their decision that he cannot ride his bike today. He experiences their decision as being "unfair" and "mean." They experience his leaving his bike in the rain as being "irresponsible" and his anger at the discipline as being "unreasonable," "disrespectful," and "a sign that he is unwilling to accept responsibility for his behavior." The family therapist needs to help both the parents and child to see that the same event can be validly experienced as both "appropriate discipline to teach you the need to take care of one's possessions" as well as "a source of frustration that I do not believe to be necessary." For one experience to be valid the other one need not be invalid.

In this example, if the therapist first helps the parents and child "hold" both differing experiences within the same intersubjective experience, then she will be helping them to integrate the break–repair sequence into the fabric of their relationship. In doing so, the parents will develop confidence that they can discipline their child, he can be angry about it, and at the same time they can maintain an open, deep, and comprehensive relationship with him. The child will develop confidence that his parents can limit him, he can be angry with them, and still remain in the same open, deep, and comprehensive relationship with them. His attachment behaviors will reflect security and the family's intersubjective experiences will remain vital and meaningful.

The therapist speaks openly of the fact that all secure attachments involve countless times when the usual state of feeling close and safe is followed by a break, which requires a repair. The therapist strives to help the family to maintain a commitment to identifying the break and need for repair, and then doing it. Breaks that are repaired are very beneficial to secure attachments as they insure the continuing balance between autonomy and intimacy that is present in well-functioning families. The therapist makes this clear through simple dialogue about the process. She does it more experientially and therapeutically when she addresses the breaks that are certain to occur within the sessions themselves among family members and between herself and family members. Through her playfulness, acceptance, curiosity, and empathy she is able to demonstrate to all family members how such breaks are able to be integrated into the relationships, and how they actually strengthen rather than weaken them.

When employing an attachment/intersubjective model to family treatment, the therapist is faced with a crucial task that is not present in individual treatment. While she is engaged intersubjectively with one member of the family, this act of engagement may activate a break in her relationship with another member of the family or a break in the relationships among members of the family.

For example, when the therapist is showing empathy for an adolescent who feels that his father is "mean," the father may become annoyed with the therapist for not challenging his son, and the mother might become annoyed with the son for being critical of his father. The therapist then needs to decide if she should continue to develop her intersubjective experience with the son, attend to the break in her relationship with the father, or explore the emerging break in the mother's relationship with the son. Or she might decide to explore the relationship between the mother and father, in which the mother supports her husband when an emerging conflict between her son and husband appears. Deciding among such possibilities involves considering many factors in which the immediate intersubjective experiences are embedded. Whichever direction the therapist decides to follow, she will need to explore the meaning beneath the interaction patterns that she experienced.

Her choices include the following:

Remaining with the son. What is it like for you when it feels to you that your father is being mean to you? When you think that, what are your guesses about why he might be mean to you if he is?

Turning to father. You seemed to be a bit annoyed with me for trying to understand your son's experience of your recent conflict with him. What was that about? Did you think that I might be agreeing with his experience and deciding that you are "mean"? Or that he is now distorting what happened in an effort to make me think that you were being "mean"? Or something else?

Turning to mother. You seemed to become annoyed with your son when he was telling me about his experience of his conflict with his father. What was that about? Were you upset that your son's experience might be presenting an unfair picture of your husband? Or that his saying that he thought his dad was "mean" might trigger a conflict between them? Or that your husband might react harshly to your son unless you correct your son first? Or something else?

When the therapist chooses to continue the dialogue with one family member, she might also show some recognition of the experience of another family member prior to that or at the same time through a gesture or eye contact, or through a short empathic/informational comment, given with a quiet tone of voice.

Turning to father. I can see it is hard for you now, listening to what your son is telling me. Would it be OK for me to continue to better understand your son's experience now and then try to understand what is hard about this for you? Thanks.

In family treatment such breaks are certain to occur frequently between and among all members present. The therapist's inviting attitude toward them will be crucial in enabling the sessions to continue within an atmosphere of safety for all. By focusing on the breaks with an attitude that regulates the emerging affect and cocreates the meaning of the breaks, she is modeling a way of relating within the family that will create the intersubjective skills needed to repair breaks and facilitate attachment security. Her basic message is that breaks need not represent an overwhelming problem. Breaks can become an opportunity to deepen the relationship by understanding the experiences that caused the break and resolving the conflict.

The following represents a general guide for the therapist in initiating repair within the session:

1. The therapist notes the nonverbal (or verbal) expression that suggests a break and then accepts it and acknowledges it nonverbally. The break may then dissipate if the person becomes aware that his or her nonverbal communication was recognized and accepted by the therapist.

2. The therapist notes the nonverbal expression and then verbally explores it with PACE.

3. If PACE is not sufficient, the therapist might then clearly communicate her thoughts and intentions behind her actions and elicit a response to this new information, again with PACE.

4. The therapist acknowledges that the break is continuing and she invites exploration about ways that the break might lead to a resolution or she explores the possible implications if a resolution is not possible. She accepts the break; no one need be right or wrong.

5. At any step the therapist may express sorrow that the client is in distress over something that she said or did. If she thinks that her actions did represent a mistake on her part, she will apologize for her actions.

BREAKS AS A NATURAL PART OF THE ATTACHMENT/INTERSUBJECTIVITY SEQUENCE

From the broader perspective of attachment and intersubjectivity, breaks represent a natural feature of ongoing, intimate, relationships. At times, affect, attention, and intentions between two or more people are not in harmony. There are countless reasons why this would be the case, including the nature of each member's affect and cognition at the onset of the interaction, differing meanings that each might give to the communications of the other, and differing intentions for the interaction. None of these factors assume the presence of psychopathology on the part of the other. None of these assumes that one person is "wrong." From the perspective of this model of family therapy, such breaks are also likely to be natural components of the sessions. This is due to the intersubjective nature of the therapy, but also to the focus of attention during treatment. The therapist and family are not meeting to discuss the weather. The topics of discussion are often permeated with shame, fears, or conflict. These affective states make the intersubjective experience more difficult to maintain for all members of the dyad or triad. These moments of lapses in intersubjectivity may be called "breaks" rather than "resistance." The interactions following such breaks may be referred to as "repair" rather than "working with the resistance."

When breaks occur within the intersubjective, a/r dialogue, they are met with the same playfulness, acceptance, curiosity, and empathy that are given to any other experiences that emerge in the dialogue. Through maintaining this attitude, the break is more likely to be repaired and the dialogue more likely to continue. When playfulness is appropriate, the stress that caused the break is often winked and smiled at and a return to the dialogue frequently follows naturally. Through acceptance, the therapist is conveying the stance that no one is to blame for the break. The break is not "wrong." Through curiosity, the therapist is conveying a desire to understand the reasons for the break, without any evaluation of the reasons. When the break is caused by the distress that was inherent in that particular part of the dialogue, empathy naturally follows.

In determining *when* a break occurs, the therapist notices:

1. Changes in vitality affect.
2. Nonverbal expressions (changes in facial expressions, voice, gestures, posture, breathing, movements, eye contact).
3. Attentional shifts.
4. Apparent misattunements.
5. Onset of a judgmental, defensive, aggressive or withdrawn stance.
6. Apparent intention to focus on another matter before resolving the current one.

In determining *why* a break occurs, the therapist begins by wondering:

1. Was the break associated with a given topic, or affective state, or intention?
2. Was the break associated with a particular person expressing his or her subjective state?
3. Was the break one of a pattern around a particular topic, state, intention, or person?
4. Did the break dissipate spontaneously?

5. Was repair necessary to end the break?
6. Was the repair an easy or difficult process?

Some common reasons for these breaks during the treatment session are the following:

1. Breaks are natural phases of intersubjective processes.
2. Breaks are likely to be more common when the attuned affect is more intense.
3. Breaks are likely to be more common when the attuned affect involves affective states that are more difficult to integrate.
4. Breaks are likely to be more common when the demands on attention span related to a given topic increase.
5. Breaks are likely to be more common when the topic is difficult to integrate into the narrative of one or more of those engaged intersubjectively.
6. Breaks are likely to be more common when the intentions of the participants are ambiguous or ambivalent.
7. Breaks are likely to be more common when the intersubjective history of one of those engaged is restricted in terms of affective states, memories, and readiness to enter intersubjective states.

When breaks are met with PACE both parents and children are more likely to give expression to their experience of the break. The theme may have created a sense that she or he was being blamed for an event in the family. The child might have felt alone in the distress and unable to turn to either the parent or therapist for support. The parents may have felt that they failed their child or that the therapist thought that they had. When the parent or child is critical of the therapist and is able to address it with her, the therapist is in an excellent position to model how to repair the break. The therapist has an opportunity to clarify her thoughts, affect, or intentions. She also is able to apologize if her statement elicited shame or fear in the client(s), regardless of whether or not the client had "projected" onto the therapist aspects of his or her past. After the apology, the therapist can easily be curious about the client's similar past experiences that may relate to the intensity of the client's response to the therapist's statement. The therapist's intention is not to shift responsibility for the client's distress back onto the client, but rather to understand the distress more fully.

CHILDREN REQUIRE MORE BREAKS

It is crucial in family work to remember that children generally need more breaks from intersubjectivity than do adults. This is quite evident when observing the attuned interactions between parent and infant. Frequently the infant looks away, decreasing movement and vitality. The parent too then becomes quiet, waiting patiently for the infant to rejoin the dance. This is also the case with older children. They are likely to withdraw from dialogues with their parents before their parents are ready to do so. This is especially true during discussions of stressful themes, but is also the case when talking about enjoyable themes.

When a child, throughout the family session, becomes somewhat distant or distracted, it is wise to simply accept that response, possibly explore something else that is lighter, and then casually go back to the original theme (i.e. "What were we talking about before? Oh, yeah!") Interpreting the child's behavior as meaning that he or she "is not working hard enough," or "changing the topic to avoid (the theme)," or "distracting whenever it gets hard," is likely to be counterproductive. What the parent or therapist is likely to accomplish through such a statement is an increase in the child's shame, fear, or resentment.

In contrast, when the therapist accepts the break initiated by the parent or child, and when the therapist and parent accepts the break initiated by the child, the momentum of the a/r dialogue is likely to continue forward, though possibly at a slower pace. The child quickly learns that she or he will not be "trapped" in discussions of conflict or shame. There is no need to guard against such discussions because when they become stressful, the child knows that if she or he disengages from the discussion, this will be accepted and understood.

The therapist conveys *acceptance for a break* in a variety of ways:

1. She might choose to change the topic to a less stressful theme. In changing the subject of their attention, she will also be changing the vitality affect so that it is more congruent with the child's change in vitality. Often the child will fairly quickly join in this new inter-subjective dialogue or a related one. As this topic winds down and there is a natural pause, the therapist then can casually return to the original dialogue, possibly with an unfinished question. Frequently the child will then rejoin that discussion without "resistance."

2. The therapist may also continue discussing the original theme, but directing the discussion to the parent alone, communicating implicitly

that the child is not being asked to reply or even listen if he or she chooses not to do so. Again, the therapist changes her vitality affect to match the change in the child's vitality affect. Frequently, when the child is given the opportunity to be an observer of the dialogue rather than a participant, he or she is likely to rejoin when ready to do so.

3. When the theme continues to be discussed, with the child being an "observer," the therapist may choose to speak *about* the child to the parents, implicitly communicating that the child need not respond. This gives the therapist an opportunity to communicate understanding and empathy for the child to the parents. The child hears the dialogue and is free to agree or disagree as he or she chooses. The therapist also is able to communicate empathy for how hard the exploration of the theme is and how strong the child is to be able to participate in the dialogue when it is so stressful. Such comments will help the child to feel accepted when he "takes a break" and it will help the parent to accept her child when he takes a break. Often when the therapist communicates to the parents or child the impact that one or both of them is having on her, the intent of the communication is to have complimentary impacts on both the parents and child. When the therapist "sees" and "responds to" something in the parents or child that she is describing as "positive," both parents and child are likely to "see" and "respond to" that quality with the same subjective lens.

4. While the therapist is speaking *about* the child to the parents she may also choose to facilitate more engagement by the child in the dialogue, without asking for the full engagement that would be created by asking the child to directly participate. She may do this by speaking *for* the child to the parents. At other times, the therapist speaks for the child because the child is not able to name the unclear, possibly disruptive, experiences of his or her inner life. In this instance the therapist's intention is to gradually bring the child back into the dialogue. The child may have the words already, but is not ready to join the dialogue. When speaking for the child, the therapist uses the first person, often with the child's own words and intonations. For example, the therapist, speaking to the parents, says:

> I think that when we speak about some of the problems at home, and especially those times when Susan becomes very angry with you, it seems to be pretty hard for her. I'll bet she might be thinking something like "OK! I get it! Why do we have to talk about it

again. Why don't we just forget it!" Because we all feel kinda uncomfortable when others are talking about our mistakes.

Another example:

> Mary, you mentioned the other day that you lost your son's CD, and he became very angry with you . . . which then led to a big conflict. Do you think he might have been thinking something like, "Mom, that CD was very special to me! Sometimes I think that you get so busy with other stuff you don't think much about me and what is important to me." I know he didn't talk much then, but maybe he was so upset that he just couldn't think of the words that would have told you why he was so upset.

5. Finally, silence is another way to convey acceptance while the child takes a break from the discussion. In a family session, more so than individual treatment, silence is likely to have to be brief. It serves to acknowledge the value in "catching my breath" as well as reflecting on what was just discovered or experienced. The therapist needs to insure that all present are accepting the need for and value of silence or it may be experienced as conveying a pressure to speak and irritation with the family member's withdrawal from the inter-subjective experience. In many nonverbal ways of communication, "acceptance" might exist in name only because there are nonverbal expressions of dissatisfaction with what is occuring. This then changes the entire meaning of the silence, of the break in dialogue, and of the intentions of those present. When this occurs at least one of those present will be likely to feel judged by the others, and be at risk to enter into shame, defensiveness, and anger.

It is important that when the therapist moves into a theme of shame or other negative affective states, experienced by one or more of those present, she maintains a similar stance of acceptance and curiousity that she held while speaking about more neutral or positive themes. Yet, even when she does so, often the client will still pull away from her into an isolated, self-protective state. The therapist needs to immediately recognize, accept with empathy, and validate this break in intersubjectivity. It is framed as being a natural response to discussions of stressful experiences. The crucial therapeutic stance remains one of PACE. The therapist is not judging the client, nor trying to convince him that he should talk about this. With some clients, the therapist's empathy is experienced more deeply if the therapist guesses what he might want to say, using the client's words. For example, the therapist might say: "Wow, it looks like you want to say to me now, 'Allison, why did you bring that up? Don't you know I don't want to talk about it.' Is that what you were just thinking?" Or: "You seemed to be ready to say, 'Allison, I'd rather not talk about that now in front of my mother. I'm not sure how she will answer and I don't want to chance it.'"

If the client senses that the therapist accepts and understands his or her withdrawal from exploring a traumatic or shameful theme, he or she is more likely to remain engaged with the therapist if she goes deeper into the withdrawal in order to understand its presence and strength: "I can really see how much you'd rather not talk about this. You really, *really,* don't want me to bring this up . . . What, do you think, makes this so hard for you to discuss?"

The therapist must be careful to maintain the nonverbal communication of acceptance when asking this question or the client may experience the question as being judgmental and critical, and frequently will not answer such a question. It can be helpful for the therapist to offer a suggestion about the meaning of the client taking a break.

> That is such a hard thing to think about. I know that you used to get nightmares about what happened. You might think that you're going to have more nightmares! If that's so . . . no wonder you wouldn't want to talk about it!
>
> You might be feeling upset that you yelled at your mom yesterday. You might be worried that if she thinks about it she'll get mad at you now. Maybe you worry that she'll think that you're a bad kid and she won't want to be near you.

At times children attempt to use words, not for the purpose of communicating and being understood, but rather to compel their parent or someone else to give them what they want. In such times, the child does not initiate and then wait for an attuned response but rather makes a demand and then expects consent. When agreement does not follow, the child simply restates the demand, usually with greater intensity and insistence. The parent/therapist then often attempts to redirect the conversation to something else, delay, or deny the request. Such a tactic usually brings even greater intensity and insistence.

One effective way to lead the child into dialogue rather than react to his or her demands is to match the vitality of the child's affective expression, with the same rhythm and general contour of the expression. Such matching conveys empathy for how much the child wants something to happen and how worried or angry he or she is likely to feel if a request is turned down. In matching the vitality of the expression the therapist may be able to catch the child's attention and direct it toward the reason why he or she would be very upset if a request is denied. For example, such a dialogue might proceed as follows:

Client: (to parent) Let me go to my friend's house after school!
Therapist: You really want to be able to go to your friend's! (same intensity, intonations)
Client: Yeah, they never let me. They treat me like a baby!
Therapist: No wonder you get so upset about it! It seems to you that your parents see you as a little kid who doesn't know what is best for him!
Client: Yeah, they never let me decide what I can handle!
Therapist: Yeah, it seems to you that they think you can't handle much at all! Have you told them? Have you said something like, "Mom, dad, sometimes it seems like you don't think I can ever make the right choice. I think that you think I'm 10 years old."
Client: It's true! You often treat me like a baby!
Father: Son, thanks for telling me that. I didn't realize that you think we see you as being a baby. No wonder you get so angry when we say no.

When the therapist is able to move the discussion to what is under the behavior or demand so that the family is ready to explore what the expression represents, a/r dialogue is being created that is likely to lead to repair of the relationship break.

The therapist may note that the parents have often used words to make demands of their child in an angry, authoritarian way. While the parents may insist that the child is being "disrespectful" to speak with them with a similar demanding tone, they may not see the parallels with a tone that they routinely take in speaking with their child. This is a clear example of primary/secondary intersubjectivity that has often been overlooked because it is so prevalent in parent–child relationships over the generations.

At times, a family member, often the child, will not become reengaged in the dialogue, regardless of how accepting of the break the therapist is. On these occasions, the entire meaning of the session may hang in the balance of the therapist's next responses. Other family members are likely to be ready to interpret the break as being due to an unwillingness to try, pervasive anger, rejection, their own failure, or the failure of the treatment. Words such as, "That's just how he is at home too! This is a waste of our time!" are about to descend over those present and color the session, the course of treatment, and the meaning of the family relationships.

The therapist, in contrast, begins to color the break with the same attitude of PACE that she brought to the fully engaged "moments of meeting" in the intersubjective matrix. She has a variety of options, often expressed in the following order:

1. She might begin by inviting the child back into the dialogue. She could say: "Robert, I've been wondering if what we've just been saying makes any sense to you."

2. If the child refuses the invitation, she could acknowledge the refusal and address it with the same attitude:

> Thanks for letting me know that you don't want to say now what you think about what we were saying. Would you be willing to help me to understand what makes you not want to talk about it now? I worry that your parents or I may have said something that bothered you, but I'm not sure what. Would you tell me why you don't want to talk now?

3. If the child refuses to discuss his motives for not talking she might guess the motives with the same attitude, to determine if the child will speak if he is given some help getting started or finding the right words:

> Susan, I think that your son, Robert, might be telling us that this discussion has gotten pretty hard and he might want to set it aside today. Or he might not trust that we will really understand what was going on with him and we might just criticize him, as if we're trying to make him feel awful. If that's what he's thinking, I can sure understand why he doesn't want to talk anymore about it. Is that about right, Robert?

4. The therapist might skip that final question, and even some of the guesses about Robert's motives. She might go directly to accepting the decision, giving empathy for whatever motives are behind it:

> Susan, I think we need to listen to Robert now. He's saying that he doesn't want to talk about the conflict yesterday anymore in

this session. I'm not sure why, but I know that he is clear in his mind about this and let's accept his decision.

5. The therapist and parent may continue to explore the theme without any efforts to reengage Robert. The therapist insures that any future discussion does not contain negative guesses about the child's motives. The therapist also insures that the discussion does not then lead into other examples of the "problem" which would only prove to the child that his withdrawal from the dialogue was the right decision.

6. The therapist might change the focus to another area of discussion, generally one that is characterized by little or no apparent shame or fear for the person who withdrew from the dialogue. The child will then be more likely to reengage. If he does not, and there was no expectation that he do so, the session is more likely to end without "failure" being given to the meaning of the session.

ADULTS NEED BREAKS, TOO

Both the parents and the therapist are certain to also periodically take breaks from the intersubjective presence during the treatment session. It is the responsibility of the therapist to notice such breaks and to respond to them with playfulness, acceptance, curiosity, and empathy.

The parent may initiate a break from the intersubjective process for reasons similar to those of her child. Family treatment asks parents to expose themselves to areas of potential shame and fear that are often likely to be very difficult to explore. They are being asked to become vulnerable and to express their own experience while at the same time maintaining attachment security for their children. Our society has a strong taboo against others questioning how parents are raising their children. Though parents may choose to enter family treatment and can choose to leave as well, it is nevertheless often very difficult for them to expose themselves to the perspective of another when it involves how they care for their children. The therapist owes the parents her commitment to maintain a strong, clear intention to relate with them with acceptance, curiosity, and empathy.

The therapist's own breaks from intersubjectivity must be recognized and addressed or they will risk greatly impeding the treatment process. It is crucial that the therapist is able to invite and explore within the intersubjective dialogue the full range of memories, affective states, and parent–child interactive patterns that are likely to emerge within a given treatment session. Self-reflection abilities are crucial if the therapist is to guide and serve as a model for the family through the intersubjective integrative process.

The following reasons represent the therapist's own break patterns that require her awareness.

1. Personal events outside of the treatment session are compromising the therapist's affective states, attention, and strength of intention throughout the session.

2. A given topic, affective state, or motivation manifested by a family member is difficult for the therapist to respond to with acceptance, curiosity, and empathy.

3. The therapist is not able to identify with the narrative of the parent or child, due to an overidentification with the narrative of the other.

4. The therapist is reluctant to address breaks of members of the family out of anxiety over the conflict, disapproval, or the distress to self or other that might follow.

5. The therapist is not able to accept that she will make mistakes or be misattuned. Rather than respond with simple awareness or realistic guilt to these situations, she reacts with shame.

The above break patterns (especially numbers 2–5) are likely to relate to features of the therapist's own attachment history that have not been resolved and integrated into her narrative. When the therapist is not able to address and resolve them through self-reflection, it is likely that resolution will require that the therapist participate in similar intersubjective experiences to those that are described in this work. These experiences may involve the therapist exploring these patterns of breaks with her own attachment figures, her supervisor, or her therapist. Her goal is to be able to respond with acceptance, curiosity, and empathy to whatever emerges intersubjectively within the treatment session. She may require similar intersubjective experiences with her own attachment figures to attain such a goal.

By accepting these breaks in the dialogue the therapist is conveying her belief that her intention during the session is to create an intersubjective matrix for the family over a wide range of memories, events, and affective states. In doing so, these themes are invited into the intersubjective context where affect is mutually regulated and meaning is mutually created. By accepting these breaks she is conveying her belief that therapeutic change will not occur as a result of giving one member of the family a lecture. Nor will it occur by seeking to elicit shame in those members who will not remain in the dialogue.

By accepting these breaks, the therapist is standing beside intersubjectivity—not problem solving—as the primary change agent. Having the a/r dialogue is more important than the content of the dialogue. When the child or parent refuses to remain in one area of content, another is found, such as the refusal itself. Over time, the range of memories, recent events, and affective states that are able to be addressed intersubjectively expands and deepens. As the sense of safety within intersubjectivity increases, the themes associated with dysregulating shame and related affective states decrease.

By accepting these breaks, the therapist is free to focus on the intersubjective dance, not the content. The content will take care of itself, as the sense of safety within states of intersubjectivity increases. If an area of content was not explored, the session is not a failure. As the areas that are safe to explore increase, all contents will gradually be welcome into the a/r dialogue.

By accepting these breaks, the therapist is not avoiding them. In fact, she may often address the reasons for the breaks. She makes the reasons explicit so that their meaning may be understood and the affective states associated with them may be regulated. By addressing the breaks with acceptance, curiosity, and empathy, she is making it clear that the breaks themselves need not be avoided. The client is never going to be trapped within intersubjectivity.

In family treatment breaks are presented not as failures but as natural and important parts of all attachment relationships. If they are avoided, the attachment becomes limited and increasingly formal and rigid. If they are not avoided but also not repaired they are likely to create dysregulating anger, fear, hopelessness, or shame. Members then relate with each other in either an inhibited and cautious way or a volatile and impulsive way. Either way, many unrepaired experiences become excluded from intersubjective engagement.

For breaks to be seen as natural and important their deeper meaning and function needs to be made clear. Since the meaning of subjective experience must vary between unique individuals, there will necessarily often be differing experiences of the same event by members of the family. The presence of these differences need not indicate that one is right and the other wrong. Rather, their presence may suggest that the functioning of the family allows for differences to be acknowledged, and even more, for the uniqueness of each individual to be respected and encouraged.

A composite case example:

> Kevin was a 9-year-old boy initially described by his parents as being quiet, anxious, unwilling to try anything new, and under-achieving at school. These qualities all contrasted sharply with the presentation of his parents, Rachel and Don. Both were "strong personalities" by their own admission, and very active in their careers and community. They also were quite "active" in their son's life, having many expectations for him that he was not meet-ing. What frustrated them the most was how he would not look at them or talk with them, when they tried to talk with him about his "difficulties." They assured me that they accepted that he had a "different personality" from theirs, but that they just wanted him to be happy and successful in his life, "at whatever he chooses."

I spent four sessions with Rachel and Don before bringing Kevin into the sessions. I spoke with them about PACE and the need to understand their son's inner world before being able to guess what the "problem" might be and how they might address it. They acknowledged that the way I was suggesting we speak with their son was not how they usually spoke with him, nor how they were raised. They gave the therapist a summary of their attachment histo-ries, both of which were characterized by conflicts that were not well resolved and were often followed by emotional withdrawal.

At one point, Don exclaimed, "I'm not Mr. Rogers, Doc." I replied that it never occurred to me that he might be, and we all laughed. They were somewhat disappointed that I was not taking a more directive approach, but agreed to follow my lead in our efforts to develop an a/r dialogue with their son. They also seemed to value that I spoke quite directly with them, initiating discussions about areas where we seemed to disagree regarding child rearing, and recognizing their commitment to do what was best for their son, even if it proved to be difficult.

In the first joint session with Kevin, I initially focused on his daily routines and a friendship that he had with a boy who shared his interest in collecting a series of figures that were connected to a pop-ular movie. He had spent the night at the boy's house recently, one of the few times in his life that he had ever slept over. Kevin spoke softly, responding easily to my questions but initiating little. I decided to explore that experience with him:

Therapist: What was that like, sleeping at John's house?

Kevin: OK.

Therapist: Stay up late?

Kevin: (smiles) Yeah.

Therapist: Talking a lot?

Kevin: Yeah.

Therapist: Seems like he's quite a friend and you guys got a lot in common.

Kevin: Yeah.

Therapist: (laughing) And how many times did his parents tell you to stop talking and go to sleep?

Kevin: (laughs) His mom did the first time and then his dad. John said we better stop when his dad told us to.

Don: I wish Kevin would talk more at home! He doesn't talk enough. (laughs) (Kevin immediately looks down and his face becomes expressionless.)

Therapist: (to Don) My worry, Don, is that the way you said that, your son might be experiencing you as being disappointed in him. That he's not OK to you.

Don: I just wish he'd talk with me more.

Therapist: Because.

Don: Because?

Therapist: Yeah, it would help me to know, and maybe Kevin too, why you want him to talk with you more.

Don: Why wouldn't I? He's my son.

Therapist: Yes . . . he's your son . . . and . . .

Don: I'd like us to talk more.

Therapist: Because . . .

Don: So I know what's on his mind. So we can share things. Is that asking too much?

Therapist: I'm sorry, Don, you seem to be getting a bit frustrated at my questioning. I don't want to be difficult, I just think it might be helpful to make your motives more explicit. I was worried that Kevin might have taken your words as a sign that you were disappointed in him, not about your lack of talking together. I think that you're now saying that this is not about your thoughts about your son, it is simply your wish that you'd talk more together.

Don: Yeah.

Therapist: And do you want more talking so that you two would be closer . . . feel closer.

Don: Yeah, of course.

Therapist: Because you love your son?

Don: Of course I do.

Therapist: Ah! Have you ever told him that . . . have you ever said, "Kevin, I love you so much and sometimes I wish that we were closer to each other."

Don: (more quietly) No, I've never said that.

Therapist: Did you have this kind of close relationship with your dad? (I knew the answer but saw value in Don acknowledging this to his son.)

Don: No, he was always working.

Therapist: So you hope to be closer to Kevin than your dad was with you.

Don: Yeah.

Therapist: But it does not come that easily, I'd guess, since you don't have experiences with your dad to draw upon.

Don: That's right, but I'm doing my best . . . but sometimes it seems that Kevin . . .

Therapist: (interrupting) I hope you don't mind my interrupting, Don, I'd just like to stay with your experience now and not guess about Kevin's. Is that OK?

Don: Yeah.

Therapist: I really sense that you are doing your best. You want a close relationship with your son a lot and you fear that it is not happening as you wished it would. And you think maybe if you two talked more . . . and you don't and you think that maybe if Kevin were not as quiet when with you, that you would be closer. And you are doing your best . . . you know you are . . . and you fear that maybe Kevin is not trying as hard as you are . . . or maybe if he just talked more to you.

Don: (quietly) Sometimes I'm not sure if he does want to be with me.

Therapist: That must be hard . . . if it seems to you . . . that Kevin does not want to be closer you . . . sort of like it was with your dad . . . all over again.

Don: Yeah.

Therapist: Yeah. (followed by 15 seconds of silence) (Turns to Kevin, in the same quiet tone that was present at the end of the dialogue with Don.) I noticed that you were listening real well when your dad and I were talking about you and him . . . and your relationship. I hope that you were OK when I guessed that when he spoke about your not talking at home, that you might think that he was disappointed in you. (Kevin is silent). I was glad that I did . . . because as we talked your dad said real clearly that he is not disappointed in you . . . he worries that the relationship that you have is not as close as he hoped that it would be. And he worries at times that you might not want to be closer to him . . . almost like he worries like you might be disappointed in him . . . I also was glad that your dad said—I think it was hard for him to say it but he did anyway—that he was not close to his dad and hoped that you and he would be closer. (Kevin now looks up into therapist's eyes.) And I think he's not sure quite how to be closer, since his dad never taught him . . . But I think he wants to learn . . . He wants you . . . and him . . . to . . . be closer. (said quietly and deliberately) Do you want that too?

Kevin: Shakes his head "yes."

Therapist: Yeah, I thought so. You both want that . . . I'm glad . . . since you both want that . . .you'll both be able to do it. Be closer to each other. Dad and son.

Therapist: (to Don) Would you hold your son's hand while I talk with Rachel for a minute. (Don takes his son's hand, they look at each other and smile.)

Therapist: What do you think, Rachel?

Rachel: Don's a good man.

Therapist: Why did you say that?

Rachel: Because he is.

Therapist: Why did you think it was important to tell me that?

Rachel: Sometimes he does not show what's inside and I'm not sure if others know him like I do. He's a good father and husband.

Therapist: I'm sorry if I said something that made you think that I thought that Don was not a good father and husband.

Rachel: No, it's just . . . it's hard for him to talk about his feelings.

Therapist: I thought that he did well. He showed courage. I could tell how much he wants to be a good dad to Kevin.

Rachel: He just doesn't talk that way.

Therapist: Do you two talk that way much with each other?

Rachel: No, I guess we don't. But we love each other.

Therapist: Yes, I can see that . . . But . . .

Rachel: But what?

Therapist: I wondered if you were saying that you wished at times that you both had an easier time talking with each other about what you think . . . and feel . . . about each other . . . that if you did . . . maybe it would deepen that feeling of love that you know is there.

Rachel: Yeah, I guess so.

Therapist: (smiles) OK if we ask Don if he would like to talk more about your relationship with each other in ways that would deepen that love feeling?

Rachel: (smiles) OK.

Therapist: Do you want to ask him or do you want me to ask him for you?

Rachel: (to Don) What do you think? Maybe it would help if we worked on getting closer too. You and me.

Don: (smiles) You got it! (Short silence while all convey happiness.)

Therapist: (smiles and turns to Kevin) And why don't you tell your mom that you would like to be closer to her too?

Kevin: (smiling and speaking loudly for the first time) I want us to be closer to you too, mom!

Rachel: I love you, Kevin. (She leans over and kisses his cheek.)

Therapist: Wow, what a hard working family! This is so great! You all want the same thing! And you can do it too! I know it!

In the final minutes of the session the therapist suggested that each evening Don and Kevin take turns choosing a game to play. He then suggested that Rachel speak with each of them individually about how the games went, and then report to us all in the next session what each said to her. Over the following two months the family all learned to relax more together and engage in reciprocal enjoyable activities. Kevin became more assertive as he felt more confident about his parents' acceptance and love for him. Sessions involving Rachel and Don focused on some unspoken areas of distance in their relationship which were addressed fairly openly once they entered the a/r dialogue.

Family treatment is often brief and the results lasting when the therapist focuses under the symptoms at the related affect and meaning states. When these are explored the experiences themselves become reorganized and are much more easily acknowledged, repaired, and integrated into the family narrative.

Chapter 9

EXPLORING AND RESOLVING
CHILDHOOD TRAUMA

Being able to acknowledge these experiences, accept them, and investigate
them in terms of their meaning and what they reveal about the conditions
with which one has to deal, and being able to communicate about them to
oneself and to trusted others, is the deepest undoing of pathology. —Diana
Fosha, The Transforming Power of Affect (2000)

Childhood trauma, when addressed in this model of family therapy for
either the children or for their parents who were traumatized as
children, benefits from principles of attachment and intersubjectivity at
least as much as do less extreme types of dysregulation and interpersonal conflicts. The principles of basic safety and then safe exploration
through intersubjectivity prove to be an excellent context from which
to approach and resolve trauma. Repetitive, intrafamilial trauma is
responsible for much more severe and comprehensive psychological
symptoms than is trauma that occurs apart from the family (van der
Kolk, 2005). These "domains of impairment" can be found in areas
of attachment, bodily functioning, affect regulation, consciousness
(including dissociation), behavioral control, cognition, and self-concept
(Cook et al., 2005).

When the parents' abilities to provide good care for their children
are compromised by their own childhood trauma, it is crucial that

this be addressed if they are to provide the safety and intersubjective experiences necessary for them to meet the needs of their children. This may necessitate working with the family therapist in some depth prior to the onset of the joint sessions with their child, or it may require a referral to a separate therapist for the parent(s). When the child has experienced trauma, this can be addressed in the family sessions so long as he is able to experience safety through the presence of his parents. If his parents were the source of the trauma, then it is crucial for the parents to have resolved the factors that led to them traumatizing their child, to accept full responsibility for their acts, and to be committed and able to not traumatize their child again.

At other times the child may have been traumatized by his or her parents and no longer be living with them. This model of family treatment is very appropriate for that child and his or her current caregivers, whether they be adoptive or foster parents, or direct care providers at a residential program or group living situation. In these situations the therapist must expect and insure that the adults serving as attachment figures are able to provide a presence in the sessions that is similar to what is expected from the parents described throughout this work. In these situations it is also important to ensure that the adults have a level of commitment to remaining as the child's caregivers for a sufficient length of time to enable the attachment to take on meaning.

Within intrafamilial trauma (various acts of abuse and neglect):

1. Safety is destroyed and developmental patterns become disorganized.
2. Intersubjective explorations are reduced and avoided.
3. The self is an object to the other, not an intersubjective partner.
4. Traumatic events are not explored and experienced in an integrative, coherent, intersubjective manner. They are not assimilated into the autobiographical narrative.
5. Traumatic events create dissociation, as do subsequent memories of such events, causing rigid avoidance or the risk of "retraumatization."

Given the severity of these "domains of impairment," it is very likely that the child's or parents' ability to feel safe and turn to others for safety is greatly impaired. A similar deficit is likely in the experience of self and other and in the ability to become engaged with others intersubjectively. As a result, this process of family treatment is likely to require a longer length of time with a more extensive reliance on PACE for the momentum of the sessions.

When a child is being traumatized by a parent or caregiver the resultant overwhelming affects of terror and shame are likely to create a dissociative reaction to the event that serves to attempt to create some semblance of psychological and physical safety. Through extreme withdrawal from the event, the child is able to diminish the affective and cognitive impact of the event on the self. The child is likely to be unable to experience his or her parents as a source of safety—an attachment figure—placing him or her at risk for attachment disorganization, which is itself a risk factor for psychopathology (Cassidy & Mohr, 2001; Lyons-Ruth & Jacobvitz, 1999). The child is certainly also likely to greatly avoid intersubjective experiences with his or her parents because such experiences increase the impact that parents have on a child's affective and cognitive development. The traumatized child is likely to be very motivated to reduce the impact that his or her parents are having on him.

The traumatizing events are not able to be integrated into the autobiographical narrative. Any associated event is likely to be strongly avoided, generating hypervigilance and a lack of the types of experiences likely to generate trauma resolution and narrative coherence. Psychotherapy is itself likely to present obstacles to the resolution of the trauma given the perceived lack of safety and the avoidance of intersubjective experiences. There is danger that the processing of the trauma might be retraumatizing in itself. There is also the danger that waiting for the child to initiate the exploration of the trauma will result in the trauma never being explored. The "therapeutic window" (Briere & Scott, 2006) within which the awareness of the trauma is neither being compulsively avoided nor is it dysregulating, may be very small for some clients. Treatment guidelines have therefore been developed to enable the treatment of such complex traumas to facilitate integration and resolution while not retraumatizing the client. These guidelines have six components: safety, self-regulation, self-reflection, traumatic experience integration, relational engagement, and positive affect enhancement (Cook et al., 2005).

The following represents the steps whereby attachment and intersubjectivity may facilitate the exploration and resolution of childhood trauma. This process is very similar to the above guidelines as well as to this general model of family therapy. However, at each step in the process it is crucial that the therapist's intention is to attend to every break in the relationship as evidenced by the intersubjective moment or its absence. At every break, the therapist stops further exploration until the break naturally ends or has been repaired. While the therapist must take an active lead in this process because of the intensity of the child's avoidance defenses, the therapist also *always* follows the child's response to the lead, continuing or stopping as the response dictates.

STAGES OF TRAUMA RESOLUTION

1. The therapist and other adults present need to serve as the source of *attachment security.* The key factors in attachment security, being available, sensitive, responsive, and committed to relationship repair, must be consistently present during the treatment sessions. The therapist must not assume that if she demonstrates these traits that her client will experience them as well. Her expressions to facilitate safety may either go unnoticed, be misinterpreted, or in themselves generate anxiety. Signs of caring and interest will not necessarily create a sense of safety.

The therapist initially focuses on light, neutral, and positive themes and notices whether the exploration of these themes generates an intersubjective experience with its matched affect, joint awareness, and complementary intentions. If it does, she makes her experience very clear to reduce the anxiety that comes from ambiguity. She develops a reciprocal, positive affective experience. If it does not develop, she accepts the response, repairs any relationship break, and invites a new intersubjective experience. She is persistent; her message being that she will not be impatient, she will not give up.

2. As pockets of safety begin to emerge she attempts to deepen and broaden them by moving into mildly stressful themes and then facilitating an intersubjective exploration of them as well. Increasingly she finds success in the discovery of qualities of self in the child or adult that have been hidden and are probably unknown. These qualities include courage, honesty, resilience, strength, being a person of worth, and a person committed to a life better than what he or she has known. Within these experiences of *primary intersubjectivity,* the child begins to experience herself tentatively in positive ways. These experiences also generate an additional sense of safety.

She also begins to experience the therapist as a person who truly is interested in her well-being, who has confidence in her abilities to improve her life, who values and is committed to her. More and more in the session, the rhythm and momentum of a/r dialogue is occurring and generating a reciprocal, experiential, positive, and hopeful state.

3. Once primary intersubjectivity is established, the child is more likely now to become engaged with the therapist in experiences of *secondary intersubjectivity.* The child is now becoming open to allowing the impact on the therapist of the past events now being explored to have a similar impact on her. She is receptive to beginning to reorganize her experiences of the past events, based on the therapist's experience of them in the present. Once the therapist notices that this is occurring, she turns her attention to the past traumatic events as well.

4. Through secondary intersubjectivity the child is beginning to again experience the traumatic events of the past through the experience of them that the therapist has. She is much safer in doing so, being able to *coregulate the affect* associated with the event based on the therapist's affective response to it. The therapist did not experience the terror and shame that the child originally did when exposed to the event. The child is now approaching the event from the safety of the therapist's affective response to it.

5. With the associated affect no longer consisting in dsyregulating shame and terror, the child is able to reexperience the event, combining her experience and the therapist's experience—two perspectives— and so *cocreating new meaning of the event.* It is not enough that she experiences the therapist's experience of the event. She must, herself, reexperience that past event now in the present, being influenced by the therapist's experience of it.

6. As the child is now fully creating the meaning of the event, affectively and reflectively, she is able to begin to assimilate the event into her *autobiographical narrative.* The child had dissociated from the original traumatic event so that it had not entered the flow of her subjective experience. She is now sufficiently able to organize the experience of the event so that it is able to enter the narrative.

7. As the event is being assimilated, it is able to be impacted by, and impact in turn, other events in the narrative. She is now in position to develop a *coherent narrative* in which certain events no longer remain rigidly isolated from other aspects of the narrative.

The following is an example of the treatment of an 11-year-old girl, Rebecca, who experienced considerable abuse and neglect while residing with her biological family. She was placed in foster care when she was 6, and after two foster placements, moved to her adoptive family when she was 8. She manifested significant difficulty turning to her adoptive parents for comfort and support and she frequently engaged in oppositional behaviors in response to routine expectations and discipline. During the fifth session she was receptive to exploring her early experiences of abuse and neglect with her therapist, Allison, and her adoptive mother, Jean. These experiences had been briefly explored in earlier sessions but she had quickly focused on other areas of discussion.

Therapist: Could you help me to understand . . . how did you make sense of your dad beating you with a belt. You were only a little kid, 3, 4, 5, 6.
Rebecca: I was scared of him. I never knew what he'd get mad about.
Therapist: You must have been so scared! He was so big and you were so little!
Rebecca: I tried to stay away from him. I'd try to keep quiet and not bother him.
Therapist: I'm so sorry that you had to do that, Rebecca. Your own dad. Someone that at first you would have wanted his attention . . . hoped that he would smile at you, play with you, hold you, and read you stories . . . and you had to hide from him!
Rebecca: I didn't know what else to do!
Therapist: Of course not. I wasn't saying that you could have prevented being beat . . . you were so little . . . how could you stop him?
Rebecca: My mom said that I was too noisy.
Therapist: Noisy?
Rebecca: She said that if I would just be quiet he wouldn't hit me.
Therapist: Did she ever tell him not to hit you.
Rebecca: No. She never did . . . She never said anything to him . . . She got mad at me for making him mad! She never . . . she never . . . did anything.
Therapist: She never kept you safe from him.
Rebecca: She made me think it was my fault! If I had been a better girl I would not get beat.
Therapist: That must have been so hard. Your mom . . . not defending

you . . . instead she blamed you. So hard . . . you were all alone when he would hurt you.

Rebecca: Nobody helped me.

Therapist: All alone . . . how sad . . . and you were just a . . . little . . . girl.

Rebecca: Why didn't she take care of me?

Therapist: Oh, Rebecca, I'm so sorry . . . I don't know why she didn't . . . I don't know why. But I know that you needed someone to keep you safe . . . someone. (Rebecca begins to cry. Jean puts her arm around her and Rebecca leans against her shoulder. Jean begins to rock her.)

Jean: You're safe now, honey. I'll never let anyone hurt you. Never.

Therapist: Why will you keep her safe, Jean?

Jean: Because she's my daughter . . . and I love her . . . and she does not deserve to be treated that way. Never. By no one.

Therapist: I'm afraid that Rebecca must have thought that it was her fault. And she did not deserve to be kept safe. What you are saying may be confusing to her.

Jean: But I'm telling the truth. She never deserved to be treated that way.

Therapist: But she did not feel that . . . and that made it all the harder. And she still may doubt it at times. Doubt that she is lovable and deserves to be safe and protected.

Jean: (to Rebecca) Some day, honey, I hope that you believe me. You are lovable and do deserve to be protected. (Jean still rocks her slowly and kisses her hair.)

Therapist: But you get angry with her sometimes.

Jean: Angry yes, but I'll never hit her, never hurt her. Sure she does things that I don't like sometimes and I do things that she does not like at times. So what! That's how all families are. And I'll still always protect her and never hurt her. No matter how mad I get at Rebecca at times, I'll still love her. (to Rebecca) I'll still love you.

Rebecca: (very quietly) I know mom.

Not only was Rebecca beginning to reorganize her early experiences of abuse and neglect, she also was beginning to accept her mother's comfort and love. As the trauma was being resolved, the attachment with her adoptive parent was beginning to move toward security.

EPILOGUE

By now, I hope that the reader will concur that concepts of attachment and intersubjectivity have clear relevance to the field of family therapy. Given the rapid emergence of congruent findings from the field of neuroscience, I am convinced that these same concepts will play a central role in the development of many diverse fields involving mental health, education, parenting, health, and social services. Our understanding of human development and relationships will be increasingly indebted to both attachment and intersubjectivity in the years ahead. I would like to turn briefly to future directions of attachment-focused family therapy as well as psychotherapy in general, based upon recent findings of neuroscience and related disciplines. In doing so I am heavily indebted to the very comprehensive and integrative theories of Allan Schore regarding these emerging findings (1994, 2003a, 2003b).

The initial organization and regulation of the infant's physiological and behavioral processes depend on the infant's physical proximity and interaction with his or her mother. These processes are being coregulated by the mother. Without her active involvement, the infant is unable to autoregulate such fundamental processes as activation, rhythmic sucking behaviors, sleep–wake states, warmth, growth hormone levels, basal corticosterone levels, and responsiveness to new situations (Schore, 1994).

The coregulation of basic neurological and physiological states also involves the coregulation of affect. When the infant and parent are engaged in an affective/bodily rhythm, the internal state of the infant is becoming able to inhibit responses and regulate its level of affect. Within these states of affect attunement, the infant's neurological development becomes organized and develops the ability to begin to autoregulate these states.

As the infant develops so too is her brain developing. Safety and regulation are primary concerns of first the amygdala, and shortly thereafter the anterior cingulate, and by 8 to 10 months of age, the prefrontal cortex. As the brain is developing during the first year of life and beyond, it is increasingly able to insure safety and regulation through increasingly subtle discriminations and resonance between the organism and the environment, enabling more flexible responses to specific environmental variations.

At the core of these increasing skills of maintaining safety and regulation are the ongoing communications between the infant or toddler and the primary attachment figures. Near the attachment figure, the child feels safe and is motivated to attend to her eyes, face, voice, movements, and touch. These reciprocal and attuned interactions—the original intersubjective experiences—facilitate the development of the prefrontal cortex, which, in turn, is necessary for the development of these skills. According to Schore (2003b),

> dyadic communications that generate intense positive affect represent a growth-promoting environment for the prefrontal cortex . . . orbital prefrontal areas are critically and directly involved in attachment functions. This cortical area plays an essential role in the processing of social signals and in the pleasurable qualities of social interaction. Attachment experiences (face-to-face transactions between caregiver and infant) directly influence the imprinting or circuit wiring of this system. (p. 15)

The prefrontal cortex provides a depth and breadth of integrative and meaning-making abilities that the amygdala and anterior cingulate lack. It is both the most dyadic and also the most integrative structure of the brain. The prefrontal cortex blends cognitive, affective, and bodily awareness. It incorporates past knowledge from both implicit and explicit memories and utilizes this knowledge in working to understand the meaning of the present. It brings the reflective skills of the cortex to identify, regulate, and express the affective states that the infant is experiencing. It brings the overall integrative skills—affect, cognition, and body sensation—and enables the infant and young child to begin to make sense of the mother's congruent, contingent communications. In time, the toddler is able to understand the mother's mind and to have empathy for her inner state just as she has empathy for his or hers. In time, the child becomes increasingly able to experience the world as she does, recall past experiences, notice repetitive and novel aspects of the present, and respond in a flexible, best-interest, manner.

It is important to note that much of the social and affective developments that comprise the sense of self are centered in the right hemisphere of the brain, including that part of the prefrontal cortex lying within the right hemisphere. To quote Schore (2003b) again:

> Confirming earlier proposals for a central role of the right orbitofrontal areas in essential self-functions, current neuroimagining studies now demonstrate that the processing of self occurs within the right prefrontal cortices, and that the self-concept is represented in right frontal areas. (p. 46)

The intersubjective experiences that have been described in detail throughout this book are considered by Schore to lie at the heart of the therapeutic relationship (2005). He notes: "at the psychobiological core of the intersubjective field is the attachment bond of emotional communication and interactive regulation" (p. 15). He goes on to conclude: "The essential biological purpose of intersubjective communications in all human interactions, including those embedded in the psychobiological core of the therapeutic alliance, is the regulation of right-brain/mind/body states" (p. 16). These communications are reciprocal, affective, contingent, and experiential (as opposed to conceptual). These communications are nonverbal at their core, but may become more elaborate and "meaningful" when made along with the "unique affectively charged language that occurs in the therapeutic intersubjective context" (Schore, 2005, p. 12).

Where do the emerging findings such as these described by Schore lead us? Our understanding of intersubjective communication and its impact on human development is only in its infancy. As we know more we will be increasingly able to understand how to utilize its power in all helping relationships as well as in human interactions and relationships in general. These understandings and implications have been described by Cozolino (2002) and Park (2004) among others. Schore himself offers us 20 principles of psychotherapeutic treatment that naturally follow from our new understandings of the developmental structure and functioning of the brain (2003b, pp. 279–281). In a similar vein, I would propose that in the years to come:

1. There will be an increasing awareness of how the range of non-verbal communications convey empathy and understanding in a manner that enables the experience to be intersubjective. The words that we use in therapy and in any significant relationship need to be embodied communications, emerging from the right hemisphere and manifested in the subtle, unique expressions of our bodies.

2. We will see a deepening understanding of not only the importance of psychological safety, but also of how such experiences of safety are generated through intersubjectivity, with its resonating qualities of joined affect, awareness, and intention.

3. Helping professionals in all fields will be expected to develop their abilities to remain intersubjectively present with their full range of clients. The training of these professionals will incorporate the same intersubjective skills that are required for their successful practice in their field. Such training must necessarily involve the energy and bodily awareness of the right hemisphere and not be restricted to abstract concepts and lectures.

4. Family therapy will move beyond strategies and structures, systems and generational boundaries, and incorporate more of the neuropsychological research that demonstrates how families are naturally suited for the coregulation of affect and the cocreation of meanings, which creates the capacity for autoregulation of affect and reflective functioning. A family therapy that builds on these principles will prove to be the most effective.

5. Prevention and early-intervention programs will emphasize the development of the affective communications of attachment and foster such developments through providing attuned relationships and videotape review where the moment-to-moment interactions can be reexperienced and reflected upon (Marvin et al., 2002).

6. Parenting practices congruent with neuroscience and attachment research will be incorporated to a much greater extent in parenting manuals and programs (Sunderland, 2006).

7. Interventions that incorporate these principles will be developed for specific populations (Dozier, Stovall, Albus, & Bates, 2001; Trevarthen & Aitken, 2001).

8. Our understanding of child abuse and neglect will deepen and the devastating effects of the lack of intersubjective

experience will be more fully understood. Prevention, early intervention, and treatment programs for both the parents and their children will become more congruent with neuropsychological research.

The dyadic nature of brain development (Siegel, 1999) will increasingly turn our attention back to the central importance of nourishing, developing, and maintaining the intersubjective relationship in both therapy as well as other settings. Developmental neuroscience is showing us that there are unique features of relationships which facilitate safety and learning about self, other, and world. Creating such relationships with clients who manifest reduced motivation or ability is not as easy as some would suggest. It is hoped that the interventions suggested in this work will add to our abilities to become successfully engaged with these individuals and families.

For decades there have been divisions in the therapy field (thought vs. emotion, intrapsychic vs. interpsychic, insight vs. behavior, individual vs. family treatment, dependence vs. independence, nondirective vs. directive). Findings of neuroscience suggest that such distinctions within the brain are artificial at best. The integration and coherence of the brain through its intersubjective engagement with another brain is the fundamental reality that needs to guide all of our interventions (Siegel, 1999, 2001, 2007). This is a perspective that requires reciprocity, nonlinear contingency, as well as the interwoven nature of past and present, nonverbal and verbal, and affective and reflective modulation.

Schore has vividly demonstrated to us that as we understand the structures and functioning of the brain more fully we will not be able to ignore the pivotal place of safety, affect, and intersubjective engagement in the development of individuals and cultures. As the applications of these exciting research findings become better established and integrated into our view of human nature, the concepts of attachment and intersubjectivity are certain to emerge from their philosophical and scientific texts. When that occurs they are likely to enter into our experiential world more deeply and comprehensively and so facilitate the further development of our nature.

Appendix 1: Case Study 1

SHAMEFUL TRAUMAS

Tonglen (the Tibetan word that means "to give and to receive") consists of accepting another's suffering and distress, and making an offering in return for all the confidence and serenity one can muster. This simple sharing of someone else's suffering means being with him or her, not leaving that person alone. —M. De Hennezel, Intimate Death

Paula, age 40 and her husband, Jonathan, age 42, sought treatment out of concerns for their relationship with their son, Ron, age 12. During the previous 12 months Ron had appeared to be increasingly unhappy, irritable, and withdrawn. He became difficult to engage and his academic performance at school had also began to deteriorate. When his parents approached him with these difficulties, he would only lash out at them that they should leave him alone. Jonathan and Paula also had a 9-year-old daughter, Trista, who did not manifest any noticeable psychological problems in her functioning.

During the assessment, Paula indicated that she had more difficulties with her relationship with Ron than did her husband. When she corrected Ron or even tried to have a discussion with him, they often ended by screaming at each other, with Paula then experiencing anxiety and despair. Paula was very ashamed of her response to Ron, which had not been present in the early years of their relationship. She actually thought that in earlier years she and Ron had a closer relationship than did Jonathan and Ron. When asked if she thought that Ron's entering adolescence might be contributing to the difficulties, Paula indicated that she did think that his increasing tendency to argue and withdraw from her was related to his adolescence and that it was particularly difficult for her. She added that it some ways it reminded her of her relationships with her parents and siblings in her family of origin. She went on to describe a childhood characterized by abuse and rejection within her family. Her father and older siblings were very abusive to her and her mother failed to protect her from the abuse. Paula indicated that she had sought treatment in the past regarding her maltreatment within her family and she had thought that she had resolved it. She believed that her relationship with Jonathan was stable and she had believed that she was proving to be a much better parent than were her own parents. However, Ron's increasingly negative behaviors, especially those directed toward her, often left her experiencing feelings of despair, anxiety, and anger, similar to, though milder, than her habitual emotional states throughout childhood.

The therapist asked if Paula saw value in again seeing the therapist that she had worked with in the past. She saw value in that course of action, but indicated that her previous therapist was no longer practicing in the area. Paula, Jonathan, and the therapist then decided that they would meet for a series of sessions before considering joint sessions that would include Ron and possibly Trista. The purpose of the sessions would be to attempt to reduce the impact of Paula's past family relationships on her current relationship with Ron.

During the first session with Paula and Jonathan, Paula readily explored her horrific childhood that included acts of abuse involving her father. She could never recall feeling safe or becoming engaged with her parents in mutually enjoyable activities. The therapist asked her if she would tell her husband about one specific memory from her past. When she did so, she avoided looking at Jonathan and she spoke of the event without any affective expression in her voice. Paula was asked to tell her husband about the incident again, but this time while looking at him. Paula did so. This time her story was much more detailed and took longer to tell. She cried throughout, while staring into her husband's eyes. When asked to explain the difference between the first telling of the story and the second, Paula replied that she anticipated at any moment that she would see "a look of disgust or rejection" in Jonathan's eyes. Jonathan reassured her while he embraced her as she cried. They both said that Paula had never told him about the abuse in as much detail as she had just done.

At the onset of the second session Paula indicated that she felt closer to Jonathan and more confident that he was able and willing to support her in her efforts to resolve her childhood years of abuse and neglect. However, since that session she had some misgivings about having shared those experiences with Jonathan. At one point she indicated that she had somehow violated his "spirit" by sharing those "gross" experiences with him. The therapist then attempted to understand the nature of her reservations about the disclosure to Jonathan.

Therapist: Is it that you love him and don't want him to experience the horrible experience that you went through?

Paula: What I'm feeling right now is the sense that at a very deep level I continued to carry myself as having been deeply damaged. (tears) . . . it took me years to recover . . . (more tears)

Therapist: I'm sorry, I don't understand . . . I understand the words but do not understand the meaning. Can you help me? (The therapist did not understand the connection between the response and the question. It is difficult to acknowledge not understanding the meaning of such an affectively intense expression. To pretend that one understands when one actually does not is likely to create uncertainty within the client of an experience, a feeling of not being heard with its associated lack of feeling felt.)

Paula: That having gone through this past stuff, I got . . . torn right in half, part of me was over here (holding arm to the left) . . . part of me was over here functioning (moving arm to right) . . . so . . . it's been years trying to pull myself back together again . . . sort of . . . bringing myself up (raising arms in front of herself) . . . (more tears) I don't think (trouble talking and breathing at same time) . . . it would have been as hard if in that entire hierarchy of a family, I had

had one person . . . but because they were all that way . . . it skewed my reality so severely . . . that it was about me (crying with hands on face) Oh!

Therapist: Probably that reality that was about you . . . from your perspective . . . you walked into that room . . . you were responsible for ruining the lives of your family.

Paula: Oh yeah! That was a constant theme! (The client remains in the past. Possibly she is making a connection to her husband and now, by commenting on how alone she was in her family and how as a result, she thought it was all her fault.)

Therapist: Your presence shattered their spirits. Constantly giving you feedback that you were a burden to them, made their lives difficult. And still do, you talk about true things. (The therapist is gently making a connection through the word *spirit*.)

Paula: (nods head, breathes deeply) Yep!

Jonathan: So your relationship with them will never get better . . . not that it matters I guess. (long pause, husband and wife staring downwards)

Therapist: Any possibility about Jonathan's spirit . . . I know I'm harping on this. (Paula laughs) . . . but the way you said that was really powerful, seemed very important . . . that its much of that to Jonathan, he will be brought down. He will be compromised . . . what he has in the world . . . his spirit, his joy, interests, love . . . somehow won't be the same because you will have harmed him (Paula staring at therapist deeply, rubbing finger over her lower lip) . . . and that reminds me of the message you experienced from the members of your family . . . that you harmed them . . . and my fear is . . . somehow you think this will harm Jonathan, just like they said you harmed them, even though your brain knows that he's different from them.

Jonathan: Yes, you said that . . . that you don't want to bring me down. That's accurate.

Therapist: What happened to his spirit since last session? (said quietly)

Paula: Nothing! He's the energizer bunny! (laughs)

Jonathan: (laughing) Is that all you got? All you got? Come on! What was that? Nothing!

Therapist: Come on (smiling), tell her the truth . . . what happened to your spirit?

Jonathan: It's fine, it's healthy. It didn't go anywhere. It got better!

Paula: (raises eyes in surprise, almost shock) Got better?

Jonathan: In terms of us. No problem.

Therapist: (to Jonathan) Elaborate, what do you mean "got better"?

Jonathan: Like . . . sharing something, that delicate . . . kinda made me feel closer to you, as another human being . . . I know you, you have properties that are not perfect, as I do (laughs), but you said yourself, we felt closer afterwards like you gave me a part of yourself, you weren't holding back. When someone opens up and shows something they are afraid of . . . and shows that with you, its like, not a favor, like a gift. (They stare deeply at each other and smile.)

Therapist: Do you hear what he just said?

Paula: Yeah, it's pretty amazing.

Therapist: Would you repeat it?

Paula: It was a gift!

Therapist: How does that make sense?

Paula: We know you don't make sense (looks at husband and laughs) . . . Ah! (deep sigh) It makes sense, he's everything my family isn't.

Therapist: Not good enough. (laughs) (Laughter may often be seen as a means of avoiding difficult affect. At this time, however, the therapist thought that Paula and Jonathan were regulating the difficult affect through laughter—setting a slower pace so that they could stay in the dialogue. This is evident throughout the entire sequence. Without the laughter it is unlikely that Paula would have been able to remain present [affectively and reflectively] throughout the entire painful dialogue. The therapist laughs along with them, while gently remaining focused on the stressful themes.)

Paula: (laughs, sighs, sits quietly for 20 seconds) I don't know. I don't know. (quietly)

Therapist: By exposing what you said is gross . . . what shattered your spirit . . . somehow giving that to him is a gift to him. Is that comprehensible? What sense do you make of that?

Paula: I don't know. What I feel is almost nausea. How does that make sense? (closes eyes, putting finger on abdomen) The whole thing . . . I have to leap from one thing to the next. (moves arms back and forth) I get it on the cognitive level . . . How does it make sense . . . his acceptance of me . . . (closes eyes, holding finger to chest) . . . who I am as a gift . . . I can't explain it. (Breathes deeply, closes eyes, is silent for 15 seconds, then opens eyes.)

(The client is showing her deep distress in her body, touching her chest as she speaks of feeling "almost nausea" and then moving her arms, while "leaping from one thing to the next," similar to how she had earlier described being "torn right in half." Now her arms seemed to be trying to integrate the two halves. This physical level of expression could have been focused on at that time but the therapist chose to continue with the meaning of the word *gift*.)

Therapist: Can I share how it makes sense to me? (The therapist may have been responding to the client's distress—shown physically, affectively, and in her confusion—by rescuing both Paula and herself with a cognitive explanation. Paula's declining the offer supports this possibility.)

Paula: Can I have one more guess? (laughs) Ah (with evident confusion), the other thing I just think of is . . . love?

Therapist: What does love have to do with it? (Possibly again, the therapist's phrase seems to be too casual for the client's evident distress and may reflect the therapist's discomfort with this ongoing distress that they are both experiencing.)

Paula: He loves me and who I am and all of who I am and all I've been through and how I've come through it.

Therapist: So how is that a gift to him? (quieter, with greater curiosity and empathy)

Paula: I share what's happened. (breathes deeply, staring at Jonathan) About closeness . . . and connection and not just . . . (sits quietly and then looks to therapist, seemingly for aid in finding the words).

Therapist: Not relying on yourself . . . relying on him . . . letting him love you . . . when someone loves someone and the person lets them love them . . . that is a gift. . . . in some sense he experienced your pain and it was hard . . . in another sense, he soared because somebody he loves said "I need your love."

Jonathan: I got more of you! More of you! (smiles gently then laughs) I want more!

Therapist: You really, really trusted. (Not responding to the laughter but staying in the vulnerable state that Paula was showing.) He felt great that you were that open . . . you were that vulnerable, you needed him . . . you gave him so much power to destroy you . . . or to love you.

Paula: (Staring, shaking head, breathing deeply, and then staring at husband.) It feels kind of crazy, feels like a whole other language. Just that . . . opening, surrendering, and allowing that caring, closeness is a . . . very different . . . than what I'm accustomed to (Moves hands, turns them over and over in front of her, staring at them. Paula appears to be truly absorbed by a new "reality" reflected in "a whole other language" regarding self and other.)

Therapist: (more reflective) You had said in the last meeting that in some ways you worried that you were too much of a burden . . . What I saw during that meeting . . . from my experience . . . the word *burden* had no relevance to what I saw . . . how vulnerable you were and looked to him for affirmation and acceptance and he was clearly loving you then and I saw you letting him love you, giving him permission to . . . being vulnerable . . . at that level of a relationship . . . who's loving who . . . total reciprocity . . . pain was generating from you so he was absorbing it, containing it, helping you to integrate it, so you didn't have to split yourself . . . at a real basic gut level, he was feeling wonderful that he had the opportunity to do that for you. In a way . . . a gift of the magi . . . who was giving the gift?

Jonathan: And where is the burden . . . no burden, just life. You give your story and I give my story. No burden . . . and then we die. (laughs)

Therapist: Thank you Jonathan, for that summary of love (all laugh). What sense do you make of this discussion (quietly again, to Paula)?

Paula: It's a different quality of what we were talking about . . . a very nice openness that . . . it's like confusing and changing all at the same time . . . feels like another language.

Therapist: Another definition of family . . . love in a family . . . another planet from . . . your first family which was a total negation of you.

Paula: (nods) Yeah. (quietly and with sadness)

Therapist: The concept of Jonathan—existing—is a stretch for you . . . a human being actually would . . . when you walk in the

room, a human being happy, excited, comes closer to you . . .
beyond your comprehension when you were 14 years old. (Paula
nods her head)

Jonathan: (Jonathan then talks of coming to know and love her
over the years. Paula sits and listens with a blank look.)

Therapist: Is there a "but" to Jonathan's comments?

Paula: No. Did you hear one? (laughs) . . . I think I've been so
absorbed with this newness—your (turning to Jonathan) feeling
that . . . like what I said was a gift . . . being able to see that was a
gift . . . trying to understand . . . keep hearing it, listening to it. (20-
second pause) I'm reminded of a dream that I had when I was 15
or 16. I was sitting on the couch in my mother's house where I
lived . . . in the dream I . . . my body went bolt upright, I gave a
horrible scream and fell lifeless to the floor. I remembered it while
you were talking . . . not sure that it was abuse that made me feel
lifeless . . . it was loneliness . . . (deep tears, breathing deeply) . . .
the sense of expectation, entitlement, I see in people . . . I've never
had that.

Jonathan: Why?

Paula: I'm so aware of that body state of aloneness . . . it would
never occur to me that my sharing what had happened to me . . .
would be possible . . . that you would not be infected by me,
would stay connected to me. . . . It's like a mind blower! (seems
sad, then wipes tears and laughs) . . . and I'm glad that you (looking at Jonathan) want more cause I got more and want more!
(laughs)

Therapist: You said, "give me more." (smiles)

Jonathan: Oh, well! (laughs)

Therapist: (in a reflective tone) I have a final question. You've said
some intriguing things . . . you just said that Jonathan's not infected . . . that was your realization . . . that implies something . . .
why is he not being infected? Love . . . he takes it as a gift. Why is
he not infected?

Paula: (laughs) You ask some very hard questions.

Therapist: And another question . . . what does that say about
your immune system? (The therapist's choice of "immune system" had the unfortunate result of moving Paula's focus back to

herself rather than on her effects—or lack of effects—on her husband.)

Paula: (long latency) It is pretty infected . . . that's what it says to me.

Therapist: But you still have an immune system. I can see why it says that to you. To me it says that it is not contagious! Jonathan's immune system . . . is fine, getting stronger. To me it means that the conclusions you draw about the deadly disease you have—that you have to be quarantined . . . may be invalid.

Jonathan: I think that's why I'm not infected, it is not infectious. It does not come out, not hurt me.

Therapist: Which suggests—you are part of the human race—it is based on a lie.

Paula: What's a lie? (almost a startle response) Say that again!

Therapist: That you have a deadly disease.

Paula: (Stares, seems stunned, has trouble breathing, becomes tearful, then stares quietly and begins to withdraw into herself.)

Therapist: Are you OK? Do you need Jonathan's arm around you? Are you doing this by yourself?

Paula: I am! Totally by myself! (Responds quickly and loudly, and begins to cry. Jonathan slides next to her and places his arm around her. Paula covers her face with her hands.)

Jonathan: What are you doing by yourself? (quietly)

Paula: (long pause) Freezing . . . reminding myself to breathe . . . taking it in . . . feeling joy as well (takes her hands off her face and takes her husband's hand in hers and looks at him)

Jonathan: That invalid assumption . . . what he said, it was based on a lie . . .

Paula: That all of this disease that I'm carrying is all based on a lie . . . (laugh) I like "lie" better (than invalid assumption)!

Therapist: And I like your feeling everything now . . . the terror and confusion . . . and you also said you're feeling joy . . . and joy!

Paula: Sighs.

Therapist: A good one . . . discovering the lie.

Paula: All I can feel myself doing now is skipping . . . like a little kid . . . just skipping! . . . This feels really big! That it is based on a lie! I'm going to be absorbing this awhile.

Jonathan: We can skip around the trees outside when we leave.
Therapist: (following a period of silence) Much to feel and think about.

Following a small amount of reflection on the session the therapist ends it. There were three additional sessions during which Paula and Jonathan consolidated the powerful work that they did during the initial two sessions. Paula had already seen an improvement in her overall relationship with Ron whose negative affect had much less power to activate her own childhood memories. She no longer responded intensely, but rather could see Ron's state as reflective of him, not her, nor their relationship. As a result, joint sessions with the entire family were never begun.

CLINICAL COMMENTS

In this treatment, Paula was able to revisit the aspect of her history that had not been fully resolved in her prior therapy and which had become activated again due to factors in the developmental journey of her son, Ron. If the treatment had begun by focusing directly on the conflicts between Paula and her son, the underlying factors that caused the dysregulating features of their conflicts would not have been addressed. Specific strategies might have helped to reduce their intensity, in the short-term at least, but their risk for returning would most likely remain. Within a few weeks after the above two sessions, Paula's relationship with her son, and her ability to foster the coregulation of their anger, was significantly improved. By beginning treatment with the parents alone, often the need for the joint family sessions is greatly reduced.

It seemed to be apparent in the first session—when Paula did not look at her husband out of fear that she would experience his "disgust and rejection"—that while she may have resolved significant aspects of the early trauma, she had not addressed the underlying shame that resulted from the trauma. This was confirmed further in the second session when Paula spoke of having "contaminated" her husband, similar to how she felt that she had "contaminated" the members of her family during childhood. Paula was able to discover "another reality" with its own language following Jonathan's statement that her sharing her trauma was actually experienced as being a gift to him. This intense sequence demonstrates the need to treat both the terror and the shame that jointly define the experience of a trauma. Shame is especially damaging to successful trauma resolution because it jeopardizes the client's ability to become intersubjectively engaged with her partner or therapist. The client's shame-based instinct is to hide. Without intersubjectivity, it is hard to coregulate the affect associated with the trauma, and cocreate new meanings of the traumatic event.

Paula moved to an even deeper reality when she then discovered that her "horrible disease" was based on a lie. Paula was able to cocreate an integrated sense of being a self with value through her relationship with her husband. Her journey led her through experiencing her husband's intersubjective presence in response to all aspects of her, to experiencing herself as being both not contagious, and also not having a deadly disease. She could not create this new meaning alone. Jonathan and the therapist, together, cocreated with her a new reality of self and other. Paula demonstrated again that her first tendency was to rely on herself at that crucial time when she had difficulty breathing, gasped, cried, and stared into the distance. With the therapist's comment, she was able to allow herself to rely on her husband so that she could stay present while experiencing the "lie" rather than withdrawing into a dissociative state.

For these two sessions to be transforming—as they appeared to have been for Paula—the therapist and Jonathan needed to coregulate the intense negative affective states that were associated with the exploration of her story. Paula was able to remain present—affectively and reflectively—to self, Johnathan, and the therapist during long periods of tearful sadness, fears of rejection and abandonment, and numbing shame and aloneness. She was able to do so because the therapist and Jonathan were also experiencing those affective states with her, coregulating them with her. They all took breaks at times, especially through laughter, but returned to the core of her story with openness and vulnerability. At times the therapist and Jonathan may have had difficulty staying present in the affective states as well. However, they were able to return to the states, or lead her back to them when necessary, within an atmosphere of acceptance, curiosity, and empathy (and occasionally playfulness). From there, it was not long before Paula became aware of a new affect, joy, bursting forth. Which also was coregulated by Jonathan who suggested that they skip around the yard after the session.

Appendix 2: Case Study 2

ROBERT'S ANGER

It's the people we love the most who can make us feel the gladdest . . . and the maddest! Love and anger are such a puzzle! . . . It's a different kind of anger from the kind we may feel toward strangers because it is so deeply intertwined with caring and attachment. —Fred Rogers, The World According to Mr. Rogers

Judy, a 37-year-old teacher and her husband, Dave, age 39, the owner of a small business, sought treatment for their 14-year-old son, Robert. They were seen together in the first session, without Robert or their other child, 10-year-old Melissa. Judy, who spoke more than did her husband, was the one who had taken the initiative to seek treatment. She indicated that Robert frequently argued with her and her husband. At times he would scream that they were not fair and refuse to talk with them. He often teased his sister, sending her running in tears to Judy. When Judy then corrected him, another outburst was certain to follow. She also expressed concern that Robert was not achieving at school, doing a poor job with his homework, and being described as "unmotivated." Judy often tried to speak with Robert about these problems but that would only lead to another argument.

Dave agreed with his wife about their difficulties with Robert, though he thought some of it simply reflected that "he's a growing boy." He also tried to talk with Robert about his need to control his "tongue" and just do what he is told. He did not know what to say to him beyond that point. He went on to say that the hardest thing for him was his feeling that he was letting Judy down by not being able to help her with their son's anger. Both Judy and Dave described Melissa as being an easy-going, seemingly happy child, apart from her bouts of tears following Robert's teasing her.

During the first session the therapist, Anne, asked Judy and Dave to describe their lives within their families of origin. Judy stated that she was the third of four children, having an older brother and two sisters. She described her parents as being hard-working, "good people" who did their best to provide their children with "a good upbringing." Her father worked long hours and her mother, who held a part-time job outside the home, was the primary caregiver. She described herself as having been "the good girl." Her older brother and sister were both rebellious and at times defied their parents. Her younger sister was "the baby." Judy reflected that she often saw herself as her mother's "helper." She tried to make her life easier when her mother was upset over the behavior of her older siblings and she also tried to help her with the care of her little sister. She did not want to be "a problem." This aspect of her relationship with her mother carried over into the present. Judy still was more helpful to her parents than were her siblings. However, she was not aware of resenting her role. She also said that she always felt that she had a close relationship with her father. She might even have been his "favorite." She was attracted to Dave because he seemed to be a gentle and honest person who seemed to be committed to being an active husband and father.

Dave's life as a child was quite different from Judy's. His parents divorced when he was young and he never had a very close relationship with his father. His mother worked hard to support them and Dave relied on himself a great deal, both in practical and emotional matters. He did not feel particularly close to his mother, but he appreciated all that she had done for him. He did not have any significant behavioral problems as a child. He did have a group of friends, played sports, and held part-time jobs throughout high school. He was attracted to Judy because of her "warmth" and because he knew that she would be a good mother.

The therapist suggested that she meet with Judy and Dave for a few more sessions in order to develop a deeper understanding about the underlying patterns that might contribute to Robert's behavior problems as well as to give them some initial suggestions about directions that she would most likely be suggesting for the treatment.

In the next session, Anne (the therapist) focused initially on the changes in the parents' relationships with Robert over the past 14 years. Within minutes Judy became tearful as she recalled how happy she was being pregnant as well as being his mother during the first few years of his life. She could not recall ever having felt "so close to a living person" as she was to Robert when he was a baby. When she became pregnant with Melissa she felt some ambivalence, out of concern that a second child might take something from the intense bond that she felt with her son. When Robert began school she felt both relief and sadness that he would become more independent. However, over the years she began to worry because he seemed to be changing in ways that were hard for her to understand. He seemed to be unhappy, irritable, and more distant from her. He had not seemed jealous of his little sister during the first few years after her birth, but now he seemed to genuinely dislike her. As she spoke she became more discouraged. She became aware of how long she had had her current concerns about Robert and how she had failed countless times during the past few years to help him and to improve their relationship. The therapist expressed empathy for her continuous efforts that felt like failure. Experiencing empathy, Judy was able to experience her shame and accept comfort. This led her to asking why Robert did not respond to her:

Judy: Can't he see how much I love him?
Therapist: It must be so hard—you love him so much—and it seems like it's not getting through, you're not able to make him feel it . . . or even harder . . . like he's turning away from your love.
Judy: Yeah! Why doesn't he let me help him!
Therapist: (quietly) I wonder, Judy, if at times Robert reminds you of your older brother . . . when he would give your mom a hard time . . . when he seemed to be turning away from her . . . not letting her help him.
Judy: (immediate puzzled look, followed quickly by recognition) He does! It's just the same! Mom tried so hard with Jack but she never got anywhere! He never listened!

Therapist: Oh my! No wonder it's hard for you! You're worried that all the problems that your mom had with Jack are going to happen again with you and Robert! No wonder you get discouraged . . . and frightened . . . and maybe angry at Robert . . . why can't he just see you love him and want to help!

Judy: It's like he doesn't care!

Therapist: How hard that would make it too . . . if he didn't care! (silence follows, with Judy clearly in distress and Dave showing concern for his wife but not speaking) I was wondering, too, Judy (quietly) if sometimes Jack gave you a hard time. If Jack would tease you and when your mom corrected him he didn't listen and kept doing it.

Judy: He seemed to tease me for years. I still have a hard time being close to him because of those memories. But he didn't get into that much trouble about that . . . I often didn't tell.

Therapist: You didn't tell?

Judy: No, I didn't want mom to get upset . . . She'd just yell at him and he'd yell back, it would just seem to get worse . . . I didn't want her to be upset.

Therapist: You must have felt trapped. He was being mean to you, but if you asked your mom for help, it would be like . . . you were being mean to her . . . because he would give her a hard time . . . Like you had to take care of her by not asking her to take care of you. So you were all alone with it . . . all alone.

Judy: And I hated him! (cries and Dave puts his hand on her arm) I know I shouldn't but I did . . . and still do when I think about it.

Therapist: (very quietly with gentle voice tone) And I wonder, too . . . if once in a while you find yourself with the same feeling toward Robert when he's upsetting you.

Judy: (silence and then a whisper) I do. (more tears)

Therapist: (following extended silence as Dave comforts his wife) That took such courage to say . . . to let yourself be aware of . . . You try so hard to be a good mom, and you often don't feel like you are . . . it's so hard not to feel anger toward your son . . . especially when he reminds you in some ways . . . probably the most when he is teasing Melissa . . . of Jack teasing you . . . and your not feeling that you could get help from your mom . . . and you were left all alone with-it . . . and it went on for so long . . . so long . . . (very quietly) and in some ways it's like it still is going on.

Judy: (more crying, with deepening sadness and anxiety in her face.) What can I do?

Therapist: (pause of 10 seconds then she responds quietly) You are doing it, Judy. You are letting us know—Dave and me—you are letting us help you with these very painful thoughts and feelings. Something that was hard for you to do when you were a kid because of your concern for your mom . . . you are letting Dave take care of you now.

Judy: (She looks at Dave and tears come to his eyes as he pulls her arm to him and holds her hand.) Don't.

Therapist: Don't?

Judy: I guess it's OK for him to cry. But I wish he wouldn't.

Therapist: Because?

Judy: I don't know. (silence, puzzled and staring at him) I'm not used to someone crying for me. I feel like a burden.

Jonathan: You're not a burden to me, Judy. You're my wife (stare at each other, both crying). I want to help you.

Judy: Thank you. (smiles and reaches toward him and they embrace)

The therapist then reflected on Judy's insights and experiences regarding Jack, Robert, and Dave. She then turned to Dave and explored how his attachment history might be influencing the current situation. He fairly quickly offered that he was similar to Judy in some ways. He said that he too did not want to be a burden to anyone. He thought that he might have taken that stance with his mother because of her difficulties as a single parent and provider. He tended to avoid stressful situations. As a result he was not sure how to respond when Judy or one of his kids was in distress. He did not have confidence that he could meet their emotional needs at those times. He thought that he became angry with Robert too, though maybe for different reasons from Judy. Robert's behavior made him feel inadequate as a husband and father. He did not know what to do to make the situation better. When the therapist commented that he never had a father to help him with his distress and to show him how to be a husband and father, he became tearful. Judy then comforted him in a manner similar to how he had supported her. Toward the end of the session the therapist commented:

> You two are something! You are both so honest . . . so committed to doing it right! To be the best parents you can be . . .

> To learn how to better help each other! You're willing to face some really painful things to help your son who seems to be struggling with his life too. You're not coming in here just blaming him and asking me to fix him. You're coming here . . . wanting to learn what you can do to make it work . . . your family . . . and I'm so glad to have a chance to help you with this . . . to work with you.

As she spoke the therapist had tears in her eyes and a respectful tone in her voice. She was experiencing with them their shame, fear, anger, and discouragement. She also was experiencing their courage, honesty, commitment to each other and their children, and their readiness to find hope and strength to do what was necessary. By her experiencing those features in their experience she was helping them to discover those aspects of themselves and join her with openness and trust in the treatment process.

In the next two sessions the therapist focused more on Dave's history and its influence on his current functioning as a husband and father. It was harder for Dave than it was for Judy to explore his background without eliciting a strong sense of shame. With the active presence of Judy, he was able to give expression to his sense of abandonment following his parents' divorce and his father's lack of interest in remaining in his life. He also was able to express the loneliness that he felt when his mother did not appear to be responsive to his distress and unhappiness. He was able to acknowledge how he thought that he needed to manage his distress on his own or he would be "selfish," given his mother's many responsibilities. In the second of these two sessions, Dave was able to give expression to his disappointment that his mother was not more affectively present, while not "blaming" her. Again, with the empathic presence of Judy, he was also able to say that he thought that Judy and their two kids had a close relationship and he often felt like an outsider. He acknowledged that he tended to "drift away" from interactions and he thought that Judy might be making it too easy for him to do so—not expecting enough. When Judy replied that she feared at times that she might be "expecting too much" they both laughed and decided that they needed to become more able to talk about this theme so that they would both understand each other's motives.

In the next session, the therapist spoke with Judy and Dave about what they could expect in the treatment sessions to come. She spoke about "the attitude" of playfulness, acceptance, curiosity, and empathy. She described a/r dialogue, contrasting it with lectures, "reasoning," and giving advice. She spoke about the need to discover the meaning under the behaviors, to encourage the communication of the meaning, and to cocreate new meanings. She gave examples of how the dialogue might go in the sessions ahead and reassured them that she knew that she will be asking them to be, relate, and talk in ways that were not part of their upbringing. She expressed confidence that if they trusted her that she really did see their strengths and commitment, they would be able to develop the skills that would facilitate their relationships with their kids, and especially with Dave. She said that she would coach them whenever they got stuck and she encouraged them to tell her whenever she had some suggestions that did not make any sense to them.

In the sixth session, the therapist met with all four members of the family. She directed Judy and Robert to sit on the couch. Dave sat in a chair next to Robert, and Trista sat in a chair near Judy. The therapist chose this sitting arrangement purposefully. She often has the child who is identified as the client on the couch next to the primary caregiver, with the other parent on the other side of the identified client. If Trista had not been present, she would have had both parents on the couch, with Robert between them.

The therapist spoke easily with Robert and Trista about their daily lives. She discovered that Robert really enjoyed playing soccer, had a friend named Jeremy with whom he spent a lot of time, and knew more about computers than did his parents. Trista volunteered that she was learning to stand on her head in gymnastics class and she refused when asked to demonstrate. She laughed easily and often looked to her mother for encouragement. The therapist then explained who she was and why the family was present. She indicated that she met with many families who struggled at times with how they talked about things, solved problems, had fun together, and divided up the chores. She asked Robert and Trista if they wanted to give their thoughts about any of those topics or if they would like to bring up something else that they thought was important in their family. Trista quickly said that she would like more dessert, especially after lunch.

The therapist then said that she had met with Judy and Dave for a few sessions to understand their worries. She mentioned that they said that sometimes members of the family become angry with one another and they're not sure how to be the most helpful. Immediately Trista said, "That's Robert, he can really get mad!" Robert looked at his sister with annoyance but said nothing. The therapist directed her attention toward Robert:

Therapist: You seemed kind of annoyed with your sister for saying that, Robert. (when he did not say anything, she added) It's OK for her to say that Robert, she's just telling us what she thinks. That doesn't mean that you're doing something wrong.

Robert: (under his breath) Yeah, sure.

Therapist: (in a supportive tone) I mean that Robert, it's OK for her to say what she thinks.

Robert: (louder) Whatever!

Therapist: Now you seem kind of annoyed with me, Robert. Maybe you think I'm taking her side already. (When Robert does not respond, the therapist does not think that she is going to get an a/r dialogue started with him by continuing along that line of discussion. Still she does not want to avoid the "break," as if it is too difficult for them to repair.) But I don't know you very well, so maybe I'm wrong. (turning to Judy) What do you think?

Judy: I think Robert is mad at Trista for saying that he gets mad a lot. And she's not lying about it. She's not just trying to get him into trouble. (Robert now looks away, looking more annoyed, now at his mother.)

Therapist: So you think that Trista was trying to be helpful when she said that . . . and not trying to have us scold Robert?

The discussion did not lead anywhere and the therapist decided to direct the conversation to another topic, after first saying that it did not seem that she was being very helpful with the first thing that was brought up, so maybe they should try something else. Dave then spoke about Saturday morning chores and how he wished there was a way for everyone to do their chores without a lot of arguing. While he was speaking about "everyone" it seemed evident to the therapist that he was mostly speaking about Robert. His refusal to discuss chores confirmed her impression. The rest of the session went much the same and the therapist was thinking that she had not done a good job of helping Robert to feel safe enough to explore his difficulties within the family.

As the therapist was "winding down" at the end of the session, she tried to reflect on what she might have done differently. She recalled her first comment to Robert: "You seemed to be kind of annoyed with your sister for saying that, Robert." That was accurate but was it too soon to notice his irritation with his sister; too soon to expect him to be able to address his anger toward her, which certainly went further than that one comment? Maybe. And then she recalled saying, "It's OK for her to say that, Robert . . ." Of course! Why did she say that? Robert clearly was saying nonverbally that it was *not* OK for Trista to have said that. In Robert's judgment, Trista saying that would only lead to trouble for him. He did *not* think that it was OK. And the first thing that the therapist did in developing her relationship with him was to try to talk him out of his judgment—even worse, to tell him that his judgment was wrong. The therapist was standing with Trista regarding her expression of her experience and standing against Robert regarding his nonverbal expression of his experience. Anne realized that she wanted to address that immediately and not end the session without trying to begin the process of repair in her relationship with Robert.

Therapist: Robert, I'm sorry that our first meeting was hard for you. And I'm sorry about what I said to you before. I told you that it was OK what your sister said when I saw that you were feeling that it was not OK to you. I'd just met you and I started an argument! Just what you need! I didn't try at all to get to know what you were feeling about what your sister said. I didn't even get to know you! I just said that you were wrong in feeling that way! I am so sorry, Robert. (turning to Judy) I'm sorry Judy and Dave that I was not more helpful for you all today. I made a mistake and I'll really try to not do it again. Please understand Robert if he says that he did not like our meeting. I can understand why he might say that. I messed up.

The meeting ended shortly after that. The therapist did not make any effort to have Robert respond to her. It most likely would only come across as her expecting him to forgive her.

After the family left the therapist tried to understand why she had not responded in a manner that she thought might have been more therapeutic. She might have said a number of things in response to Trista's statement and Robert's nonverbal response.

She might have said:

Wow, Robert, looks like you might want to say, "Thanks, sis, that's just what I need! Why not tell her that I'm Freddie Kruger!"

Or: Robert, I think you might want to say, "And my problem is my little sister who talks too much!"

> Or: Robert, I think you might be thinking now, "Sisters! See what a big brother has to put up with!"

Then she could easily have moved into a quieter, more empathic response to Robert's nonverbal response to Melissa:

> It seemed hard for you when your sister said that. Could you help me to understand what made it hard?

> Or: I think you might wish that your sister had not said that. How come, do you think?

Anne felt confident that Robert would have responded to her empathy, first given by matching the intensity of his nonverbal vitality affect and then by finding words to more quietly invite him to express his distress over her comments with his own words. He might well have responded if she had shown acceptance and empathy for his response, followed by curiosity about what motivated it.

The question remained for her: Why did she try to tell him that his experience was invalid? Robert quickly was demonstrating his "symptom," he became annoyed at criticism directed his way; he was angry because he was the first one in the family identified with a "problem." And it was his little sister who did it. He most likely was aware that the family sessions were motivated by his behavior. He was not "buying" the therapist's generalities. He was defensive when he entered. He most likely was feeling shame as "the bad one" and he protected himself at the first sign of criticism.

As the therapist reflected she became aware that she had felt mild anxiety when she saw Robert's annoyance. She had become uncomfortable with it and had wanted it to go away. She felt frustrated with herself because she had noticed a similar response to anger in other therapy sessions over the years. She knew where it had come from. She had been a peacemaker in her family. She was the one who tried to get her siblings to get along, who tried to distract her parents when they became angry with each other. She thought that she had resolved that issue and there it was again. Maybe it was activated in response to Judy. Judy's childhood and her manner of adjusting to the family problems were similar to her own. The therapist became aware that her response was both to her own anxiety and also to Judy's anxiety. Judy did not feel safe when her son became angry. Now that she knew what happened, the therapist felt relief. She was confident that if the circumstances recurred she would be able to utilize a different response. She would be able to regulate the affect of the family and her own and help to bring out the meaning under Robert's anger. Then maybe she would be able to help him to communicate it and cocreate new meanings with him and his family.

In the following session, Robert related in a manner similar to the onset of the previous meeting. He was reserved and not pleased to be there, but he did not appear to be angry. He might have been suggesting that if the therapist, his parents, and sister did not bring up his anger, he would be agreeable. After the first 10 minutes of small talk, the therapist chose to address the prior session. She restated her sorrow for not getting to know Robert better and for suggesting that his annoyance with his sister had been uncalled for. Robert responded as if he had not given it any thought and he said that he was not angry about it anymore. His nonverbal voice tone and facial expressions suggested that though he might not be angry, he did not want it to happen again.

Therapist: Oh, good, Robert. I'm glad that you're OK about it now. (gently) Would you help me to understand today what it was last time that bothered you about what she said? I'd really like to know.
Robert: It seems like she just wants to get me in trouble. She's always going to mom and dad about me. She's always telling them that I'm doing something to her.
Trista: You do!
Robert: Shut up!
Anne: (Slowly putting up her hand to Trista while continuing to talk to Robert in a quiet voice.) So it seems that you get into trouble a lot about your sister. (some sense of sadness, but not disapproval, in the therapist's voice)
Robert: They always take her side! (with anger and frustration)
Therapist: After most of these hard times with your sister, it seems to you like they are angry with you and not with her. (both reflective and affective)
Robert: All the time! They *never* yell at her!" (Robert is trying to convince the therapist that this problem is extreme and unfair.)
Therapist: So it seems to you that they *always* become angry with you! And *never* with your sister. That *must* seem so unfair to you!
Robert: It is! They *do* always yell at me! (both anger and discouragement)

Therapist: Robert, tell me please—if your parents always yell at you, and never at your sister—what does that mean? What would make them do that? (some quiet anguish is evident in the therapist's voice)

Robert: I don't know! Ask them! (a bit less anger, along with some uncertainty)

Therapist: But what do you think, Robert. What do you think? (more quietly still)

Robert: They think that she's good, and . . . (quiet too, with some distress in his voice)

Therapist: Oh, Robert, it seems to you that your parents think that Trista is good, and . . . you are bad. Oh, Robert if that what you think that must be very hard . . . very hard . . . very hard for you. (The therapist is now speaking slowly, quietly, and with sadness over the meaning that Robert has given his perceptions of his parents' behavior involving his conflicts with his sister.) Robert, that must be so upsetting to you if you think that your parents think that it is your fault. That you are bad and your sister is good. (Robert does now appear to be "upset," and it is important to note that for him. His affect about this experience is deeper and more complex than his initial expression of anger.) I wonder Robert, have you told your parents that . . . told them that sometimes you think that they think that you are bad and your sister is good? Have you told them, Robert. (Gentle, quiet, question, with emphasis on the therapist's deep interest in his response.)

Robert: No. (very quietly, looking down with apparent sadness and probable shame)

Therapist: Would you tell them now, Robert . . . would you tell them now. (very quietly)

Robert: You *do* think that it's always my fault. (more loudly, with a fleeting glance at his mother, a mixture of anger and unhappiness in his voice)

Judy: Robert, thank you for telling me that (clear empathy and sadness in her voice). I didn't know that you thought that I always think it's your fault. Oh, Robert, that must be hard for you if you think that I think that. (This is close to what the therapist had asked the parents to say if their son shared something about his experience of their discipline of him. Empathy is the focus, not explanation or justification. Mom speaks quietly, matching the tone that existed prior to Robert's statement to her.)

Robert: You do mom! (More anguish than anger. Some tears appearing.)

Judy: I'm sorry Robert if I made you think that! I really am! (Empathy for her son's distress evident in her voice. There is almost a minute of silence, which gives focus to the sadness and empathy shown between mother and son, with dad's quiet support in the background.)

Therapist: I'm glad you told your mom that, Robert, I could see that it was hard . . . it took courage to say that. . . . Good job understanding your son, Judy . . . I think he needs that . . . Would he let you squeeze his arm for a second? (Voice demonstrates compassion for both with tentative question at the end.)

Judy: (quietly, moving closer to her son) I think so. (Both are tearful. Both have a few tears and Judy's hand rests on her son's arm. After a minute of silence, the therapist faces dad and reflects quietly over the present moment. She wants to reduce the focus on Robert and make it easier for him to regulate the affect that he is experiencing.)

Therapist: I think that Robert just showed you and his mom why it is so hard for him when one of you becomes angry with him when you think he is teasing his sister. He loses confidence in what you think of him.

Jonathan: I hadn't realized that. I'm glad that he told us. (Dad seems to be touched by the interchange between Robert and Judy.) (looking at Robert) Son, like your mom, I didn't know that you think that we favor Melissa over you—that she is more special to us. I'm sorry that you got that message from me and your mom. (Dave seems to struggle with a new awareness) Son, when I think about it maybe you and I are a bit alike. Sometimes I think that your mom is more important to you than I am. That I'm letting you down as a father.

Robert: You're not dad.

Dave: Well I now feel like it son. I have to get my act together and let you and your sister know better how important you both are to me. And maybe show it more (shows a few tears that leave the rest of the family speechless).

Therapist: That took courage, Dave. You and your son are really working hard at this.

Dave: And I'm going to keep at it till I get it right. Being a dad is something that I didn't learn much about as a kid.

Therapist: Trista, I can see that you feel sad too. (Trista has tears in her eyes as she stares at her mother and brother embracing.) Could you tell us why?

Trista: Bobby's not bad! (She begins to cry. Mom puts her arm out toward her daughter and Trista jumps from her chair, runs to her mother on the couch and is embraced by her while Judy continues to touch Robert.)

Trista: (As she cries and hugs her mother tightly, she looks at her brother who is still close to their mother.) I'm sorry, Bobby.

Robert: It's OK, Trista. You didn't do anything (compassion for his sister's distress).

Dave then leaves the chair for that spot on the couch next to his son. He leans over and places his arms around all three members of his family.

The family came for six additional sessions with a significant improvement in Robert's functioning. His reduction in angry outbursts reflected his having been heard as to what his anger represented. It also reflected the fact that his parents were less anxious in response to it. His anger was less able to activate their attachment histories. Finally, it reflected the therapist's readiness to reflect on her own affective/reflective responses in order to remain intersubjectively present for the family and to repair the relationship when necessary.

CLINICAL COMMENTS

This is a composite case of a fairly brief family treatment. It represents many similar cases of both my own and other therapists who have used this model of treatment. The sequences described are common. When the treatment is able to be brief, the therapist is likely to have been able to successfully help the parents to understand and begin to address how their own histories are having an impact on their relationships with each other and with their children.

The therapist is not judging the parents, but rather is conveying PACE. Because the therapist is not "blaming" the parents, they often do not feel "blamed." If they do express an experience of being blamed by the therapist, she is then able to express the same attitude of PACE, welcoming this new and troubling experience into the intersubjective context.

In this composite case, I also chose to include a pivotal sequence in which the therapist failed to respond with PACE to the identified client's first expression of his experience of the session. The need to identify and repair such relationship breaks is crucial if therapy is to be successful. Such breaks are not all that uncommon, given the nature of the influence of one's attachment history—including the therapist's—on current significant relationships. The therapist's reflection on her own anxiety at the early sign of Robert's anger enabled her to remain present with him in his angry state so that he could access its meaning and communicate it to his parents. Her initial difficulty may have served as a model for the whole family: when you make a mistake, repair the relationship. She felt some guilt over her failing and so was able to address it and repair her relationship with Robert. If she had felt shame instead, she would have been likely to find some reason to blame Robert or one of the other family members for the sequence. That would most certainly have led to an unproductive course of treatment.

When the therapist has had success in coregulating the parents' shame, fear, anger, and discouragement, and cocreating the meaning of the current family problems—often by understanding connections with their own attachment histories—a similar process is repeated with the children and parents together. In this way the parents are likely to be able to give expression to the same qualities of PACE that they have experienced, as well as supporting the therapist's intent to provide that experience for their children. When the therapist and parents are together able to provide safety and communicate an open intersubjective stance characterized by PACE, very frequently the children respond quickly. When their anger, oppositional, or dismissive behaviors are not reacted to in kind, but rather are responded to with the focus on the child's experience under the behavior, frequently the child's symptoms find nothing to maintain them.

Often an attachment-focused family treatment requires more sessions than the 12 described here. However, for some families, even such few sessions can be transforming when they enable all to go under their symptoms and discover their motives and strengths that were unseen and unexpressed.

Appendix 3: Case Study 3

SAFE ENOUGH TO BE A MOTHER

When attachment figures cannot support the individual so that he feels safe in feeling his feelings, affective experiences can threaten to overwhelm the integrity of self and relationships; when faced alone, they can be unbearable. —Diana Fosha, The Transforming Power of Affect (2000)

The following case involves, Laurie, a 27-year-old mother of a 9-year-old boy, Tim, and Laurie's husband, Eddie. Tim manifested a variety of oppositional-defiant features that often left her feeling overwhelmed. She would scream at him, he sometimes screamed back, and then she would withdraw for fear that she might abuse him. She worried that as he entered adolescence his anger might become much more intense than it was now. Her relationship with him was beginning to remind her of her life with her family when she was a child. She had been physically abused at times by her own parents. She also was now afraid that her intense problems with her son would cause problems in her marriage with Eddie, the boy's stepfather. She also reported that the boy's father had physically abused her. She felt both rage and fear toward her son, who at times reminded her of his father.

The therapist, Anita, met with Laurie and Eddie together for the first eight sessions. During those sessions Laurie expressed terror that she would hurt her son the way that her parents had hurt her. She had grown up in a very dysfunctional family, the third of six children, characterized by substance abuse and domestic violence. She saw her mother as generally having been passive and avoidant of the volatile outbursts of her father that occurred often when he was drinking. She had four brothers who were verbally and emotionally abusive to each other and especially to her and her younger sister. When she became pregnant with Tim, she married an older man who quickly began reminding her of her father. She fled from him with her infant son, with no support from her family. She became involved with a group for battered women who, in Laurie's words, "saved my life." They helped her to get an apartment, her high school degree, and she eventually got a part-time job when her son entered a Head Start program.

Laurie met and married Eddie when Tim was 6 years of age. Eddie was calm and quiet, the opposite of her father and ex-husband. His parents were much more stable than were Laurie's, without major conflicts or substance abuse. He described himself as being similar to his father. Neither talked much about what they thought or felt. Both worked hard. His father was not active in his upbringing, but Eddie expressed a desire to be an active father for Tim. He tended to be patient with him, but often did not initiate much, seemingly out of uncertainty about what to do and not being confident that Tim would want to do things with him.

Laurie spoke of times when she screamed at her son, threatened, and spanked him. She had felt impulses to slap him and swear at him but had never done so. When he did something wrong she had great difficulty being patient with him. She would respond in anger and often regret the intensity of her reaction. At times she would feel very hurt if he was not affectionate with her, did not want to play with her when she set aside some time for him, or if he did not talk with her about something that was bothering him.

Given Laurie's history and the intensity of her emotional and behavioral dysregulation, the family therapist suggested that she see another therapist for herself, while the family therapist continued to work with her, Eddie, and Tim. Laurie agreed to do this and within a few weeks began individual treatment. At the same time the family therapist met with Laurie and Eddie, to explore practical ways that Eddie might be able to assist Laurie. Initially family treatment was successful in having Eddie reassure Laurie that their marriage was stable from his viewpoint and that he was very willing to help her more in raising Tim. He expressed a commitment to both assume some discipline responsibilities as well as become engaged with Tim in some out-of-home activities without Laurie. This assistance and reassurance from Eddie immediately helped Laurie to feel more hopeful and patient with her son's behavior. The therapist also focused with her and Eddie on establishing a more consistent daily routine, predictable rules and consequences for Tim, and beginning efforts to communicate empathy during discipline. This proved to be harder for both Laurie and Eddie than they had thought it would be. The therapist then suggested that Tim begin attending the sessions. She indicated to Laurie that she would try to model for her ways of speaking with her son that might be different from what she generally did. She also asked Laurie permission to interrupt her if Anita (the therapist) thought that Laurie was saying something that might hurt her relationship with her son. The therapist would suggest another way of addressing an issue. Laurie agreed.

During the first session with Tim present, he was fairly quiet and anxious. He responded briefly to questions and did speak somewhat about his sports interests. At one point Laurie became impatient with him and asked him to tell the therapist what he thought. Anita gently told Laurie that it was understandable that Tim would be more quiet than usual because this was his first session and he probably was not used to sitting and talking with three adults under any circumstance. Later in the session when the therapist began speaking generally of some of the family's conflicts, Tim withdrew further as if he anticipated that he would be scolded. The therapist then led a dialogue into that theme:

Therapist: Yeah, Tim, that's what I do. Sit and talk with families about what their life at home is like and try to be helpful. Try to find ways that might help things to work out better. Are you OK with that? If I can find some ways?

Tim: (Nods yes)

Therapist: Great! That's great, Tim. This is such a good start. I asked the same question of your mom and Eddie when I met them before and they said the same thing. All three of you do! Wow! With a family like yours my work should be easy . . . Tell me, Tim, what would you like me to help you folks with?

Tim: I don't know.

Therapist: Oh, OK. Yeah that is a hard question, not having much time to think about it.

How about if I give you some thoughts? Would that be OK?

Tim: OK.

Therapist: Great! OK, now what might be a place to start . . . I wonder . . . Oh, yeah, your mom was saying that she was sad that there
is more anger between you two than you both wanted. She was
hoping that I might help you and her with the anger you both have.
Would you like some help with that too?

Tim: Yeah.

Therapist: Wonderful. You both, and my guess Eddie too, would
like help with the same thing. That's great! Now, I wonder why.
Why would you both want help with that? Maybe . . . let me
guess . . . maybe . . . when you are both angry with each other . . .
maybe then you both don't feel close to each other! Maybe then it
gets kind of lonely. Yeah, maybe that's it. (quietly and slowly)
Tim, when you and your mom are angry with each other . . . do
you feel . . . kind of all alone. Like there's no one to talk with . . .
or laugh with?

Tim: Yeah.

Therapist: I thought so . . . I thought so. You're a 9-year-old boy, and
it's hard then when you're not feeling that close with your mom.
When you and she are just so angry . . . and then! Mom tells me that
sometimes the anger takes so long to go away! *So long!* She says that she
doesn't know how to make it stay short then, and you don't either! Of
course you would feel kind of lonely when it lasts real long! Of course
you would! Tim, would that be something that maybe I might try to
help with first? Maybe, that when you two are angry, maybe I can help
to find ways to make it be shorter, and then you two could be close
again a lot faster! That's it! Closer again a lot faster! What do you think?

Tim: Yeah.

Therapist: You'd like that?

Tim: Yeah.

Therapist: How about you mom, would you like that too?

Laurie: I sure would!

Therapist: You would?

Laurie: Of course I would.

Therapist: Why would you?

Laurie: Because I love Tim.

Therapist: You do?

Laurie: Of course I do!

Therapist: Do you tell him?

Laurie: Every day!

Therapist: Even when you're angry.

Laurie: No not then. It's hard to say that when I'm angry.

Therapist: Why?

Laurie: I don't know. I'm just angry and I guess I don't think of saying it.

Therapist: But do you still love him when you are angry even if you don't say it?

Laurie: Of course I do.

Therapist: Oh! Wow! I'm so glad that you said that. I thought that you did, but maybe at those times . . . when you are both angry . . . maybe Tim has some doubts about if you are still loving him then.

Laurie: He knows that I love him! (somewhat defensively)

Therapist: Laurie, I would agree with you that if I saw Tim alone and asked him if you still loved him when you were angry he would tell me that you did. But, I'm talking not about what he knows in his brain but what he feels . . . and right then he may feel not close with you . . . and maybe in his heart there is a doubt or two . . . especially if you two are angry with each other for a long time . . . not feeling close. That's a hard time for you both. I'll bet even though you know that Tim loves you . . . at those times when you are both angry . . . you might not feel his love and it might be a bit scary for awhile. Is that true?

Laurie: Maybe a bit.

Therapist: Scary?

Laurie: Yeah.

Therapist: That's what I thought. When two people . . . mom and son . . . love each other and they don't feel the love for awhile . . . it is scary for awhile . . . till they feel close again . . . and that's why we have to find ways to make the anger be shorter! Do you both agree?

Laurie: Yes!

Therapist: Tim?

Tim: Yeah.

Therapist: I thought so! How about you Eddie? Do you want to help to find ways to make the anger in the family shorter when it comes out?

Eddie: I do too.

Therapist: Why?

Eddie: Because I don't like anger.

Therapist: OK, I understand that. But we're not going to make it go away. Just shorter.

Eddie: Yeah, shorter.

Therapist: Do you think Laurie and Tim love each other?

Eddie: Yes.

Therapist: Do you love them both?

Eddie: Yes I do.

Therapist: I knew it! You all love each other and you all want the anger to be shorter . . . so that you will not feel alone so much and so you will feel the love more often. I get it! Now, Tim, we adults are doing most of the talking. Is there anything that you disagree with?

Tim: No.

Therapist: You're OK with all this love stuff we're talking about?

Tim: Yeah.

Therapist: Great! So tell me Tim, when your mom is mad at you do you sometimes feel that she doesn't love you right then?

Tim: Yeah.

Therapist: Wow, Tim, that must have been hard to say. That must be such a hard feeling to have. Thanks for being honest about it. Have you told your mom that?

Tim: No.

Therapist: Would you be willing to tell her now? To say, "Mom, sometimes when you are angry at me I worry that you might not love me."

Tim: (Shakes his head "no")

Therapist: I can understand that. That would be very hard to say. Would you mind if I spoke for you? Would you let me speak for you to your mom?

Tim: (Nods head "yes")

Therapist: Thanks, Tim. I'll speak in your voice. If I say something wrong just tell me. If you want me to stop just tell me. OK?

Tim: Yeah.

Therapist: (turning to Laurie who is smiling; adopting a more child-like voice tone) Mom, sometimes when you are mad at me, I feel that you don't love me.

Laurie: Of course I love you Tim!

Therapist: (speaking for herself) Laurie, would you not tell Tim what you feel just yet. Would you be willing to express understanding for what he is feeling, what he just told you.

Laurie: But I do love him when I'm mad. I always love him.

Therapist: Yes, Laurie, I understand, but right now I'd like you to try to just tell him that you now understand why it is so hard, why you two are angry. That he feels that you don't love him right then.

Laurie: But I do! (increasingly frustrated over therapist's request)

Therapist: Yes, and I can now see that you are a bit annoyed with me. Maybe you fear that I don't think that you love him then and that it's OK that he has this feeling.

Laurie: Well, why don't you want me to let him know how I really feel about him?

Therapist: Later, I want you to tell him . . . but now I want you to tell him you now understand his feelings better . . . and you know why the anger bothers him so much.

Laurie: I don't know what you want me to say.

Therapist: Would it be OK if I spoke to Tim for you? That I pretend that I'm you just like I pretended that I was him?

Laurie: OK.

Therapist: OK, why don't I start over. First I'll be Tim and then I'll be you, Laurie, answering him. OK?

Laurie: OK.

Therapist: Tim?

Tim: OK.

Therapist: OK, here we go. (looks at Laurie, speaks with child voice) Mom, sometimes when you are mad at me I don't feel that you love me. (looks at Tim, speaks with another feminine voice) Oh, Tim, I didn't realize that. Thank you so much for telling me. It must be so hard . . . so scary if you think that I might not be loving you right then. So scary. Oh, Tim, I'm so sorry that you have that feeling. So sorry. (Tim now has some tears in his eyes; resonating with him, the therapist feels her own eyes becoming tearful. She glances at Laurie, who is also tearful.)

Laurie: I'm sorry honey. (Tim looks down.)

Therapist: May I speak a little more for you to Tim, Laurie?

Laurie: (Nods "yes")

Therapist: Tim . . . (waits for eye contact) I am so sorry that sometimes when I'm mad at something you do, you begin to feel that I might not love you then. I'm so sorry that you feel that then . . . Tim, I have to work hard . . . *so very hard* . . . to find a way to let you know that I love you even when I'm mad . . . And maybe find a way to make my mad smaller and shorter. I want to do that, Tim . . . for you because I love you so much . . . I want to do it for us.

Laurie: That's true, Tim. What she said is true.

Therapist: Thanks for saying that Laurie. I think it helped him a lot that you just said that.
Laurie: Come here and get a hug! (Tim and Laurie embrace)
Therapist: Well, Eddie, I am so impressed with this family. Tim and Laurie both just worked so hard, feeling hard things, letting me speak for them, being sad together. And I noticed you were sad too. You were working hard to; being with them.
Eddie: Like I said before. I love them both.
Therapist: Great. I'm glad that you told them and are with them now.

In the next few sessions, the therapist would begin each session speaking with Laurie and Eddie alone for about 20 minutes and focus with them on ways to convey empathy and understanding. She spoke of the value of helping Tim to express what he thought and felt—without any judgment—before expressing their own thoughts and feelings or their reasons for a rule or consequence. This proved to be very difficult for Laurie. Her immediate reaction was to judge whether or not Tim's thought or feeling was "right" and try to correct it if it differed from what she wanted him to think or feel. Laurie acknowledged how hard this was and indicated that she was trying to make sense of it in her talks with her individual therapist.

Two months after the onset of Laurie's individual treatment, her therapist attended a family session. Laurie thought that the therapist's presence would assist her in understanding why the conflicts with her son were so difficult for her. Given Laurie's difficulty manifesting empathy for her son, the family therapist had been careful to address Tim's oppositional-defiant behaviors in a very gradual manner. Laurie was now more able at home to control her intense anger toward her son, but it continued to be a struggle for her. Her individual therapist was able to see Laurie relate to Tim in a manner that seemed somewhat similar to how she related with her father and her first husband. She often wanted her individual therapist's approval to validate that she was a good mother. This facilitated progress in her individual treatment. During the family session Laurie was more able to tell her son about her own difficulties. She acknowledged her responsibilities in parenting him that she was working hard on, in both family and individual treatment. She did this without any efforts to blame her son or to give him a lecture that he needed to work hard too. She was able to tell him that she was going to make sure that he had a better life than she had as a child. She would learn to parent him better, no matter how difficult it was. In responding to her vulnerability, Tim was able to acknowledge that at times he thought that it was his fault, that he was "just too bad." Laurie was able to express empathy before crying and reassuring him that he was "not a bad boy." They embraced with mutual tears, reassurance, and commitment. Laurie then looked at her therapist with pride and joy. Her therapist responded by taking her hand, smiling, and acknowledging her work with "well done!"

The family and individual .treatment for Laurie, Eddie, and Tim lasted for another six months before there was sufficient stability in Laurie's functioning to permeate the functioning of the whole family. Eddie's active participation and commitment was central to the success. Periodic sessions without Tim, which focused on their marital relationship, were also instrumental in the success. Laurie's commitment to Tim to do whatever it took to give him a life better than her parents had given her was the foundation of all the progress. The presence of the second therapist was able to assist Laurie in knowing that she—along with her son—deserved care, empathy, and acceptance. She then was more able to focus more clearly on Tim's best interests. Laurie remained in individual treatment for herself another eight months after the last family session.

This excerpt is from the third to the last family treatment session, which was about nine months after the onset of treatment. Changes in the a/r dialogue between the earlier excerpt and this one seem to be quite evident.

Therapist: So this week . . . how were you guys able to work out this week the problem that you were having with choosing what you would do Friday nights?
Tim: It's no problem! She always gets her way!! (laughs)
Laurie: (laughing) Now you tell her the truth, Tim. Tell her what we really decided!
Tim: Well you did. You wanted to watch that dumb movie and Eddie and I didn't get to watch what we wanted. We had to watch what you wanted!
Laurie: (laughing) Now, Timothy! You lie! You know we all agreed to take turns!
Tim: Yeah, and who got to go first!
Eddie: He's right!
Laurie: (laughing) Now you better tell the truth! Why did I go first!
Eddie: Cause you're the boss! (Tim and Eddie laugh)

Laurie: You're both liars! Because we rolled the dice and I got the highest roll!

Therapist: Who picks the movie this Friday?

Tim: I do! I rolled an eight!

Therapist: So your mom was telling the truth! You two are liars! (laughs) OK, now how about a struggle. What was something hard this week? Laurie?

Laurie: Tim wanted to go out and play ball. I said no because he hadn't finished his chore and he yelled and threw the ball against the wall.

Tim: My friends were starting the game and if I didn't go right then I wouldn't be able to play!

Therapist: Ah!

Laurie: Yeah, he was really mad at me.

Therapist: And.

Laurie: I told him that it was OK to be mad but not OK to throw the ball in the house and because of that he couldn't go out when his chore was done.

Tim: I didn't get to play that whole day!

Therapist: That must have been hard!! How did you handle it?

Tim: OK? (looking to Laurie)

Laurie: She asked you. How do you think you handled it?

Tim: OK.

Therapist: What did you do?

Tim: Let me think. I ran to my room and slammed the door. I thought that she was really being mean. Then I came into the kitchen and she *still said* that I had to do my chore.

Therapist: And you did?

Tim: I did my chore.

Therapist: And then?

Tim: I don't know. You tell her.

Laurie: Well what I remember is we had a snack and I got out a deck of cards and we had a game of rummy.

Tim: And I won!

Laurie: No you didn't, I won!

Tim: Liar! (laughing)

Laurie: You watch your mouth, boy. Just because the therapist is here doesn't mean you can get away with that.

Tim: You called me that!

Eddie: You did. And me, too!

Laurie: But you are and I'm not!

Therapist: Wait a second. Let's get back to the story. Tim got really angry that you would not let him play with his friends and he threw the ball in the house . . . and my guess is that you got angry at his ball throwing, Laurie . . . and kept him inside . . . and Tim got more angry and went to his room and slammed the door . . . and then Tim came down, did his chore, and you two had a snack and played cards, and I don't care who won! Is that about right?

Laurie: That's it.

Tim: Yeah.

Therapist: Wow, that's great you guys. Really great! You both handled that so well! The throwing the ball was dealt with and then it was over. Way to go! Why do you think, Laurie, why do you think it worked out so well?

Laurie: I think it's like we've been talking about when we've come here. I can let Tim be angry about something. It's really OK now. I don't think it's the end of the world and I'm failing him or he hates me or I'm a rotten mom. It's just a disagreement and we can handle it. And we did. And most of the time we do.

Therapist: Wow! It sounds like it. Would you agree Tim?

Tim: I guess.

Therapist: I guess, is that all?

Tim: Mom's right. We get mad at each other and it's no big deal anymore like it used to be.

Therapist: Why do you think that is?

Tim: I don't know. Because we love each other better?

Therapist: Wow! What a kid! How old are you? You are really figuring it out. Yes, you both are figuring out that you can argue, disagree, and not like something the other does, and you still love each other! The love never gets lost anymore! So the disagreements, the mad feelings stay small and go away quickly! Wow!

Laurie: You're right, Tim is a bright boy! My bright boy! Cause he has a bright mother!

Tim: Yeah, right! (laughs)

Laurie: You do!

Therapist: And a hard working mother! Who is going to do whatever it takes to be the mom that Tim needs her to be!

Laurie: I'm doing my best!

Therapist: Yes you are! Yes you are (smiles). So is this why you love her Eddie?

Eddie: You bet! And Tim, too!
Therapist: And Tim, too (smiles). Thanks, guys.

CLINICAL COMMENTS

This case demonstrates how a parent who has had a very difficult childhood may need a referral for individual therapy in order to be able to be a source of attachment security for her child in the family sessions. Providing nonjudgmental curiosity and empathy for Tim's experience of her proved to be very difficult for Laurie because she had so infrequently experienced such unconditional presence from her parents. She strived so hard to be a "good" parent for her son, that when he said that he disliked her or something that she did, she was quick to feel shame and then react with anger. She experienced his experience of her as being "unfair" or "wrong" and had almost a compulsion to change it. Tim had no freedom to be angry with her because in her view his anger would prove her failure as a parent. Within individual therapy Laurie was able to begin to experience her worth as a person. Her therapist was able to coregulate the affect and cocreate new meanings regarding her traumatic childhood. With increased acceptance of self, Laurie was able to accept her son's criticism of her.

With Laurie having difficulty maintaining PACE throughout the family sessions, the therapist took a more active role in providing safety for Tim, while modeling and coaching Laurie in relating with him in a more therapeutic way. Having developed a working alliance with Laurie, Anita was able to address with her the comments to Tim that were creating relationship distress and affect dysregulation. Over the course of the sessions Laurie was increasingly able to give expression to the attitude of PACE.

Due to Laurie's own history, emotional communication did not occur regularly between her and her son. As a result, both had great difficulty finding the words for their experiences that lay under their behaviors. When Tim was not able to tell his mother what the therapist asked, the therapist was then willing to speak for him. By doing so, she provided him with modeling for emotional communication while also giving him a place of safety while the words were being spoken. When the therapist speaks for the child (or parent) his vulnerable affect is being coregulated while deeper meanings regarding his behaviors are being cocreated.

REFERENCES

Becker-Weidman, A., & Shell, D. (Eds.) (2005). *Creating capacity for attachment*. Oklahoma City, OK: Barnes 'N' Wood.

Beebe, B., & Lachmann, F.M. (2002). *Infant research and adult treatment: co-constructing interactions*. Hillside, NJ: Analytic Press

Bowlby, J. (1982). *Attachment and loss: Vol.1. Attachment*. New York: Basic Books. (Original publication 1969)

Bowlby, J. (1988). *A secure base*. New York: Basic Books.

Briere, J., & Scott, C. (2006). *Principles of trauma therapy*. New York: Sage.

Buber, M. (1965). *The knowledge of man*. New York: Harper & Row.

Cassidy, J. (1999). The nature of the child's ties. In J. Cassidy & P.R. Shaver, (Eds.), *Handbook of attachment* (pp. 3–20). New York: Guilford.

Cassidy, J., & Mohr, J.J. (2001). Unresolvable fear, trauma, and psychopathology: Theory, research, and clinical considerations related to disorganized attachment across the life span. *Clinical Psychology: Science and Practice, 8*, 275–298.

Cassidy, J., & Shaver, P.R. (Eds.) (1999). *Handbook of attachment*. New York: Guilford Press.

Cook, A., Spinazzola, J., Ford, J., Lanktree, C., Blaustein, M., Cloitre, M. et al. (2005). Complex trauma in children and adolescents. *Psychiatric Annals, 35*, 390–398.

Cozolino, L. (2002). *The neuroscience of psychotherapy*. New York: Norton.

Dozier, M., Stovall, K.C., Albus, K.E., & Bates, B. (2001). Attachment for infants in foster care: The role of caregiver state of mind. In *Child Development, 72*, 1467–1477.

Field, T. (1996). Attachment and separation in young children. *Annual Review of Psychology, 47,* 541–561.

Fonagy, P. (2003). The development of psychopathology from infancy to adulthood: The mysterious unfolding of disturbance in time. *Infant Mental Health Journal, 24,* 212–239.

Fonagy, P., Gergely, G., Jurist, E., & Target, M. (2002). *Affect regulation, mentalization, and the development of the self.* New York: Other Press.

Fosha, D. (2000). *The transforming power of affect.* New York: Basic Books.

Fosha, D. (2003). Dyadic regulation and experiential work with emotion and relatedness in trauma and disorganized attachment. In M.F. Solomon & D.J. Siegel, (Eds.), *Healing trauma: Attachment, mind, body, and brain* (pp. 221–281). New York: W.W. Norton.

Freeman, J., Epston, D., & Lobovits, D. (1997). *Playful approaches to serious problems.* New York: Norton.

Ginsberg, B.G. (1997). *Relationship enhancement family therapy.* New York: Wiley.

Greenberg, L. (2002a). *Emotion-focused therapy: Coaching clients to work through their feelings.* Washington, DC: American Psychological Association.

Greenberg, L. (2002b). Integrating an emotion-focused approach to treatment into psychotherapy integration. *Journal of Psychotherapy Integration, 12,* 154–189.

Greenberg, L., Watson, J.C., Elliott, R., & Bohart, A.C. (2001). Empathy. *Psychotherapy: Theory, Research, Practice, Training, 38,* 380–384.

Hayes, S.C., Strosahl, K.D., & Wilson, K.G. (1999). *Acceptance and commitment therapy.* New York: Guilford.

Hesse, E. (1999). The adult attachment interview: Historical and current perspectives. In J. Cassidy & P.R. Shaver (Eds.), *Handbook of attachment.* (pp. 395–433) New York: Guilford.

Hobson, P. (2002). *The cradle of thought.* London: Macmillan.

Hughes, D. (2004). An attachment-based treatment of maltreated children and young people. *Attachment and Human Development, 6,* 263–278.

Hughes, D. (2006). *Building the bonds of attachment* (2nd ed.). New York: Jason Aronson.

Jaffe, J., Beebe, B., Feldstein, S., Crown, C., & Jasnow, M. (2001). Rhythms of dialogue in infancy: Coordinated timing in development. *Monographs of the Society for Research in Child Development, 66*(2).

Johnson, S.M. (2002). *Emotionally focused couple therapy with trauma survivors: Strengthening attachment bonds.* New York: Guilford.

Johnson, S.M. (2004). *The practice of emotionally focused couple therapy: Creating connections* (2nd ed.). New York: Brunner-Routledge.

Kaufman, G. (1996). *The psychology of shame* (2nd ed.). New York: Springer.

Kirschenbaum, H., & Jordan, A. (2005). The current status of Carl Rogers and the person-centered approach. *Psychotherapy: Theory, Research, Practice, Training, 42,* 37–51.

Kobak, R. (1999). The emotional dynamics of disruptions in attachment relationships. In J. Cassidy & P.R. Shaver (Eds.), *Handbook of attachment* (pp. 21–43). New York: Guilford.

Kohn, A. (2005). *Unconditional parenting.* New York: Atria Books.

Linehan, M. (1993). *Cognitive-behavioral treatment of borderline personality disorder.* New York: Guilford.

Lyons-Ruth, K., & Jacobvitz, D. (1999). Attachment disorganization: Unresolved loss, relational violence, and lapses in behavioral and attentional strategies. In J. Cassidy & P. Shaver (Eds.), *Handbook of attachment* (pp. 520–554). New York: Guilford.

Marvin, R., Cooper, G., Hoffman, K., & Powell, B. (2002). The circle of security project: Attachment-based intervention with caregiver-pre-school child dyads. *Attachment and Human Development, 4,* 107–124.

Norcross, J.C. (2001). Purposes, processes, and products of the task force on empirically supported therapy relationships. *Psychotherapy, 38,* 345–356.

Omer, H. (1997). Narrative empathy. *Psychotherapy: Theory, Research, Practice, Training, 34,* 19–27.

Park, J. (2004). Walking the tightrope: Developing an attachment-based/relational curriculum for trainee psychotherapists. *Attachment and Human Development, 6,* 131–140.

Rogers, C.R. (1951). *Client-centered therapy.* Boston: Houghton Mifflin.

Schore, A.N. (1994). *Affect regulation and the origin of the self.* Hillsdale, NJ: Erlbaum.

Schore, A.N. (2001). Effects of a secure attachment on right brain development, affect regulation, and infant mental health. *Infant Mental Health Journal, 22,* 7–67.

Schore, A.N. (2003a). *Affect dysregulation and disorders of the self.* New York: Norton.

Schore, A.N. (2003b). *Affect regulation and the repair of the self.* New York: Norton.

Schore, A.N. (2005). A neuropsychoanalytic viewpoint: Commentary on paper by Steven H. Knoblauch. *Psychoanalytic Dialogues, 15,* 829–854.

Siegel, D.J. (1999). *The developing mind.* New York: Guilford.

Siegel, D.J. (2001). Toward an interpersonal neurobiology of the developing mind: Attachment relationships, "mindsight," and neural integration. *Infant Mental Health Journal, 22,* 67–94.

Siegel, D.J. (2007). *The mindful brain.* New York: Norton.

Siegel, D.J., & Hartzell, M. (2003). *Parenting from the inside out.* New York: Tarcher/Putnam.

Sroufe, L.A. (1995). *Emotional development: The organization of emotional life in the early years.* New York: Cambridge University Press.

Stern, D. (1985). *The interpersonal world of the infant.* New York: Basic Books.

Stern, D. (2004). *The present moment in psychotherapy and everyday life.* New York: Norton.

Sunderland, M. (2006). *The science of parenting.* London: Dorling Kindersley.

Tangney, J., & Dearing, R. (2002). *Shame and guilt.* New York: Guilford.

Trevarthen, C. (2001). Intrinsic motives for companionship in understanding: Their origin, development, and significance for infant mental health. *Infant Mental Health Journal, 22,* 95–131.

Trevarthen, C., & Aitken, K.J. (2001). Infant intersubjectivity: Research, theory, and clinical applications. *Journal of Child Psychology and Psychiatry, 42,* 3–48.

Tronick, E. (1989). Emotions and emotional communication in infants. *American Psychologist, 44,* 112–119.

Van der Kolk, B. (2005). Developmental trauma disorder: Toward a rational diagnosis for children with complex trauma histories. *Psychiatric Annals, 35,* 401–408.

Vygotsky, L.S. (1962). *Thought and language.* Cambridge, MA: M.I.T. Press.

Weininger, O. (2002). *Time-in parenting.* Toronto: Rinascente Books.

Index

Page numbers followed by a "t" denote tables.

Index

affective/reflective (a/r) dialogue
    with adolescents, 114
    characteristics, 100–102
    with children, 99, 107–18, 172–76
    content, 209
    and empathy, 87–94, 104, 106
    eye contact only, 107–10
    finding words, 110–12
    focus, 99, 113
    and meaning, 101–5, 112
    and narratives, 105
    nonverbal cues, 57, 98, 101, 112, 115
    openings, 113–14
    PACE, 105–10
    and repair, 100, 192
    sequence, 102–7
    and shame, 114–18
    therapist stance, 98, 110–20
aggression, 107–10
Aitken, K. J., 19, 225
Albus, K. E., 225
amygdala, 223
anger
    in abused parent, 256
    in adolescents, 133–35, 239–54
    and attachment security, 25
    coregulation, 51, 136–39
    and discipline, 142, 148
    as disrespect, 141
    example dialogues, 57–60, 92–94
    isolation response, 137
    and meaning, 55
    in parents, 125, 242, 258
    and shame, 178, 182
    in therapist, 86
anterior cingulate, 223
anxiety
    after excitement, 138
    in breaks, 24, 28, 30
    laughter as, 74
    and parent history, 135
    in parents, 30, 41
    and playfulness, 66
    in therapist, 70, 86, 246–48, 253
    and trauma resolution, 218
attachment
    avoidant style, 74
    and family, 1–2, 21
    insecure, 21–22

    and motivation, 14
    and shame, 178
    in therapeutic relationship, 2–6
attachment bond, 14
attachment disorganization, 217
attachment history
    of parents, 30, 44, 92–94, 131–36,
        141, 153, 161, 239–54
    of therapist, 44–45, 208, 248, 253
attachment security
    and affect coregulation, 33, 53
    and anger, 25
    and a/r dialogues, 105
    and conflict resolution, 148
    definitions, 13, 27
    description, 139–43
    family therapy role, 2–6
    insecurity, 21–22
    and intersubjectivity, 14
    and parenting, 13, 126, 148,
        150–51t
    and repair, 22–26, 192, 196
    and self, 35
    and trauma resolution, 218–21
attachment theory, 40, 137
attention, 48
attunement, 47, 139–43, 180, 222
    see also breaks; repair
authority, 141, 142
avoidance
    as attachment style, 74
    of breaks, 191–92
    and shame, 22, 178, 186
    and traumatic events, 216

bad breath example, 65
Bates, B., 225
Becker-Weidman, A., 7
Beebe, B., 25, 26
behavior, 36, 129t, 130t, 144–47, 166
blame, 155, 177, 182, 246–52
Bohart, A. C., 87
borderline personality, 67
Bowlby, J., 15, 40, 45
brain, 50, 222
breaks
    with angry adolescent, 246–52
    avoidance of, 191–92
    child need, 200–207

272

Index